The Early Sunset

MAGAZINE

1898-1928

An Anthology edited by
Paul C. Johnson
Director of Publications
California Historical Society

CALIFORNIA HISTORICAL SOCIETY

SAN FRANCISCO • SAN MARINO

PUBLISHED BY THE CALIFORNIA HISTORICAL SOCIETY
2090 Jackson Street, San Francisco, California

Composition by Dharma Press, Emeryville, California
Lithographed and bound by Graphic Arts Center, Portland, Oregon

The Early Sunset Magazine

*Selections
from Sunset Magazine's
first 30 years*

Preface

IN 1973 *Sunset Magazine* celebrated its 75th anniversary. It is the West's oldest popular magazine and the only one ever to achieve large circulation. It is also one of America's oldest magazines.

Sunset has had three phases to its history. This new book deals with just the first two. It contains excerpts from the "discover the West" phase of *Sunset* from 1898 to 1914 under the Southern Pacific Company's ownership, also excerpts from the "literary *Sunset*," published from 1914 to 1928 following the magazine's sale to Woodhead, Field & Company.

The "literary *Sunset*" published many great writers of its day, but public support was never sufficient to make it a financial success. By 1928 the magazine was floundering. Stage for the third *Sunset* phase was set late in 1928 when the L. W. Lane family bought the magazine, assumed its debts, changed its direction and focus, and relaunched it with the February 1929 issue as The Magazine of Western Living.

It was the conviction of L. W. Lane, Sr., that life in the West was different enough from the rest of the nation to justify and sustain a magazine designed to serve Western differences.

History has indeed proved that reasoning correct. But the early going wasn't easy nor was success achieved quickly. The stock market crashed with only the tenth Lane issue on press. The following months and years saw losses mount but also saw public support for the basic Lane idea strengthen. The corner was turned in the late 1930s. World War II with its paper rationing only served to delay an inevitable broad popular acceptance of *Sunset*. This began more than 25 years ago and has continued steadily since then.

In the Lane years the magazine's approach changed drastically. The Jack London and Bret Harte bylines became a thing of the past. Staff research and staff writing took over. Advertising became as carefully controlled as the editorial content.

Sunset opened branch offices in Los Angeles, Honolulu, Seattle. The magazine split into four different regional editions—Northwest, Central, Southern California, and Desert—with a sizable portion of content changed to fit climate and other local conditions.

Today *Sunset* has wide-ranging circulation in the nine Western states (currently more than 1,100,000). *Sunset* also publishes books (in 1973 about seven million copies of 120 different titles) and special interest magazines (four currently, more in planning). And it produces films (about a dozen so far) for clients and for *Sunset's* own marketing and promotion.

In addition to serving readers' needs around the home and away from home, today's *Sunset* is paying increasing attention to actions affecting community quality as well as to growing environmental concerns. Often these areas are controversial. *Sunset's* role is not one of crusading but rather one of showing its readers ways in which they can inform themselves and take action.

Sunset's next 75 years should be interesting. We hope the California Historical Society—which recently celebrated its hundredth anniversary—will continue to keep a scholarly eye on our performance.

PROCTOR MELLQUIST
Editor, Sunset Magazine

Contents

Introduction

I N May 1898, a slim new magazine appeared in San Francisco under the sponsorship of the most unlikely of publishers—a railroad. The magazine was *Sunset.* The railroad was the Southern Pacific.

There was little physical resemblance between this 16-page pamphlet, named for the company's crack train, the *Sunset Limited,* and its plump descendant of today, but in terms of content, the lineage is self-evident. Then, as now, the magazine was committed to exploring the challenges and opportunities of life in the land west of the Rockies. Then, as now, the editors devoted a generous proportion of the magazine's pages to photographs—under the precept that "pictures speak all languages" —and exploration of little-known scenic treasures of the West. Half of the first issue was devoted to Yosemite—then a formidable travel destination—and the pleasures of packing into the High Sierra, illustrated by photographs by Professor Joseph N. Le Conte, distinguished geologist on the faculty of the University of California in Berkeley.

Sunset's initial mission was to publicize for the Easterner the "resources of this great western empire for the husbandman, stockman, and miner, and for the tourist and health seeker, as fully as space will admit, as concisely as the subjects will warrant, and at all times— truthfully." It was sold at 5 cents a copy, 50 cents a year. It was hawked aboard trains, sold in all the railroad's depots and in a selected group of stores, half of them east of the Rockies.

Although the first issue contained no advertising—"and comes to you unbiased"—the restriction was soon lifted, and the lean little magazine began to take on weight as it filled with advertisements for land developments and, seemingly, every county and irrigation district in the West. As the magazine grew in stature and circulation, it began to attract national advertisers, many of whom are in its pages today.

In the beginning, *Sunset* was edited by a small staff attached to the Passenger Division of the railroad. For more than a year, its sole fiction contributor was an executive, Paul Shoup, who later became president of the company. The only true literary light in its first issues was kindled by David Starr Jordan, the president of Stanford University, which was also launched by one of the Big Four of the Southern Pacific railroad.

In due time, a professional staff was recruited under the editorship of Charles K. Field, a talented member of Stanford's first graduating class (which also included Herbert Clark Hoover, a later contributor to *Sunset*) and a man with wide acquaintance among San Francisco's literati. Field soon drew into the *Sunset* fold such associates as Charles G. Norris, author of the realistic novels, *Salt, The Pit,* and numerous short stories; Gelett Burgess, a perceptive writer and versifier with talents far beyond his notorious *Purple Cow;* the prolific poet George Sterling, who published thirty-one poems in the magazine between 1904 and 1920; Mary Austin, well known for her *Land of Little Rain,* who contributed articles, poems, and a serialized novel, *The Blue Moon;* Ina Coolbrith, poet laureate of California, who published seven poems in *Sunset;* and, of course, the redoubtable Jack London, whose muscular stories gave solid substance to a half dozen early issues, beginning in 1903.

Other well-known writers—some of whose work is included in this book—included Bret Harte, Sinclair Lewis, James Hopper, Gertrude Atherton, Kathleen Norris, Witter Bynner, Vachel Lindsay, Joaquin Miller, Charles Warren Stoddard of "Mission Trails" fame, Luther Burbank, Samuel Hopkins Adams, Frederick Lewis Allen, Senator William Borah, Aubrey Drury, Hamlin Garland, Helen Hunt Jackson, Hiram Johnson, Stewart Edward White, Frank Taylor, Damon Runyon, John Muir, and hosts of others.

In time, the magazine outgrew the needs of the Southern Pacific. After absorbing a Portland, Oregon, journal, *The Pacific Monthly,* in 1912, the scope of the combined publication moved far beyond the original mission and the Southern Pacific arranged to sell the publication to the magazine staff in 1914.

When the new publisher, Woodhead, Field & Company, took over, it introduced significant changes. No longer influenced by railroad corporation policies (or benefiting from its financial support), the magazine brashly tackled controversial topics that the editors conceived to be of relevance to the Pacific Coast, fearlessly taking on organized labor, crime, movie immorality, drug traffic, despoliation of the forests, and congressional ineptitude. Hiram Johnson, Senator Borah, and David Starr Jordan wrote at tedious length on national and international problems.

Alongside this new political awareness, the editors maintained their historic preoccupation with the "beauties and opportunities" of the West and shopped for "the best fiction that money can buy." Under the new policy, the magazine shifted towards a journal edited for westerners rather than easterners, but it still regarded itself as a national magazine. By 1923, it carried a subtitle, "The West's Great National Magazine." In its closing years under the Woodhead-Field regime, it was edited by Joseph Henry Jackson, noted author and book critic who inveigled many famous authors into its pages.

The revamped magazine survived until 1928 before it finally succumbed to financial anemia, and, on the verge of bankruptcy, was sold to the Lane family, its present owners.

Turning back the pages of the early *Sunsets* is a rewarding visit to a greening West, when life was simpler and filled with wonder and discovery. This first thirty years covered a period when old and new Westerners were discovering their domain. Roads and rails were being extended in every direction, opening fresh vistas to a mobile people, to whom the extravagances of nature were personal revelations.

Even the mere exercise of getting from one natural spectacle to another held a pre-smog spell. In this period, the motor car had advanced beyond the sputtering toy of the rich to Henry's millions, and people thrilled to the liberation it offered. No longer held to the channeled travel of the train or stagecoach, or the slow backbreaking discomfort of horse and buggy, Westerners whizzed over their new roads with zest. This was the start of the love affair with the automobile. Writers contributed pleasant little odes toasting the kinesthetic delights of travel by car; the hiss of the tires on gravel, the smell of hot leather in the sun, wind on the face, and the welcoming light at the end of the empty road at night. The pages reflect this period of automotive puppy love with unaffected gusto.

Sunset also reported on the dawn of the Air Age, when experimenters "pedaled furiously in the sky" to keep their home-made contraptions airborne, pilots "contemptuous of death, dare the roads between the thunder and the sun," and 14,000 spectators at an international air meet in 1910 collectively held their breath as they awaited the miraculous moment when the wheels of a taxiing plane rose above the tips of the grass blades and the plane ascended the "invisible ramp into the sky."

Nor was the grave menace of this new means of transport lost on *Sunset*. As early as 1910, articles reported the military potentiality for the new aeroplane; by 1914 the magazine was concerned about the vulnerability of the Panama Canal to assault from the air. The concept of the sitting-duck battleship, indefensible to air attack, was aired in *Sunset* some eight years before the court martial of Billy Mitchell for promoting the same heresy.

These first decades of the century also saw the opening of the wilderness to the venturesome. From its first issue, *Sunset* reported on this wide-ranging activity, which still carried with it the thrills of new discovery. As early as 1902, the magazine was advising its readers what clothes (ample!) and food (likewise—even with desiccated foods) to take on a high country tramp. A 78-year-old professor reported on his dancing a jig on the summit of Mount Whitney, a young married couple back-packed their three-month-old baby to the top of an 11,000-foot peak, and two hundred merry "Sierr-i-ans" marched to the highest of the High Country under the auspices of the Sierra Club.

During its first thirty years, the early *Sunset* offered a substantial, often lively, mix of fact and fancy. Thorough articles on the economic development of the West methodically inventoried every corner of this expanding domain.

Written in an era of long-winded literary style, with sentences that crawl by like slow freights, or, perhaps more to the point, in a time when authors were paid by the word and had to write interminably to eke out a living, most of the factual articles make soporific reading today, although they do record for the historian a valuable picture of the growth of the West.

The political polemics are likewise difficult for a modern reader to penetrate. Written in prolix style, often fuzzy in concept, the topicality of these articles makes most of them of interest mainly to political scientists. Only the women writers seem to have been able to handle political subjects with clarity and interest.

Readers of the present-day *Sunset* may be surprised to find fiction and poetry featured in the ancestral issues, but these were an integral part of the old *Sunset,* beginning with Vol. 1, No. 1, which contained a verse from *The Lady of the Lake,* a poem entitled *The Choo Choo Car,* and a short story about the biggest liar in the whole Southwest.

The stories were contributed by well-known writers—some just on the verge of becoming famous—and were largely entertaining yarns, usually set in the great outdoors, on a Pacific atoll, or aboard a troubled ship, and resolved in the final three paragraphs with a classic O'Henry snapper. A reader of today, unaccustomed to stories with a beginning, middle, and an end, may find these tales puzzling and pat, but many of them still make rousing good reading. Some of the fiction, notably the novel-length pieces by women writers, Mary Austin, Ruth Comfort Mitchell, and Rose Wilder Lane, provide sensitive portrayals of emotional relationships and a sharp understanding of people and place.

Any story worth publishing was also worth illustrating, and *Sunset* drew upon a stable of talented artists, such as Henry Bull, Edward Borein, Will James (launched by *Sunset*), and the dean of them all, Maynard Dixon, who contributed a flood of top-quality action drawings in his 22-year affiliation with *Sunset.*

Every issue likewise featured poetry, mostly light verse, contributed by well-known poets such as Sterling, Benét, Bynner, and hosts of lesser bards. The rimes were of a piece with what Louis Untermeyer has labeled the Age of Verse, an outpouring that bridged the passage between the declining romantic school and the soon-to-be-born modern school. Most of *Sunset's* poets sought meaning and symbolism in the natural world. With varying literary grace, they raised and set the sun, saluted the autumnal fall of leaves, sensed the message of the zephyr and the storm, and recorded the lamentation of the surf. In contrast, were the number of bright little verses that celebrated the commonplace with wit and occasionally sharp commentary.

Perhaps the most enchanting encounter in the old issues is the advertising—well worth a book in its own right. Even more obviously than the fiction, poetry, and essays, the advertisements clearly reflect the spirit of their day, in their typographic extravagance, the costuming of their models, and the brashness of their message. The art style ebbs and flows with the fashions, cycling back on itself from time to time, so that even today's reader may be astonished to sense a "modern" feel in ads from the 1900s and 1910s. There is also wry amusement in seeing how persistent are the buyers' dreams and fears that have been the target of the copywriter's wiles. Even in the early 1900s cars were being promoted for their reliability and "powerful performance with economy"; milady's styles were sure to resolve all personal problems and physical shortcomings; riches awaited the fortunate who invested in the Nile of the Pacific (e.g., San Joaquin Valley), rubber plantations in Central America, Zane's Steam Dirigible, eucalyptus (soon to displace hickory as hardwood), hop farms, whatever. Shredded Wheat saved families from debilitation in 1911; in 1909 you could grow five inches by sending in a coupon; in 1907 you could play your wind-up hi-fi on the deck of a yacht.

And so, from the mountainous accumulation of stories, poems, essays, sketches, travelogues, and nostalgic advertisements, this anthology has been extracted and digested. The reader will find the early follower of *Sunset* an informed and industrious soul, vigorously poking around his West, enjoying it hugely, worrying about its present and future, and commenting sometimes with tongue in cheek on the pageant around him—in other words, a profile that is not too unlike the involved reader of today's Magazine of Western Living.

Ballad of the Hyde Street Grip

By Gelett Burgess.

March 1902

Oh, the rain is slanting sharply, and the Norther's blowing cold;
When the cable strands are loosened she is nasty hard to hold!
There's little time for sitting down, and little chance for gab,
For the bumper guards the crossing, and you'd best be keeping tab,
Two-and-twenty "let-go's" every double trip—
It takes a bit of doing, on the Hyde Street Grip!

Throw her off at Powell Street, let her go at Post,
Watch her well at Geary and at Sutter when you coast!
Easy at the Power House, have a care at Clay,
Sacramento, Washington, Jackson—all the way!
Drop your rope at Union—never make a slip—
The lever keeps you busy, on the Hyde Street Grip!

Foot-brake, wheel-brake, slot-brake and gong,
You'd better keep 'em busy or you'll soon be going wrong!
Rush her on the crossings, catch her on the rise,
Easy round the corners when the dust is in your eyes—
And the bell will always stop you if you hit her up a clip;
You are apt to earn your wages on the Hyde Street Grip!

North Beach to Tenderloin, over Russian Hill,
The grades are something giddy, and the curves are fit to kill!
All the way to Market Street, climbing up the slope,
Down upon the other side, hanging to the rope!
But the view of San Francisco, as you take the lurching dip!
There is plenty of excitement on the Hyde Street Grip!

If you had to drive a penny 'bus from Chelsea to the Strand
You'd see Westminster Abbey, and you'd say that it was grand!
If you had to pass the Luxembourg and Place de la Concorde
Atop a Paris omnibus, no doubt you'd thank the Lord!
But the Frenchy'd give his chapeau and the Cockney'd give his whip
For a sight of San Francisco from the Hyde Street Grip!

Oh, the lights are in the Mission, and the ships are on the Bay,
And Tamalpais is looming from the Gate, across the way;
The Presidio trees are waving, and the hills are growing brown,
And the driving fog is harried from the ocean to the town!
How the pulleys slap and rattle! How the cables hum and skip!
Oh, they sing a gallant chorus to the Hyde Street Grip!

When the Orpheum is closing and the crowds are on the way,
The conductor's punch is ringing and the dummy's light and gay;
But the wait upon the switch above the beach is dark and still—
Just the swashing of the surges on the shore below the Mill;
And the flash from Angel Island breaks across the Channel rip
As the hush of midnight falls upon the Hyde Street Grip!

San Francisco

By BRET HARTE

October 1902

Serene, indifferent of Fate,
Thou sittest at the Western Gate;

Upon thy height so lately won,
Still slant the banners of the sun;

Thou seest the white seas strike their tents,
O Warder of two continents!

Down the Sacramento in a Skiff

By CLOUDSLEY RUTTER

June 1902

THE mere mention of a boating ex-
pedition brings up pleasant fancies to your
mind. But suppose you are in a skiff, with one
or two others, on a winding river, the water
pure, cool and clear, the current so swift that
you travel three or four miles an hour without
other exertion than merely guiding the boat.
Cover the banks with trees, and put a few riffles
or small rapids in the current to give a little
excitement, and insert an occasional stretch of
quiet water by way of variety, and locate camps
among the trees with great piles of driftwood
for bonfires at night, fill the river with fish and
cover its surface with game birds, and extend
your excursion to a hundred miles and loiter
along for a couple of weeks—the charm is
beyond description. Such is a California outing
on the Sacramento river, between Redding and
Tehama.

I have made this trip several times and always enjoy it, though any one voyage is not
exciting enough to bear describing in detail. If
it were, it would be suitable only for the few,
whereas it is an outing that even women can
take, and every moment is enjoyable.

Although there are many riffles and rocks
along the route, do not think the trip at all
dangerous. Any one who can guide a boat can
make it. The rapids and rocks can all be seen
without a chart, and are easily avoided, though
maps will be found of some advantage in
showing when and where to look for them. I
have traveled nearly eight hundred miles on
the river in a skiff without serious accident,
though I knew but little about a boat when I
began. I have never heard of a serious accident
to any one so traveling, excepting a Chinese
who went to the right of the island below Big
Bend ferry—and he died.

For making this trip a party of three persons
will need a boat sixteen feet long, and of not
less than four and one-half feet beam. It must
be well built, with a high bow and a depth of
sixteen or eighteen inches. In loading be careful
to keep the bow clear of the water, so as to
make turning easy. Oars nine feet long are
preferable, one pair only being needed. There
are no boats at Redding, though one can be
shipped by rail from Tehama. Make your
camping outfit as small and light as possible.

One starting point is the wood-jam at Keswick

Three comforters for each person are an abundance. Provisions can be secured at Redding, Anderson, Balls Ferry and Red Bluff, so that a large supply need not be taken in the boat.

The start is made from Reid ferry, near Redding. There is very little of interest outside of natural scenery, which is enough. On the right below the ferry is an old and dilapidated mill with a cable running upstream to trip up your oar. A little further down as you run in close to the bank you see a novel method of drawing in water. A wire reaches from an anchor in the river up to a tree on the bluff above. By means of a rope and windlass a bucket is lowered to and drawn up from the water along this wire.

The second riffle is quite shallow, and can be passed only at the extreme left. Keep in the rough water. On the left bank at this point you may find a few Indians if you are interested in them. Most of their habits have been changed more or less from their contact with white men, but their ancient modes of fishing are still followed. On one occasion the ferryman showed me an Indian spear that he had found the day before floating down stream fastened to a live salmon. Upon my expressing a desire for the spear, he gave it to me. Then I wanted to photograph it, and thought it would be best to have some one hold it. I saw an Indian across the river, and decided to take the spear across and have him hold it in order to have things as natural as possible. When I spoke to him, he said, "Yes, I lose him yesterday in big salmon. Some one tell me ferryman found him, and I come here now to get him." And he did. My realistic zeal lost me the spear. The Indian posed, however, and I had to be content. The spear was a two-prong affair, with a toggle on each prong. The toggles were fastened to the pole with cords "made of Indian hair."

Early on the trip, you encounter very good riffles in which to become acquainted with your boat and learn how to handle it in a current. If you go wrong there is no harm done, except that you may get scratched by the overhanging brush, as I have several times. You will also find out whether your load is properly stowed. You will find that the bow must be clear of the water, otherwise you cannot turn as quickly as you sometimes need to.

It was in passing one of these riffles in 1898,

that we, as novices, allowed our boat to turn crosswise of the current. As a consequence we shipped about a barrel of water and hung ourselves out to dry.

The high bluffs of conglomerate at Redding bend are well worth noting. They, like many others along the river, are covered with swallows' nests.

Immediately below a moderate riffle, you come to the mouth of Clear creek, on the opposite side of the river from which is a very good camping place, though the trees are at a considerable distance from the water. There are large piles of driftwood here, which make fine campfires at night. I stopped for lunch here once, and the quail annoyed me so much I could hardly eat!

A short distance below Clear creek you hear an ominous roar, which upon investigation proves to be made by a small brook entering the river over a fall. If you are thirsty, take a drink from the river; the brook water is warm.

Along the banks you will see several irrigating pumps, the only practical artificial rainmakers.

It would be a good plan to go into camp for a day or two at the head of Iron canyon. The region is interesting, and is worth exploring.

Iron canyon is very much of a joke. Before I made my first trip down the river, I was repeatedly warned of the danger in passing this terrible water. The current ran a mile a minute

and was full of rocks, which was enough to frighten any one. I got up at 4 o'clock on the morning that we were expecting to pass Iron canyon in order to equip our boat with a rudder, so that we could handle it the more easily. Before reaching the dreaded place we tied all our baggage to the boat so that we would not lose anything in case of a wreck. By a vote that lacked only one of being unanimous, it was decided that I should take the oars and be responsible for the wreck. As it was nearly noon, I decided to eat my lunch first so as to be that much ahead in case of accident. So I sat in the bow and ate chipped beef and crackers while Fred handled the oars and Mack held the tiller. My lunch was two or three miles long, for the current was pretty strong most of the time. At one place the channel was very narrow, but the water was smooth and clear of rocks, and we wished the whole river were like it.

After finishing my lunch I took the oars and Fred got into the bow with the camera in order to secure a picture of the canyon when we should reach it. There was some doubt about the wisdom of attempting to take a picture of the canyon owing to the danger of getting the camera wet, but we decided that a picture would be worth the risk. Fred crouched behind the camera a long time, and I began to complain that they had made me take the oars too soon, and Mack wanted his lunch—but we saw no canyon. Then we saw a boy on the bank and asked him how much further it was to Iron canyon. What was our chagrin to learn that we had passed it while I was eating!

Several other parties have had similar experiences, not recognizing the rapid until it was passed. It is not a canyon at all, at least not different from all this portion of the river; simply a long rapid. The channel is very narrow, at one place for about a hundred yards it is only about forty feet wide, and the current in this portion really does run at the rate of ten or twelve miles an hour; but the channel is entirely clear. There are a few rocks on the right at the beginning of the rapid, and it is a little rough there, but as a whole Iron canyon is the prettiest bit of water that you will find. The term "iron" probably comes from the lava through which the channel is cut. Basaltic columns and swallows' nests may be seen at the lower end.

The rapid is more fascinating than the scenery

This is an excellent region for ducks; also for cormorants. You soon come to Cow creek, on which stream old Fort Redding was located. From this point to Balls Ferry the river scenery is magnificent. One side is bordered by high bluffs, and both banks are forest-covered. For most of the distance there is but little current, and pleasure boats are common.

If you are to visit the hatchery at Battle creek, which I would advise you to do, you had best pull your boat over the bar at the upper mouth of the creek. The middle mouth, through which most of the water runs, is difficult of ascent on account of rapids. The creek from the lower end of Bloody island to the fishing grounds has but little current, and rowing up stream is not difficult. If you are approved, the hatchery fishermen will give you a fish from the net; otherwise you will have to wait till the spawning is over.

You will find the best camping below the mouth of the creek, on either side of the river. Battle creek water is frequently not very good on account of the large number of salmon that die in it.

Between this point and Red Bluff you will frequently have to dodge wires that are stretched across the river two or three feet above its surface. You will notice several lines hanging down to the water from each wire, and further observation will show a hook on each line. Salmon are caught on these hooks occasionally, and their jerking shakes a little flag on the wire, giving notice of the strike. Sometimes the hooks are suspended from a line lying along the wire and attached to a bell on shore, which the fish rings when it jerks. Truly accommodating!

Spanish riffle is very shallow on the left. I once saw some fishermen stranded here, but fortunately they were towed off, or at least were helped in getting off, by a five-hundred-pound sturgeon that they were taking down to Red Bluff to market, and had tied to their boat.

The river below Red Bluff is very much like that for two or three miles above, and needs no particular comment. Gravel banks are frequent, and drifts occasionally obstruct the channel. Cultivated fields adjoin the river, boatloads of grain lie at the landings awaiting the arrival of the river steamers, and cattle, sheep, hogs and turkeys are seen everywhere—all proclaiming it an agricultural region. For much of the distance, however, the banks are covered with trees, and camping places are not wanting.

There is a snag just above the west end of the drawbridge at Tehama. Look out for it. I once had my skiff twist around for half an hour on just such a snag. Here your voyage ends. #

Across The Tule

(By the Carquinez Straits)

By WILLIAM R. BENÉT

The marshes like some vast chameleon lie,
    Burnished in bronze and webbed with vivid green.
Whistling, the blackbirds wheel against the sky.
    Afar—that strip of steel—the straits are seen.

Beyond the straits, the foothills, tipped with fire,
    Signal night's closing-in, from height to height;
Till flares Diablo's titan smoldering pyre,
    Its gaunt escarpments etched in livid light.

December 1907.

Housekeeping in the Summer Camp

By KATHERINE A. CHANDLER

May 1902

CAMPING in California today is as primitive or as luxurious, as carefree or as arduous, as nomadic or as stationary as one chooses to make it. One family, I know, has all the comforts of an opulent home transferred to a forest plot they own, and there, for two months in summer, they rest in what they are pleased to style their camp. With the same trained service and the same choice menu that they enjoy during the ten months of city life, the only pretensions they can make to the title are the canvas tents that are substituted for permanent walls and the absence of elaborate dress.

Another family goes to the ocean beach and rents a tent furnished for housekeeping. With as good a market as at home, the "camping" consists of the crowded quarters and the freedom from the regular housework that a comfortable home entails.

Another family has gone to Yosemite, carrying their bedding and food. There they rented tents, cots, mattresses, stools, a table and stove, and spent a very delightful five weeks at the cost of one week's board at the hotel. They traveled by the regular train and stage and thus avoided all care of a team and vehicle.

Another party has hired a large wagon and a pair of strong horses; and with plenty of provisions and bedding, they have been independent of railroads, hotels, or any of the necessary appurtenances of modern travel. They, however, could not cut through the circumference of civilization, for a wagon must have some sort of a roadbed to pass on.

It is with none of these that this article proposes to deal, but with the most primitive campers, or we might even call them trampers.

Seeking to explore a region not yet under the dominion of man, the most independent way is afoot with pack horses, or better still, with burros. The latter do not require food carried for them and keep up their strength on any kind of pasturage, perversely preferring thistles to timothy. The fewer the animals, the less the care, so it is essential to study ahead the details and have as little baggage as possible. To get full benefit from a camping, one must have nourishing meals and warm sleeping accommodations, and both of these must be planned for, so as to demand the minimum amount of time in their preparation. Otherwise the camping will become a burden, and not a source of rest.

For the trip one wants to be as unhampered by clothes as possible. Men always seem to know what to wear; or at least, they never confess that they are uncomfortable; but all women have not learned the lesson yet. An active woman can get along well for a month's tramp with two short skirts and one jacket of some stout material, as corduroy or denim; bloomers and leggins of the same goods, or at least the same color; strong shoes, not too heavy, but with a thick sole containing Hungarian nails, for tramping, and a lighter pair to rest one's feet in camp; a sunbonnet and a soft canvas hat; a few darkish shirt waists of cotton crepe which will wash easily and not need ironing; some stout gloves; two changes of underwear; one flannelette nightgown, and a golf cape, or a heavy shawl. She will need hairpins galore to keep tidy and all the necessities of a workbag.

For breakfast one might have fried mush, bacon, pancakes, dried apricots and coffee; lunch will probably be taken off on a tramp and may consist of sandwiches of canned corned beef and hard tack, chocolate, nuts and dates; dinner, at camp, will offer soup, macaroni, galleta, the apricots left from breakfast and tea or coffee. For variety beans, rice, spaghetti and desiccated potatoes, either white or sweet, may be substituted for macaroni; prunes, dried Bartlett pears, peaches or apples take the place of apricots; raisins or figs used in lieu of the dates; and fish or game replace the bacon.

OFFICIALS
SOUTHERN PACIFIC COMPANY.

PASSENGER DEPARTMENT.

J. C. STUBBS, THIRD VICE-PRESIDENT,
San Francisco, Cal.

E. HAWLEY, ASST. GEN. TRAFFIC MANAGER,
New York, N, Y.

T. H. GOODMAN, GEN. PASS. AGENT (PAC. SYS.),
San Francisco, Cal.

S. F. B. MORSE, GEN. PASS. AGT. (ATL. SYS.),
New Orleans, La.

R. A. DONALDSON,   JAS. HORSBURGH, JR.,   H. R. JUDAH,
ASST. GEN. PASS. AGTS. (PAC. SYS.), San Francisco, Cal.

C. H. MARKHAM, GEN. PASS. AGT. LINES IN OREGON,
Portland, Ore.

G. W. LUCE, ASST. GEN. PASS. AGT.,
Los Angeles, Cal.

F. S. DECKER, ASST GEN. PASS. AGT. (ATL. SYS.),
New Orleans, La.

Galleta, hard tack and pancakes are sufficient breadstuffs; but if one wishes to make biscuits there is a convenient little oven made for camping purposes. It is of tin with sloping sides and open front. This is placed close to the blaze and it bakes by reflection. However, biscuits require carrying flour, and we have found the substitutes perfectly palatable. Hard tack is unlike the musty cracker the seamen used to grumble over, and it has great nourishing qualities. Some experienced mountaineers carry just it and cake chocolate for a long day's tramp. The galleta is a hard Italian bread, which, when moistened and heated, tastes quite like French bread. The pancakes are made from some of the patented pancake flours, and one would better try the several brands at home before laying in the camping supplies. They are not equally good.

As for mush, one can take any he prefers, but the old-fashioned cornmeal makes an excellent fried food. We cook it at night as we sit around the campfire, and in the morning cut it into slices and fry it in bacon grease. It is well to have several kinds of these breakfast meals, as variety is as necessary in them as in other foods.

It may be suggestive to quote here the quantity and cost of food for a party of five, two men and three women, for a four weeks' trip: Hard tack, 40 pounds, $1.20; galleta, fifteen pounds, 75 cents; pancake flour, 2 packages, 50 cents; breakfast foods, 3 packages, 25 cents; cornmeal, 1 sack, 35 cents; macaroni, 2 boxes, 50 cents; spaghetti, 1 box, 25 cents; desiccated potatoes, 60 cents; rice, 8 pounds, 50 cents; beans, 5 pounds, 20 cents; tomatoes, 6 cans, 50 cents; marrowfat pea soup, 6 sausages, $1.20; other soups, 12 packages, $1.60; bacon, 25 pounds, $4.50; tongue, 4 cans, $1.20; beef, 4 cans, $1; dried beef, 2 pounds, 50 cents; butter, 6 pounds, $1.20; cream, 12 cans, $1.20; milk, 12 cans, $1.50; coffee, 5 pounds, $1.75; tea, 1 pound, 80 cents; sugar, 24 pounds, $1.50; salt, 5 cents; pepper, 10 cents; mustard, 10 cents; vinegar, 10 cents; Edam cheese, 90 cents; American cheese, 3 pounds, 45 cents; chocolate, 8 cakes, $2; raisins, 5 pounds, 75 cents; figs, 9 pounds California, 75 cents; dates, 3 pounds, 45 cents; prunes, 8 pounds, $1; apricots, 6 pounds, 90 cents; pears, 5 pounds, 75 cents; peaches, 2 pounds, 30 cents; apples, 1 pound, 15 cents; walnuts, 5 pounds, 75 cents; almonds, 4 pounds, 50 cents; tea cakes, 50 cents; or a total of $34.05.

A party of four men on a two weeks' trip found the cost of their food, which was practically the same as the above, $25.20; and three women report the total cost of their food for four weeks' camping as $18.15. When we divide these totals by the number in each party, the cost per individual is so small that we wonder how our housekeeping bills at home can reach such alarming figures as they often do. #

Ever glittered on before, in anticipation, the summit of Mount Whitney

On the Tip-Top
of the United States

By THEODORE H. HITTELL

February 1903

ON June 23, 1902, we—that is to say, upward of two hundred ladies and gentlemen—started on the second outing of the Sierra Club. Our destination was King's river canyon. Part of us went by the way of Sanger and Millwood and part by the way of Visalia and the Giant Forest. I was of the Visalia and Giant Forest crowd.

From Visalia we went the next day, by stages, some fifty-five miles up the Kaweah river, to the Giant Forest, which we entered on June 25th. This forest, which is at an elevation of from four to five thousand feet above sea level and extends over many miles, is perhaps the grandest in the world. It consists of many thousands of the big trees (sequoia gigantea) and contains the finest specimens of those antediluvian vegetable wonders, besides uncountable numbers of splendid sugar pines, yellow pines, silver firs, incense cedars and other imposing trees. From there, after spending a day or two among the sequoias, we commenced our walking, and we kept on walking, at the rate of from ten to fifteen miles a day, for four consecutive days. Our course lay north and north-east over mountain ridges, most of the way through forests, across rocky slopes or along mountain meadows covered with the most beautiful flowers. On the fourth day, at the end of a steep descent of about five miles, we reached King's river canyon, in which, some six miles farther up, we made our main camp.

A long pack train, mostly of mules, carried our blankets and provisions, and every evening stopped at one of the many lovely meadows, where the cooks prepared our evening meal. After supper we built an immense camp fire, using only fallen timber; and around the blaze

highest peak in the United States, and chief object of the whole campaign

of the dry wood we would sit for several hours, entertained with recitations, stories, singing and music. We all slept under the stars, and probably none of us ever slept sounder or better. In the morning, after breakfast, we were on our way again, tramping along "with joy upon the mountain side."

King's river canyon is a sort of larger Yosemite, without its grand water falls, its El Capitan or its South Dome. It has, however, its Grand Sentinel, a huge, precipitous and beautifully colored granite cliff some thirty-five hundred feet high, which is magnificent. The whole canyon, as well as the canyons entering into it, is lined with stupendous crags, surmounted by immense pinnacles.

Our main camp was near the mouth of Copper creek, on the north bank of King's river, and directly opposite the Grand Sentinel. There, in a grove of tall sugar and yellow pines, cedars and firs, oaks and cottonwoods, we selected our sleeping places, each, as on the road, "under the greenwood tree;" there we gathered regularly three times a day in a great merry crowd for meals; there we built our nightly camp fire, and there we enjoyed life, as it only can be enjoyed, in the mountains.

From this main camp, in the course of the four weeks of the Sierra Club outing, we made numerous excursions. Much of the time, we were above the timber line and lived among

ragged peaks and pinnacles, and every move involved an ascent or a descent of thousands of feet. Of course, a mule train carrying our provisions and blankets accompanied us on every distant tramp.

About the end of July, after finishing up our King's river trip and returning to the Giant Forest, a dozen of us made up a new party for a still grander trip. This was to Kern river and the highest portions of the Sierra Nevada. The party included John Muir, the famous glacier man and naturalist; Dr. C. Hart Merriam, head of the biological division at Washington; Dr. Henry Gannett, head of the geographical department at Washington; William Keith, the artist; four ladies and three boys.

For this trip, which was into the roughest kind of mountains, we were all mounted. When we started from the Giant Forest, I supposed that I knew something about mountain trails; but I soon found that my experience was very limited. In some places we seemed to be going almost straight up a precipice, and in others, straight down. At one time we were skirting a yawning chasm and at another, threading a narrow backbone of rock. At times we were high up among jagged peaks far above the timberline and at others, down in dark gorges apparently hemmed in by over-hanging cliffs.

And so we traveled for four or five days, up to Alta meadows, under the Kaweah peaks,

Enjoyable exercise

across to Mineral King, over Farewell gap, along the Hindman trail to Coyote pass and then down into the lower end of Kern river canyon, a gorge still more extensive and grander than that of King's river. I never before saw such scenery and magnificent mountain landscapes as I witnessed on this trip. They probably equal in rugged beauty anything else of the kind in the world. Keith, the artist, who had seen but little to attract his special attention in King's river canyon, became enthusiastic with the Kern river country.

We made our main camp in Kern river canyon at Soda Springs, a couple of miles north of what is commonly in that region called Kern lake, a mere dilation of the river between stupendous cliffs, apparently caused by a rock slide at its lower end. The canyon there, as well as throughout its whole length along the river and up to the precipitous wall on either side, is well timbered. Our camp at Soda Springs and, in fact, every camp we occupied was among the trees, with arrangements much the same as on the King's river trip. At every one we had our camp fire, our talks, stories, reminiscences, songs, music and merriment. The ladies had taken along a guitar, upon which several of

them were experts; all were good singers.

In the course of the next two or three weeks we went up the Kern river canyon to its head, and made several excursions up side canyons.

The most interesting and impressive and ever-to-be-remembered, the crowning of all our mountaineering, was the excursion to Mount Whitney. We started on this trip from our temporary camp at Junction meadows, where the Kern-Kaweah and Crabtree creeks come into the main river. It took us several days to climb up on horseback the rocky and precipitous eastern side of the canyon and get around over the rough and indistinct trails, to the neighborhood of Whitney, though the distance in a direct line was only six or eight miles. But, after much work, we succeeded, on the evening of August 10th, in reaching a beautiful meadow on Crabtree creek, about four miles below its source.

On the morning of August 11th Mr. Muir, who was the leader and mainspring of the entire trip, roused us at three o'clock. We had breakfast about four, and by five were on our horses. There were ten of us, including the four ladies and three boys. It was hardly light enough to see; but we managed to follow the dark trail up the creek, mounting and climbing among the rocks and along several lakes, soon getting above the timber line, with immense cliffs on both sides, until we came to a small rocky amphitheater, hemmed in by bare crags except where we entered it. This was as far as the horses could go. There was no way of tying our animals, except by stretching a long rope from one huge boulder to another and tying to that.

From there we had to mount on foot; and in several places we were obliged to use our hands, as well as our feet, and pull ourselves up. The summit was three thousand feet above us. We started on this climb at seven o'clock. The elevation at which we left the horses was twelve thousand feet. The boys hurried on first; then Dr. Gannett. Two of the ladies followed, and I tried to keep up with one of them, but about halfway up I found her pace too fast and told her to go on and leave me to have a good rest. Mr. Muir and the other two ladies were some

Worshipper at the base of the "General Sherman," Sequoia Gigantea,
in the Giant Forest, Tulare County, California
This view is from the northwest side of one of the grandest trees in the world
Here (left to right) are Dr. J. S. Merriam, Miss Wanda Muir, Miss Helen Muir, Dr. Gannett, and John Muir.

*On the summit of Mount Whitney. The tallest figure in the center is John Muir, naturalist and mountain climber;
next him, below the flag, is Dr. Henry Gannett geographer United States Geological Survey, and
next him, with one foot on the base of the monument, is Theodore H. Hittell,
the historian and author of the accompanying article.*

distance behind, taking it more slowly. By the time they came up I was ready to go ahead again and, taking a new start, I kept up with them, and at ten o'clock reached the summit, where the boys had been for half an hour or more. No one of the party, however, touched the highest point until after Miss Marian Hooker had done so. This honor was reserved for her on account of her being a grand niece of Professor Josiah D. Whitney, for whom the mountain was named.

As I was seventy-two years of age, and perhaps the oldest person that ever climbed Mount Whitney, there was a hurrah by the party as I reached the highest point and placed my hand upon the piled-up monument of rocks erected there. I had banteringly said, when we started in the morning, that I would dance a jig on the tip-top of the United States before night. The ladies insisted that a promise was a promise, so they commenced a rag-time song. The top of the helmet-shaped summit of the mountain, next the monument, is a large flat

granite rock. I felt invigorated with the pure air, and perhaps somewhat elated at the thought of having reached so high a point. At any rate, upon their beginning to sing, I commenced hopping around on the rock and at length "shuffled and pigeon-winged," when the infection caught the others: we were soon all dancing and pirouetting, and of course nearly bursting with laughter. Finally, taking hands, we had a general whirl, as near a "ladies chain" as the rock would allow. And we all vowed that we had never in our lives before taken higher steps than then and there.

The view from the summit of Whitney is very extensive and very grand. For panoramic effect it is not excelled. One feels as if he were looking down on everything else. We had a magnificent morning and our view was not interfered with. But as we were looking, clouds began to form over Owen's lake, which lay some two miles and a half in perpendicular distance below us, and to climb up the mountain sides; and some of the rugged peaks toward the north began to take on misty hoods. Usually there is a thunder and hail storm on these mountains every day about noon at that season of the year. We had been in several of these storms on the way up from Kern river; and the day before our ascent of Whitney there had been quite a severe one, which left considerable loose snow on the summit. When we made our ascent this snow was melting, and we were much annoyed by its caking on the bottom of our shoes and obliging us to scrape it off every ten or twenty steps of our climb. As there was a likelihood of another storm coming up, we stayed only an hour or two on the summit and then commenced our descent. This was much easier than the ascent, though in some places we had to be very careful. I went down most of the way almost like an avalanche, sometimes taking three or four steps in one, and reached the horses in an hour, making as good time and with as little fatigue as any other of the party.

On returning from Mt. Whitney back to Kern river we took the usually traveled trail, over a wonderfully wild country, by way of what is known as Whitney creek, which is the home, and the only original home of the golden trout. This splendid fish is in general not more than six or eight inches in length. It resembles the common brook trout in form, but is of a brilliant golden yellow color, particularly on its under side.

Six or eight miles before reaching the mouth of Whitney creek, which enters Kern river near Soda Springs, we came to several craters of extinct volcanoes, and were much interested in the red cinder cones, which they had left, and the lava-flows issuing from them, over or along which we traveled for a number of miles. It is a wonderfully attractive region. After leaving it, which we did with regret, we hastened back to our Soda Springs camp, from which we retraced our way back to Mineral King, where four of us took the stage and had a delightful ride down the Kaweah river to Visalia, which we reached on August 16th.

This trip I regard as the most enjoyable of my experience. It seems to me that it would be difficult to find any mountain country in the world more interesting. The views are unparalleled. We all pronounced them the grandest and most magnificent of the kind we had ever seen. And I think I may safely say that the day will come—and is not far distant—when this High Sierra scenery will be regarded generally as equaling, if not excelling, the Alps in attractiveness. #

Climbing

By JULIA BOYNTON GREEN

September 1906

I sit and gaze and think an old, old thought
  Here is the autumn hush, the autumn heat;
  Yonder the purple heights, when we entreat
Substantial succor, and the spiritual, wrought
When lowly things contemplate high. If, taught
  By my heart's zeal, I set determined feet
  Upon the mountain's path, however fleet
My steps, I know the splendid peaks I sought
Would mock me and elude. If still I pressed
  Up, up, through stream and thicket where have been
Pilgrims before, ambitious to be blest,
    What should I find, where I so oft have seen
    The rosy promise of the afterglow?
Stillness, and awful solitude, and snow.

President Roosevelt in the Sierra

By CARL E. ACKERMAN

July 1903

WHEN President Roosevelt reached the Yosemite Valley on his recent trip through the West, he issued an ultimatum. He would view the wonderland in his own way and with but one companion, John Muir. And, leaving his party to enjoy themselves in their own way, he mounted his horse and disappeared for three full days. With John Muir and two guides he climbed many trails, jumped logs, waded through snow until his travel-jaded spirit had rest.

On the morning of his return from Glacier Point to Yosemite Valley, he waxed enthusiastic. "This is the one day of my life," he exclaimed, "and one I will always remember with pleasure. Just think of where I was. Up there, amid the pines and silver firs, in the Sierra solitude, in a snowstorm, too, and without a tent, I passed one of the most pleasant days of my life." #

The President talking to Mr. Jorgensen, the artist, and his wife

John Muir and President Roosevelt cantering into Yosemite Valley after a ride down from Glacier Point

The motor turned toward the sun—the boiler white from reflected heat

Sunshine as Power

By ARTHUR INKERSLEY

April 1903

MANY attempts have been made at various times to use solar heat as a source of power. A century or more ago great burning glasses were constructed both in France and England which developed a heat intense enough to melt iron, gold and silver. At the Paris exposition of 1870 an exhibit that attracted much attention was a sun engine which furnished the power for a printing press. This device was improved by the American inventor Ericsson. But though these contrivances concentrated the sun's rays, generated steam and furnished the power to engines, they failed for various reasons to be practically available for ordinary use. They were too fragile, too delicate, too costly or what not.

At last a practical solution of the problem seems to have been reached. There has been constructed and set up on Edwin Cawston's ostrich farm at Pasadena, California, a contrivance which performs its work regularly and with certainty. From one hour and a half after sunrise to half an hour before sunset it drives a ten horse-power engine, raising fourteen hundred gallons of water twelve feet per minute. This is enough to irrigate about five hundred acres of deciduous trees, or three hundred acres planted with orange trees.

In outward appearance the solar motor—for that is its name—partakes of some of the characteristics of a windmill, a steam engine, a mirror maze and a merry-go-round. It is in shape like a section of a huge umbrella of very substantial construction, having a diameter of thirty-three feet at its widest part and of fifteen feet at its narrowest. The whole inside surface is covered with mirrors, each two feet long by three and a half inches wide. Nearly two thousand of these long, narrow mirrors catch the sun's rays and reflect their heat upon a slim boiler, which is just where the handle of the umbrella would be. The great reflector is set like an astronomical telescope, the axis being north and south, and the movement from east to west. It is so nicely adjusted that one person can easily move it in either direction. The boiler is thirteen and a half feet long and holds one hundred gallons of water, with eight cubic feet of steam space to spare. It is made of fire-box steel covered with lampblack. When the reflector is not working the boiler is quite inconspicuous, but when the concentrated heat from the mirrors is focused on it, it gleams like polished silver and is the most striking feature of the contrivance. In a little while it becomes so hot that a stick held against it smokes and bursts into flame. In almost an hour steam is generated and is conveyed from the head of the boiler through a flexible metal pipe to the cylinder of the steam engine, being thereafter used in the ordinary manner.

Though the solar motor at Pasadena develops only ten horse-power, it is already clear that plants able to develop one hundred horse-power are practicable. Many improvements are likely to be made in the present machine, especially in the direction of lessening its weight and cost, thus bringing it within the reach of people of moderate means.

The immense advantage possessed by the solar motor over most other sources of power is that it requires no fuel, which in arid regions is a scarce and expensive commodity. #

Supreme Among Small Cars

MODEL M VICTORIA BODY

MODEL M COUPE

Doesn't the fact that last year the sale of Cadillacs of the 10 horse power type exceeded the combined sale of *any three* models of other makes carry a pretty strong conviction of superiority?

This record is a result of the wonderful efficiency of the Cadillac single-cylinder engine—a bit of mechanism so perfect in construction that it has successfully withstood the test of five years of severe service in thousands of cars. Thus while others were experimenting and changing, we stuck to time-tried principles we *knew* were correct, until to-day there is absolutely no question as to the supremacy of the

Single-Cylinder

CADILLAC

MODEL M STRAIGHT LINE BODY

MODEL K

It is the favorite among owners of large touring cars who want a thoroughly dependable small car for general utility purposes. It is the choice of those who know motor quality. Every day adds to its prestige and every day more forcibly proves that the Single-Cylinder Cadillac is THE IDEAL CAR for those who desire a motor vehicle which will afford the maximum of pleasure and service with the minimum of expense, the car which affords all there is in motoring—except the troubles.

Your dealer will give you a demonstration that will reveal some interesting facts.

Model M—10 h. p. 4-passenger Car, Straight Line or
    Victoria Body.   (Catalog M W)
Model M Coupe—10 h. p.   (Catalog M W)
Model K—10 h. p. Runabout.   (Catalog M W)
Model G –20 h. p. 4-Cylinder Touring Car. (Catalog G W)
Model H—30 h. p. 4-Cylinder Touring Car. (Catalog H W)

Send for Special Catalog of car in which you are interested, as above designated.

CADILLAC MOTOR CAR CO., Detroit, Mich.

Member Asso. Licensed Auto. Mfrs,

Motor Touring in California

By Arthur Inkersley

December 1903

NO state in the union offers greater variety of scenery for the automobile tourist than California. In the interior valleys he can find great stretches of level road on which he will be tempted—forgetting that there are such things as speed limits—to "let her out" for an exhilarating spin. In winter and spring he may run along highways bordered for mile after mile with orchards in all the glory of full bloom. In summer he may traverse roads which parallel vast grain fields growing yellow for the harvest, and in autumn he may see almost every product of temperate or semi-tropical climes in the perfection of maturity. If he is a lover of mountain scenery, he can find the Coast Range or the Sierras in almost every county; or, if he is in search of grades that will test the hill-climbing powers of his machine, or of deep sand that will try his temper and patience, he can find these things too. He may tour through the redwoods of Mendocino, wind his way among the sugar-pines of Siskiyou or the giant trees of Mariposa grove. The Yosemite has been entered several times by man in the motor-car. At Monterey the seventeen-mile drive along the shore of the Pacific furnishes a series of marine views that for sheer natural beauty can hardly be surpassed anywhere in the world.

A motorist who traveled about fifteen hundred miles in his Packard touring car in Southern California reports:

On Glacier Point, Yosemite Valley. Lippincott Photo

Along the Russian River

"I must say that the roads are much better than my best expectations. The condition of the roads in general is very much better than that of the roads in New England; and the village councils have not gotten the foolish idea that automobiles have no right to travel. All the inhabitants along the country roads will do anything to assist one."

The first automobile in San Francisco was owned by the late Charles L. Fair, who had a strongly-developed mania for fast traveling—a mania that cost himself and his wife their lives. Like his powerful launch Lucero, his motor-car was of the gasoline type. Then he became the owner of an electric automobile. A few months before his death, near Paris, he brought to San Francisco a fine racing machine, the product of the famous Panhard-Levassor factory, and a Parisian chauffeur to operate it. With the exception of Mr. Fair's two motor-cars, almost all the automobiles owned in California then were steam carriages, manufactured by the Locomobile, Mobile or White companies. A gasoline touring car was almost unknown, and nearly all the vehicles were light run-abouts.

At the present time however, the steam carriages, except for heavy passenger service and livery work, for which they are excellently adapted, seem to be dropping out of favor. They are being supplanted by gasoline cars, many of the well-known makers having agents in San Francisco. Of these the best known are the Winton Touring Car, the Packard, the Oldsmobile, the Cadillac, the St. Louis, the Haynes-Apperson, the Auto-Car, the Peerless and the Toledo.

The Automobile Club of California has directed its attention chiefly to securing favorable legislation in the counties round San Francisco. Half a dozen times or so in a year the club holds runs to San Mateo, Menlo Park, Haywards, or some other convenient spot. The automobile men rendezvous on Van Ness avenue and run out under the direction of a captain, who heads the line and whose car must not be passed. After the rendezvous luncheon is served, and after a rest the return trip is begun, each owner proceeding as he likes. Occasionally, a run to Cliff House and back is made in an evening. The clubmen gather in one of the large rooms, enjoy a little supper and music, and discuss matters of interest to the fraternity.

The most important and interesting automobile tournament so far held in California took place in August last at Hotel Del Monte, Monterey. It was under the management of the Automobile Club of California. The automobilists from San Francisco and neighborhood started Thursday, August 6th, reaching San Jose that evening. There they found the Hotel Vendome beautifully decorated in their honor, and were received by the automobilists of San Jose and vicinity. At various times next morning up to 10 o'clock they started on the road to Del Monte. All surmounted the steep San Juan grade and reached Del Monte that evening or early next morning. On Saturday they watched the last match of the polo tournament and the pony races, while on Sunday afternoon they went round the famous seventeen-mile drive. On Monday a program of ten races, some of them requiring three heats on account of the number of contestants, was successfully run off. The machine that attracted most attention was the forty horse-power Mors, which won the ten-mile race, open to machines of any type or power, in 13 minutes, 21 1-5 seconds, the fastest mile being done in 1:18. In a five-mile exhibition against time, it covered one mile in 1:15 4-5, winning the cup offered by the Automobile Club for a mile in 1:17 or better. The time for the five miles was 6:21. The Owners' Race, a handicap event, was won by an Orient buckboard, which seemed to be on the track all the day. The driver entered every event for which his rig was eligible and reeled off miles regularly in a second or two above two minutes.

Nearly all the other events, except those for gasoline machines only, were won by a White touring car, or a White stanhope entered by the Southern California Automobile Club. A cup was presented for the fastest mile, 1:19, made in the morning of the meet, and for covering ten miles in 14:06 1-5.

On Tuesday there was a hill climbing contest on the hill near the Military Reservation at Pacific Grove, the distance being about a thousand yards and the grade ten per cent. A Toledo car won in 2:06 2-5. #

Motor Touring to Yosemite

By WALLACE W. EVERETT

January 1905

THERE can be no description by words or pen of the pleasures of motoring to Yosemite. The canvases of a Hill have accomplished much but the motorist must guide his car up the heights, along the levels and under the spreading boughs of the sheltering trees ere he can realize what God and Nature have given him in the glories of the Yosemite.

In taking the Yosemite trip great care should be observed in the preliminary inspection of the working parts of your car; greater in fact than any other touring possibility would exact, for the grades are heavy and the strain practically unequaled. Then again see that your gasoline shipments have gone on ahead for the high altitudes demand more fuel than the sea-level stretches. You can obtain water all along the route but your telephone communication ceases between the valley and Groveland, situated between Priest and Hamilton.

From San Francisco to Oakland by boat, you commence the auto trip. Through the leafy quietude of the Niles canyon to the commodious hotel at Byron Springs, you make your first day's pilgrimage over roads without equal in this country and enjoy your night's rest with all the comforts of your home. You have been through the passes of the grain-covered Coast range over grades that cause no trouble and the morning finds you on your way to Stockton. Then on to Knights Ferry and you end your day's exertions at Chinese Camp, the scene of wide-awake mining operations. The road, ranging along by the Eagle Shawmut mine takes you to the base of Priest hill where

A party from San Francisco in the Valley—Yosemite Falls in the background

the grade is steady, steep and heavy, but, if your car be of adequate power, you ascend with low speed gears grinding out their protest at the surmounting of an obstacle which would tire the best of Kentucky's blue-grass stock and which displays to best advantage the reliability of the twentieth century auto car.

The hotel at the summit proves a godsend for the tired driver and his party, while the next morning with its invigorating mountain ozone seems to welcome the final effort to reach Nature's paradise, the Yosemite. You have your first impression of the Sierra giant redwood, which you encounter between the summit and Crockers. The grades are most exacting but surmountable with your twelve-horse-power car. Down the gradient you spin for fourteen miles when the floor of the great valley meets you with its level stretch of sandy roadway. You have reached your goal and tomorrow promises a festival of scenery unsurpassed the world over. The chuff-chuff of your car places you at the base of the falls of the Yosemite where the roar of the vast falling waters makes conversation a trial. Slowly moving down the floor of the valley, you reach the mirroring surface of the lakes at the northern end and have passed by the glistening falls of Nevada and Vernal. You have labored to place your car where it is, but that is all forgotten in the vista of attractiveness that daily opens to your amazed eyes. #

The Islands of the Blest

By George Sterling

December 1907

In Carmel pines the summer wind
  Sings like a distant sea.
O harps of green, your murmurs find
  An echoing chord in me!

On Carmel shore the breakers moan
  Like pines that breast a gale.
O whence, ye winds and billows, flown
  To cry your wordless tale?

Perchance the crimson sunsets drown
  In waters whence ye sped;
Perchance the sinking stars go down
  To seek the Isles ye fled.

Sometimes from ocean dusks I seem
  To glimpse their crystal walls
Dim jewels of mirage that gleam
  In twilight's western halls.

Sometimes I hear below the moon
  A music that pursues—
A wraith of melody, that soon
  I doubt, and doubting, lose.

Those palmy shores no prow may find,
But once it seemed to me
A ghost of fragrance roamed the wind,
  Yet was not of the sea.

What tho' my tale the seaman scorns?
  The Chart of Dreams, unrolled,
Attests their havens' jasper bourns,
  Their reefs of sunken gold.

I do not know what lonely strands
  Await the wingéd star;
I only know their evening sands
  Seem wonderful and far.

Have You a Little "Shaver" In Your Home?

We mean a

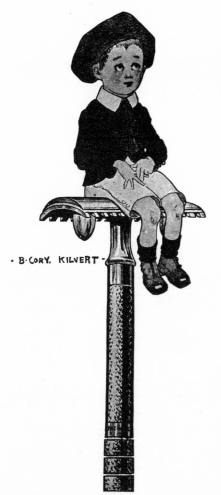

Gillette Safety Razor

of course ——

(With apologies to FAIRY SOAP.)

No Stropping, No Honing---
Just Lather and Shave

THERE are a good many reasons why there should be a Gillette in your home.

In the first place "he" ought to shave himself and you ought to see that he does. There are many reasons why — and none in favor of the barber shop habit except a mistaken feeling that it's easier that way. It used to be, possibly, but that was before the Gillette came.

A GILLETTE Safety Razor and the twelve double-edged blades that come with it will solve your shaving problem for months to come. Each blade will give from 15 to 20 clean shaves of comfort. When at last it commences to "pull" a little, throw away the blade, like an old pen, and slip in a new one. The razor itself will last a life-time—extra blades cost about 2 cents a week—50 cents for package of ten.

If your dealer doesn't keep them, send us $5 for standard "triple-silver" plated set in handsome velvet-lined, leather-covered case. If after 30 days' trial you are not satisfied we will refund your money.

WE have bought the entire edition of "Science of Shaving," a new work, the first text-book ever written, we believe, on the care of the face in its relation to shaving. It is worth a good deal to every man who shaves or lets others shave him—no matter how much he thinks he knows about it already. Fully illustrated with photographs and drawings.

In the first thousand copies of the edition we have added some pages about the Gillette Safety Razor with pictures and prices of the different styles. While these copies last, a postal card will bring you one free, with our compliments.

Send for this Book To-day

A copy will be mailed free to any man who cares for his face or his feelings, or to any woman who cares for the face or the feelings of any man.

Gillette Sales Company
229 Times Building   **New York**

SCIENCE of SHAVING

· B·CORY· KILVERT ·

Winnedumah — A Paiute Legend

By MARY AUSTIN

June 1904

This the tale of Winnedumah
Whom the Paiute clans revere,
But you must not tell the story
When the snakes can overhear,
When the tall grass makes a cover
Where the spotted snakes may hide,
For the snakes are mischief makers,
Double-tongued and evil-eyed.

But when twilights chill and deepen,
When the streams run scant and small,
When the frost has nipped the piñons
And they hear the wild goose call,
When the children by their mothers
Snuggle closer in the byre,
When the young men come from hunting,
And the old men stir the fire;

Then they tell of Winnedumah,
How he lived and what he wrought,
Dealing straightly with his people,
Speaking truth as leaders ought.
Winnedumah and his brother—
Skilled in magic arts was he—
And they taught the Paiute peoples
What a brother's love should be.

C.J Hittell.

When the warlike, fierce Shoshones
Broke their ancient metes and bounds,
Slew the red deer, chased the blacktail
On the Paiute hunting grounds,
When they stole the piñon harvest,
Stopped with earth the mountain springs,
Winnedumah put on war paint,
Put on plumes of eagles' wings;

Set his braves to track them featly,
Stalked them as they stalked the deer
By the high and windy headlands
By the passes straight and sheer.
All by night the women watching
Saw their signals in the sky,
Heard by day above the ambush
The beholding eagles cry.

When at last they drew to battle
Sped the fight in valiant part,
'Til about the hour of sunset
Flew a virus-venomed dart,
Struck at Winnedumah's brother—
Vultures wheeling heard the cry,
Heard the death wail, when the Paiutes
Saw their magic-maker die.

Then their hearts were turned to water,
Since no art the Healer saves;
Vultures wheeling slow and stately
Saw the fleeing of the braves.
Only Winnedumah lingered,
Standing on the skyline clear;
Lingered, calling for his brother
Who could neither come nor hear.

Lingered, questing through the twilight
Till he found his brother dead,
Saw the black plumes of his warriors
Through the cedars as they fled,
Saw the wattled huts of willow
Huddled on the mesa brown,
Saw the hot-eyed, fierce Shoshones
Come like wolves to pull him down.

Then the faithful Winnedumah,
Owning neither fault nor fear,
Cried to Taupee, god of Paiutes,

Saying, "Taupee, Father, hear!"
Swift the word sped, swift the answer;
Taupee touched him where he stood,
Changed him to the granite boulder
High above the swathing wood.

Gray at twilight, white at noonday,
Faithful Winnedumah stands,
But the thieving, fierce Shoshones
Come no more to vex our lands;
For the wrath of Taupee caught them,
Plunging headlong down the hill,
Changed them all to yellow pine trees,
Gnarled pine trees, standing still.

Then the little Paiute children
When the tale is ended quite,
Turn from leaning on their mothers
To look out across the night;
Then they look at Winnedumah
Darkling through the alpen glow;
Then they count the wicked pine trees
Up the stream-side all a-row;

Then they snuggle to their mothers;
Then they huddle in the byre;
Then they hear the back log singing;
Hear the pine sap in the fire;
Hear again of Winnedumah
Whom the Paiute clans revere—
But you must not tell the story
When the snakes can overhear.

Note: Travelers over Kearsarge Pass, of California's Sierra Nevada, coming from Kings river, are always impressed by the skyward pointing granite pinnacle directly on the crest of the opposite Inyo range. It stands out singly against the pale desert sky and is a conspicuous landmark far up and down Owens valley and from any point on the easterly Sierra. Just above Independence toward Kearsarge, bordering the stream that runs down from it, is a single file of pines of a variety not found elsewhere in that vicinity. The presence of both the pines and the great boulder are accounted for in the preceding legend, related by the Paiute Indians of Owens valley. Concerning the spelling of the tribal name, Paiute, in place of Pah-ute, has been adopted by the Indian commissioners, while the United States geological survey prefers Pahute. #

F O R D

PROMPT DELIVERIES

TWO ERRORS CAN'T CORRECT ONE MISTAKE

COLONEL INGERSOLL USED TO SAY "To be a successful liar one must have a good memory; for one lie will only fit another lie made for that express purpose, whereas a truth will fit any other truth in the universe."

WE HEAR A LOT THESE DAYS about "hand made" motor cars—its funny, but the same concerns who, a year ago, prated of "quality not quantity" as if the two were incompatible, now build 1,000 or 2,000 cars per year and still expect you to believe it is "hand work," "personal supervision" and all that sort of rot.

FORD CARS ARE MANUFACTURED—have been made in immense quantities and by modern American methods from the first. And the first FORD ever made is still giving excellent service—what of the "cut and try" contraptions made in that same year?

HAND WORK AT BEST is but a series of mechanical inaccuracies, each made to fit, as nearly as may be, another. Ingersoll would call them mechanical fibs; and making one mechanical fib to fit another does not cancel the error any more than two lies make a truth. And when you want to replace a part, the maker will need a mighty fine "memory" to give you one that will fit—you'll find he forgot.

WHEREVER THE "PERSONAL EQUATION" is permitted to enter, absolute uniformity and accuracy are impossible. Did you ever read a letter written on a hand made typewriter? Would you buy one for $100? Certainly not. Yet it would cost $10,000 to make one. That's the way with "hand made" cars—the only evidence of superiority is the fancy price. Superior efficiency—it is not there.

SIX-CYLINDER FORD CARS are the product of the brightest minds, the most efficient organization, the ripest experience and the most modern manufacturing plant known to the industry. Every pound of steel is made especially for the Ford Company, under personal supervision of Ford experts, from Ford formulae and finally heat-treated in Ford furnaces. No other concern in the business can make that claim.

A $5,000 CAR IN EFFICIENCY—Luxurious appointments, performance, and endurance. The Ford price is made possible by Ford methods and Ford quantity production. We could command the fancy price too—but we are looking further ahead than a year or two.

ADD TO THE QUALITY OF THE CAR "Ford courtesy"—the replacement promptly, cheerfully, gratis, of any part that shows a defect in work or material—and the value can not be equalled. "Charge it to the advertising account" is our way of disposing of this item.

1907 Ford Model K—6-cylinder motor. 40 h.p. at the wheels; will climb anything the wheels can hold on the "high;" six to sixty miles per hour by throttle control alone—no need for transmission, except for reversing; two complete and separate systems of ignition—magneto and storage battery—jump spark; two sets of plugs; 120-in. wheel base; 34-in. x 4-in. tires; all the latest features and improvements; the silence of an electric, the flexibility, the steady pulling power of a "six;" the simplicity and reliability of a FORD. In quality, performance and endurance a $5,000 car.

A DEMONSTRATION IS A REVELATION

PRICE, $2,800—with top and full touring equipment, $3,000.
FORD RUNABOUTS (4-cylinder), Model N. $600; Model R, "edition de luxe," $750.

Ford Motor Company, Factory and Main Office, Detroit, Mich.

BRANCH RETAIL STORES:
NEW YORK, PHILADELPHIA, BOSTON, CHICAGO, BUFFALO, CLEVELAND, DETROIT AND KANSAS CITY.
Canadian trade supplied by Ford Motor Company of Canada, Walkerville, Ont.

The Stanford Jewels

By DAVID STARR JORDAN

February 1907

THERE was once a man—a real man, vigorous, wealthy and powerful. He loved his wife greatly, for she, wise, loyal, devoted, was worthy of such love. And because among all the crystals in all the world the diamond is the hardest and sparkles the brightest, and because the ruby is most charming, and the emerald gentlest—the man bought gifts of these all for his wife.

As the years passed a great sorrow came to them; their only child died in the glory of his youth. In their loneliness there came to these two the longing to help other children, to use their wealth and power to aid the youth of future generations to better and stronger life. They lived in California and they loved California; and because California loved them, as she loves all her children, this man said "The children of California shall be my children." To make this true in very fact he built for them a beautiful "Castle in Spain," with cloisters and towers, and "red tiled roofs against the azure sky"—for "skies are bluest in the heart of Spain." This castle, the Castle of Hope, which they called the University, they dedicated to all who might enter its gates, and it became to them the fulfilment of the dream of years—a dream of love and hope, of faith in God and good will toward men.

In the course of time the man died. The power he bore vanished; his wealth passed to other hands; the work he had begun seemed likely to fail. But the woman rose from her second great sorrow and set herself bravely to the task of completing the work as her husband had planned it. "The children of California shall be my children"—that thought once spoken could never be unsaid. The doors of the castle once opened could never be closed. To those who helped her in these days she said: "We may lose the farms, the railways, the bonds, but still the jewels remain. The University can be kept alive by these till the skies clear and the money which was destined for the fu-

ture shall come into the future's hands. The University shall be kept open. When there is no other way, there are still the jewels."

Because there always remained this last resource, the woman never knew defeat. No one can who strives for no selfish end. "God's errands never fail," and her errand was one of good will and mercy. And when the days were darkest, the time came when it seemed the jewels must be sold. Across the sea to the great city this sorrowful, heroic woman journeyed alone with the bag of jewels in her hand that she might sell them to the money changers that flocked to the Queen's Jubilee. Sad, pathetic mission, fruitless, in the end, but full of all promise for the future of the University, founded in faith and hope and love—the trinity, St. Paul says, of things that abide.

But the jewels were not sold, save only a few of them, and these served a useful purpose in beginning anew the work of building the University. Better times came. The money of the estate, freed from litigation, became available for its destined use. The jewels found their way back to California to be held in reserve against another time of need.

A noble church was erected—one of the noblest in the land, a fitting part of the beautiful dream castle, the University. It needed to make it perfect the warmth of ornamentation, the glory of the old masters, who wrought "when art was religion." To this end the jewels were dedicated. It was an appropriate use, but the need again passed. Other resources were found to adorn the church—to fill its windows with beautiful pictures, to spread upon its walls exquisite mosaics like those of St. Mark, rivaling even the precious stones of Venice.

In the course of time the woman died also. She had the satisfaction of seeing the buildings of the University completed, the cherished plans of her husband, to which she had devoted anxious years, fully carried out. Death came to her in a foreign land, but in a message written before her departure to be read at the laying of the corner-stone of the great library, she made known the final destiny of the jewels. She directed that they should be sold and their value made a permanent endowment of the library of the University.

And so the jewels have at last come to be the enduring possession of all the University—of all who may tread these fields or enter these corridors. In the memory of the earlier students they stand for the Quadrangle, whose doors they kept open, and for the adornment of the church, which shall be to all generations of students a source of joy and rest, a refining and uplifting influence. To the students who are to come in future days the message of the jewels will be read in the books they study within these walls and the waves of their influence spreading out shall touch the uttermost parts of the earth.

They say there is a language of precious stones, but I know that they speak in diverse tongues. Some diamonds tell strange tales, but not these diamonds. In the language of the jewels of Stanford may be read the lessons of faith, of hope and good will. They tell how Stanford was founded in love of the things that abide. #

Aftermath:

Out of my life has gone
So much that made it worth living,
I watch with stark eyes for the dawn
Hoping, despairing, forgiving.

Hoping that Hope may live;
Despairing lest fate should us sever;
Forgiving what e'er is to forgive —
Forever and ever and ever.

Chas. Warren Stoddard

(Written following the recent death
of the author's father.)

September 1908

The Valley of the Shadow

A Tale of the San Francisco Fire and Earthquake

By CHARLES GILMAN NORRIS

June 1906

WILBUR CLAXTON paused at the corner of Market and Montgomery and watched a late cable car rumbling by on its way to the ferry. He was deliberating whether he should go home. Market Street, uptown, presented an inviting appearance. A number of electric signs were still glowing and there were many pleasure seekers abroad. Across the street a party came out of the Palace, where they had been supping in the Palm Garden; they clambered into an automobile and whizzed uptown, the siren of the machine wailing musically.

Claxton drew out his watch and found it was nearly one. Abruptly he turned down Montgomery towards his office. He could not go home until he had obtained a better control of himself. This news of Deering's would not adjust itself in his mind. He let himself into the big office building with his pass key and began to climb the eleven flights of massive steps. He had no difficulty in finding his own door, in spite of the fact that the lights were not on, for he could easily see his name, "Wilbur Claxton, M. D.," in the lower right hand corner of the door marked, "Private."

He went to the window before turning the button of the electric lights and leaned his forehead against the chilled glass. It felt very refreshing to his burning head. Far below him lay the city, the roofs of the houses jogging against each other, crowding and elbowing one another, some towering above the others, some hugging the lee of more substantial buildings and others clinging to the perpendicular wall of a giant sky-scraper. His office was in the rear, but he could see portions of the streets nearby which dissected the confused mass. A little further on, however, the buildings seemed to wedge themselves into a confused tangle and jam that ended abruptly at the water front.

Claxton was not in the mood to appreciate. His heart was consumed with a fierce jealousy. He had controlled himself for the last hour or so, but now, alone in his office, he gave way entirely to the agony of his pent-up feelings. It seemed preposterous that Frances should have consented to marry Deering. Deering was his best friend, it was true. All three of them had chummed together while he had lived in the East, but he had always thought that it was generally understood that he and Frances would one day marry. He had not spoken about the matter to her, but he believed that she had always known it. He considered that no man had the right to ask a woman to marry until he had sufficient means to properly take care of her. He had returned to San Francisco a year sooner than he had expected in order that this very thing might sooner be accomplished. In the last two years he had succeeded beyond his hopes and the summer was to see the fulfillment of his ambition. He had even picked out the house where they were to live. And now Deering, his best friend, came between them!

He turned from the window and flung himself into the chair at his desk, burying his throbbing head in his arms.

"Deering! Why should it have been Deering?" he found himself saying again and again. It was a real regret to Claxton that the ability to hate Deering was denied him. He struggled with himself, but to no purpose. He recalled, with no bitterness of feeling, Deering's jubilation and unsuppressed pleasure when he had broken the news to him a few hours before.

Deering had arrived that Tuesday afternoon from the East and Claxton had at once appropriated him. It was his first visit to San Francisco, and Claxton had determined that he should receive his impression of Bohemian San

Francisco under personal supervision. Of course, he could have dined him at the Palace, taken him to hear Caruso in Carmen and then to supper at Zinkand's or the Tavern, but he knew that Deering was quite familiar with that kind of life. Claxton, therefore, lured him from his hotel and piloted him towards the other end of Kearny Street, where in the midst of the Mexican quarter, opposite the old jail, he introduced him to Mathias. That restaurant keeper had immediately risen to the occasion. They dined in the back room, papered with wonderful lithographs of famous bull fights, and between the warbles of Mathias' mocking bird they had feasted on mysterious peppery Mexican dishes with odd sonorous names: chile con carne, enchiladas, frijoles, tortillas and tamales.

When the seemingly endless dinner was done and they had inspected Mathias' souvenir book and had performed all the rites which were prescribed, Claxton and Deering found themselves again in the street. It was difficult to believe the sight that greeted them was a part of a great American city. Everywhere was a strange mingling of Italians and Mexicans, a fantastic combination of foreign and American dress, and a mixed babble of unfamiliar languages. A romantic picturesque atmosphere pervaded everything; children laughed and capered in the streets; a guitar hummed in a doorway; the men lounged and smoked their cigarettes, and one felt the gaze of half-curious eyes from the shade of mantillas.

The character of the people changed farther down the street. The quaint atmosphere faded. Cigar stands and restaurants with menus on blackboards in front, succeeded. Pawn shops, saloons and shooting galleries took the place of the quaint quarters of the Mexicans and Italians. It had been noisy and crowded there, and Claxton was glad on Deering's account when they found Portsmouth Square—the old plaza—with its thick dark foliage and refreshing odor of wet grass, where always the golden ship of Robert Louis Stevenson sailed its never-ending voyage of commemoration.

They sauntered across the square, and the scene abruptly changed, as if they were in a ceaselessly shifting panorama. The streets became narrow and dingy, the houses squalid

and huddled together. Everywhere, however, bright flashes of brilliant color relieved their gloomy and sinister aspect. Large pot-bellied lanterns, red with lettering, swung from balconies; yellow and vermillion strips of paper, bearing odd symbols and characters, were pasted on windows and lintels, while queer green pottery and gay silks could be seen in profusion inside the gaudy shops. There was a strange mingling of odors, a smell of musk and incense, of fish and vegetables, of dark, uncleanly alleys, of stale tobacco and burning punk. The streets were crowded with a blue-bloused, hurrying throng that shuffled past, silent, indifferent.

This was Chinatown, a part of the city Claxton dearly loved. They visited the gilded restaurant above the plaza and had tea and then went to the Joss House and Chinese theater, and finally to Sing Fat's, where Deering loaded himself with jade rings, chiseled ivories and royal colored embroideries. When they had returned to civilization, Claxton suggested visiting the top of the Call Building, as it was early yet and he wished Deering to see San Francisco from that vantage. They found a table near a window of the restaurant that occupied the top floor, and there for two hours they had sat gazing over the city which lay below them.

It was here that Deering had told Claxton the news of his intended marriage to Frances Stanyan. The evening had been so perfect, so ideal, that the blow was all the more brutal. Deering did not spare him. Claxton listened very pale, slowly turning his spoon in his untouched coffee. Then had come the painful moment when he must offer his congratulations. He was grateful that his voice did not falter. He shut his teeth and determined that Deering should not guess his pain. But after a while the strain became too great. He complained that he was tired. Deering accused himself for being thoughtless and they walked to the Palace and parted with a final "See you in the morning." Then it was that Claxton had sought the solitude of his office.

What made Claxton's sorrow more acute was the suddenness with which the news had come. He drained his cup of bitterness and grief to its dregs and it carried him down into the pit. He was left without consolation or hope. The thought of the long, long days, weeks and months ahead of him when he would be sitting as he did then, his head bowed upon his hands, wretched and unhappy, was utterly intolerable. He could foresee the sorrow, the heartache, the unending, unallayed agony that he must endure day after day without any hope, or other interest, or surcease to his pain. His spirit rebelled. Why, he asked himself, why was this necessary, why must he go on playing a role, acting a deception, living a lie, like a Canio in another Pagliacci?

The miniature steel clock on the medicine case ticked constantly; the regular beat of the passing seconds was the only sound that could be heard. An appalling silence pervaded the office, the building, the empty street below. The moon, hidden every few minutes by patches of fog, now threw a bright square of white light on the floor and part of the desk. The hours dragged on in deep silence. There was no movement—the dark office might have been a tomb.

Abruptly the man rose, and turning on the electric light, he examined the medicine case. He read the labels on the vials. What he wanted evidently was not there. He went slowly back to his desk and dropped into his chair. As he did so he noticed his surgeon's case lying in front of him. Slowly he opened and took from the case two surgical instruments, a pair of scissors and a long steel miniature knife.

The only thing which might have sustained such a nature as Claxton's in an hour like this, he entirely lacked. So morbid and so despondent a disposition demanded the consolation of a religious faith. But this he did not possess. He had always claimed that he was an atheist, a scoffer. He frankly admitted to himself that the deed he contemplated was cowardly, but the future, the years of silent suffering, terrified him. And it was so simple and easy to end it all.

He wondered if Frances Stanyan would despise him when she heard. She could never understand the motive of his act, unless from the fact that the deed followed so closely Deering's confession. He suddenly determined to write to her and tell her how much he had loved her and how empty life seemed without the thought of sharing it with her. There was no reproach in his words, only a bitter self-accusation that he had not told her of his great love before it had

been too late. What a fool he had been! Writing down his thoughts seemed to intensify his grief, but it was still a comfort to open his whole heart to her. Once the flood gates were opened, however, his pent-up passions, his fierce staggering love rushed forth, carrying him outside of himself, breaking the bands of his self-control, crushing and beating him down until he flung out his arms and fell moaning and sobbing across the crumpled sheet of the unfinished letter.

It was sometime before he gained control of himself. The thought that he must hasten if he did not wish to be interrupted during the act he contemplated helped him. It was shortly after five and only a few hours remained. His stenographer usually came at eight-thirty. He turned to wash his face in the basin in the corner when he became aware of a low reverberating rumble; the floor under his feet began to tremble, and then—the whole building was rocking and swaying. He had a brief moment of ominous suspense, then there rushed upon him a terrifying realization that something of portentous consequence was about to occur. His mind no sooner grasped this idea than it seemed as though there began the crash of worlds. The building shook and rocked. The bric-a-brac ornaments slid from their places and broke upon the floor. He could hear the beams and girders creak and groan under the mighty strain. He staggered back to the desk and fiercely gripped it to retain his footing. The ink was slopping over. Abruptly the electric lights went out. At the same moment the massive bookcases toppled forward, their doors swung open and with a grinding sound of broken glass, snapping woodwork and falling books, the whole mass crashed down. There was a second's cessation, and Claxton had a fleeting impression that the force of the earthquake was spent. He had hardly opened his eyes, however, when there came a sudden uplift, a mighty twist and wrench, and the structure of steel and stone under him swayed and tottered. Crash after crash followed. He could hear masses of bricks falling about him, the dead impact of enormous weights, the splintering of wood and the crumbling of masonry. Claxton fell upon the floor and with his hands clasped above his head, waited for the end. "Good God! How long is this going to last?" he muttered.

As suddenly as it had begun the earthquake ceased. Claxton did not move; every moment he expected it to recommence. But as the seconds passed he relaxed his tense posture and stretched himself upon the floor in the debris of plaster, glass and broken china. He was too weak to find his feet. He knew he was safe, however, and uninjured. A dreadful fear seized him. Had San Francisco withstood the shock? Had the city survived? He struggled to his feet and stumbled to the window.

A cry of joy escaped him! There the city was—safe, uninjured, the buildings standing intact, shoulder to shoulder, unconquered and undaunted. They seemed to look back at Claxton with a glad, triumphant smile. As far as he could see, down to the ferry and the wharves and on the south side of Market, stood the brave buildings, like loyal ranks of a great army. Not one had faltered; courageous and steadfast they had stood together against the force of the destroying earthquake. They had won the fight. San Francisco, his city, was still there. A few chimneys were gone, a few cornices had fallen, but the city, the city, the heart of Bohemia still stood!

When he had recovered himself sufficiently to again look out of the window, he could see a number of half-clad figures huddling in the middle of the street, gazing in terror at the buildings about them, waiting for a recurrence of the earthquake. He could see them frantically gesticulating. A group of them were on their knees, praying.

In looking out over the city again he could see that more damage had been done than he had first supposed. The shot-tower was gone and over in the Mission he could see the shattered steeple of a church. The streets, too, were strewn with broken masonry, mortar and debris. The ferry tower was intact; he could see it plainly from his point of vantage, but the flagstaff at its top, from which the time-ball fell at noon, was badly bent and careened outward at an absurd angle.

His eye was suddenly arrested by something that he had not before noticed. A small black cloud of smoke was rising from a building on the south side of Market street. There was another beyond, and there another, and another, and another! The city was on fire! At that moment he could hear the fire bells, and a little later an engine and a hook-and-ladder dashed down Market, followed by a second and then a third. Here came a fire chief's automobile, the clang of the bell sounding clear and ominous in the early morning air. A mounted policeman galloped past. Then came the people, crowds of them, pouring down from uptown, filling the sidewalks, hurrying along to view the effect of the earthquake and the progress of the fires that had burst out simultaneously in an alarming number of places.

A mist of dark smoke hid the street from Claxton's sight. In an instant he had flung open the window and was leaning out. Yes, the building immediately below him was on fire. A smoking engine pulled up at the curb, the men tumbling from their places. In a second's time the hose was dragged from the hose-cart and the long ladders run out. Firemen armed with axes disappeared in the building and a moment later came the cry, "Turn on the water!" It was repeated again and again in the crowd that had already collected to watch the flames.

A fireman suddenly appeared on the roof below. He shouted something to the group of men about the hydrant. There was no answer.

"What's the matter?"

A man crossed the street on the run, his hands to his mouth.

"No water! The main's broken!"

It was some moments before the full significance of this burst upon Claxton. The shock of the earthquake had broken the water mains. There was no water! These flames, then, could not be checked—nothing could stop them! They would sweep from one end of the city to the other!

Claxton imagined he had been frightened when the shock of the earthquake had come, but now he knew what real terror was. He must make his escape at once if he did not wish to be burned alive. He turned swiftly from the window, hurriedly threw a number of his surgical instruments, his records and what else he could lay hands on, into his small doctor's bag and tied the balance up with a piece of window cord. Then with a parting glance he seized the knob of the door. It refused to open! Claxton dropped his bundles and put his whole strength against it, but to no purpose. He studied it a moment in perplexity, then he caught sight of the woodwork at the cap of the door and realized in a moment that he was a prisoner. The earthquake had caused the whole building to settle and the door was jammed fast.

In the next few minutes Claxton quite lost his head. He raged and stormed. He beat his fists against the door until his knuckles bled; he kicked it viciously and tore at the panels with his nails. Suddenly his strength left him. He sank down weakly upon the plaster-covered floor. What was the use? Escape seemed hopeless. His building would soon be burning, if it were not in flames already. He crawled to the window again, but below him the smoke was so dense he could see nothing. He shut the window to keep the air as free from the suffocating fumes as possible. As he did so his eyes caught the unfinished letter on the desk.

With a rush the memories of the night came back upon him. The surgical instruments still lay where he left them. What was he trying to escape from? From one agony to another? He had been planning his death an hour before, and now the instinct of self-preservation had been so strong within him that it had been the one dominating impulse. Here before him lay the means of escape. He knew that time was precious. His energy returned to him. In a moment he had removed his coat and cut away the sleeve of his shirt and laid bare his left arm to the shoulder on the desk, and without a moment's hesitation drove the blade of the surgeon's knife into the flesh at the bend of the arm and made a cut about two inches in length. A spurt of blood told him that he had successfully located the artery.

It did not occur to Claxton before that the letter he had been writing would be burned when the building went. He wished some word to reach Frances just that she might know of his great love for her. He drew a sheet of paper toward him, and while the blood spurted from the severed artery, he hurriedly wrote her a few lines. He did not write more than half a page for he feared his strength would leave him too soon. He sealed the letter and placed it with his paper weight in a larger envelope and once more raised the window.

The whole city was in flames. Three dense black columns of smoke arose lowering and menacing. Down near Front street one of the wholesale houses was a roaring furnace. Below him he could distinguish the red flames darting upward from the roof through the rifts in the smoke affectionately licking the side of his own building. As he gazed, the glass in a window some five stories below broke with a crash and the next moment he saw the window sash catch. He had acted not a minute too soon.

Far below him in the street he could see the black edge of the crowd held back by a line of soldiers. He shouted, waving his arms. They saw him. A hoarse cry burst from the watchers. Everyone was pointing at him.

Then Claxton threw the envelope containing the letter and the weight with all his might. He hoped it would fall in the street and somebody would pick it up. But even here he failed. The stone weight tore its way through the paper envelope and he saw his letter flutter down into the flames below.

An upward rush of heat drove him back into his room. For the last time he closed the window. He realized he was very weak. He sank down in the revolving chair and waited.

Suddenly above the noise in the street and roaring flames below in the adjoining building he heard his name shouted clear and distinct.

"Wilbur—Wilbur, are you there?"

It was Deering. A flood of returning hope brought back his strength. He answered eagerly. There came a hoarse reply, a rush of feet, the point of a pick through the unyielding door, a rending and splintering of woodwork, and Deering burst through into the room followed by the firemen and caught him in his arms.

Deering saw in a moment the escape Claxton had planned for himself, and quickly made a tourniquet above the elbow and bandaged it with a strip of the shirt sleeve. Then, he and the firemen carried him out through the hall, already thick with smoke, and down the steps to the street. A moment later an ambulance appeared and Claxton was driven to a private residence on Gough street, temporarily transformed into a hospital, and was given over to the nurses of the Red Cross.

Throughout the entire day, while the fire consumed block after block of the city, destroying everything within its path, leaving nothing but black, tottering walls and smoldering debris, Claxton lay on his cot, unconscious of the wholesale destruction, asleep from weariness and weakness.

It must have been some time during the very early morning on Thursday that he awoke. He had been aware even in his sleep that around him everywhere there arose harsh, discordant noises, a murmur as of distant shouting, a confused mingling of unfamiliar sounds. For a moment he had no recollection of the recent events through which he had passed. Suddenly a reverberating detonation aroused his dormant mind, and memory rushed back upon him.

The explosion he knew meant that the firemen were dynamiting. He wondered what headway the fire had made. He knew it must be much nearer, for everything in the room in which he lay, the coverlid of his bed, the arms of the chairs, the polish on the brasses, the very ceiling itself, reflected the glare of the fire. Outside, it seemed like day lighted by a deep bloodred sun. Slowly he realized what were the strange noises which he had heard in his sleep. An endless throng of people in the street were passing the open window near his bed. He could hear the shuffling of their feet, the babble of their voices, the whimpering of children, the cries of drivers to their animals, the continual harsh rasp of heavy trunks being dragged over the sidewalk, the great murmur of vast multitudes, the voice of an army on the move. It was the flight of thousands of homeless families before the menacing danger which pursued them.

The great tragedy of it all overwhelmed Claxton. It seemed the end of everything.

Parts of conversations came to him through the open window.

"The office went about ten o'clock. The Flood Building's completely gutted. Jim lost everything."

"Where are you going?"

"Holladay's Hill,—we want to watch the fire. The Staffords are up there. It's perfectly safe."

"Near Powell. They're hoping to stop it at Union Square."

"They'll never stop it, I say. I'm going to the Beach. How're you going to stop fire without water? You take my advice and get out of here while there's time."

The rest of the party moved down the street. Others approached.

"Orpheum and Tivoli are gone! They're trying to save the St. Francis, but there's no use, the dynamiting seems to make it worse."

"They won't stop it before it reaches Van Ness, and if it crosses there, the city's done for. If we only had water. There's only about two streams available."

A little later came a more desperate report. The speaker's tone was full of authority.

"There doesn't seem to be much hope. There's nothing to fight with. The fire is sweeping up Sutter street. The Synagogue is burning now and all Chinatown's in flames. Everything south of Golden Gate is totally gone. My advice to everyone is to go to the Park. The city's doomed."

Claxton shut his eyes. What was the use? "The city's doomed," he repeated to himself. Was there anything life could offer him now? All the old places so infinitely dear to him were gone forever. He would never dine again at Mathias', or visit the gilded balcony above the Plaza, or explore the dark crannies of Chinatown. The city of Zinkand's, of Coppa's, of Sanguenetti's, of the Old Poodle Dog, of Campi's, and all the rest of the marvelous places that had made San Francisco fascinating, were no more. What was the use? It was better as he had decided. He gave the bandages on his arm a twitch and loosened the twisted tourniquet. He felt the warm blood on his forearm. He knew he was facing death now for a second time. The Valley of the Shadow lay before him. Memories of the old psalm came back to him, "Thy rod and Thy staff they comfort me—"

What of the thousands of others as miserable, more miserable than he,—the fathers and mothers with those little children,—the grizzled merchants that must begin life all over again,—the destitute? They, too, were passing through the Valley of the Shadow. For the first time a great pity surged up in Claxton's heart. It had been only of himself he had been thinking. In the face of this far greater calamity, how petty seemed his own selfish emotions. Was there not something after all to live for? These homeless, wretched people, this poor, crushed and blackened city? The tears ran down his cheeks. For the first time since his boyhood his trembling hands folded on his breast and he prayed to an Unseen Being for pity and mercy and help. The prayer was never finished. The fluttering eyelids closed, the hands dropped apart. He had fainted.

When Claxton regained consciousness he found himself gazing into a pair of anxious eyes. It was a long time, it seemed to him, before things began to adjust themselves. At first he was not sure that he was not dead. The events up to the time when he had loosened the tourniquet about his arm were quite clear. He remembered the warm sensation of the blood. He hesitated before examining the bandages. As far as he could determine they had been readjusted. He was still alive, then. But somehow he seemed different, somehow he had changed; he was not the same man.

Slowly he began to realize that it was Deering who was gazing down upon him. Deering? A sudden jealous anger rose within his heart. The association of his recent suffering brought the recollection of everything back to him. The anger faded away like the ebbing of a tide. It was never to return. The great pity he had felt when he believed death was at hand came back, driving away every other emotion. About him everywhere he seemed to see the spectres of the thousands of homeless, ruined people. They stretched supplicating hands towards him. They needed him and wanted his help; some were sick,—he was a physician; some were destitute and would soon be starving,—he could provide shelter and food. Ah, here was something to live for! Here was hope and life and love. In the face of such far greater sorrow, his own selfish desires seemed puny and contemptible. That was it. Of course he felt different. He was not the same man,—he had changed. The dawn of the new day broke over the horizon of his dark and selfish life. He had walked through the Valley of the Shadow and had been comforted.

A happy smile came to his face. He was too greatly moved to understand what Deering was trying to tell him. " . . . too near the fire . . . the doctor thinks it best to move you out to the Presidio hospital."

Claxton caught the word "doctor."

He raised himself on his elbow with an effort. "Is there a doctor here?"

A man whom he recognized as being one of the attendant physicians at Cooper College approached.

Claxton spoke eagerly.

"What I want is strength. I must have it. I have got work to do and I have lost so much blood that I am not strong enough. I think that if you can give me an injection of salt and strychnine I would be all right. I've got to be able to get about at once. I've got a lot to do."

"But, Wilbur," objected Deering, "You can't do that. Why,—man—you were nearly dead when they found you. You haven't the strength."

"Give me what I want, I tell you!" he replied fiercely. "I have lain here too long. All I ask is that you give me the injection. I must do my work." #

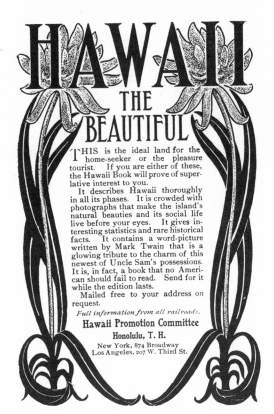

SUNSET MAGAZINE

Tells of California
and all the far West.

One Dollar A Year   For Sale by Newsdealers
Send For Sample Copy.

ARTISTIC PICTURES ON EVERY PAGE

Published   By

SOUTHERN PACIFIC COMPANY

San Francisco,   California.

How Things Were Righted
After the Fire of 1906

By SAN FRANCISCO'S MERCHANTS

April 1907

HIBERNIA BANK'S MILLIONS

WHEN the flames from surrounding buildings leaped toward the fine structure of the Hibernia Bank, between 1 and 2 o'clock on the morning of the 19th of April last, there were in the vaults more than $1,000,000 in cash, $15,000,000 in government bonds, $10,000,000 in micellaneous bonds, $30,000,000 in notes and mortgages, and all the books and accounts that related to a vast amount of business. R. M. Tobin, secretary of the bank, saw the fire draw near this great treasure. He was in the bank with faithful assistants. After the Murphy building had been saved temporarily, there appeared to be a chance that the Hibernia Bank might also be saved, but Fate decreed otherwise.

The superheated interior of the bank burst into flames. Everything that was inflammable was ablaze in an incredibly short time. "The flames from the outside," said Mr. Tobin, "did not seem to be the cause of igniting this structure. The structural granite just outside of the windows, as ascertained after the fire, was chipped by the heat from the inside. Glass fuses at a temperature of five hundred degrees. The heat must have been that in the bank interior for we found glass bottles fused with the glass of the windows.

"On the morning of April 18 I came to the bank early, but we did not open. A notice was posted on the front door notifying our depositors and all others concerned that we would not open that day. No one came to protest at that notice. In fact no one came around to see us at all."

This circumstance points out as clearly as any one of thousands that might be mentioned, that the city, on that morning had little real belief that all the business portion and a large part of the residential portion of San Francisco was doomed. It also sufficiently illustrates that the first thought of the great city was not about its money, for the Hibernia Bank has the largest number of depositors of any savings institution on the Pacific Coast, and not one of these thousands appeared on April 18 to demand his money or even to ask about it. What happened subsequently, as told by Mr. Tobin, touches current California history at several points.

"We provided temporary quarters as soon as possible where we conferred with our customers. Banks of all descriptions were for a brief time in private residences. The savings banks waited for their vaults to cool sufficiently to make it safe to open them. As savings vaults were unlocked it became evident that the treasures that had been confined to their keeping were safe. For our part, when we swung back the doors that had been closed just before we were compelled by the coming flames to go away, we found that not so much as a sheet of blotting paper in the vault had been scorched. We came back to the old place to do business and reopened May 23, just a little more than a month after the great fire.

"We at once began to pay out money, for there were many depositors—the banks having been closed for weeks, and business having been suspended generally—who needed money for their immediate necessities. Everybody was paid who came. Business soon flowed along in its accustomed channels without any limit on payments. We find that payments of principal and interest on loans in San Francisco are more prompt now than before the fire. It is also ascertained, by the prices that are refused by owners in the burned business district, that values are held strongly and that the realty security for loans is as good as it was early in 1906."

In a spirit of fun, the discommoded affected the high-sounding names of fashionable hotels

A STOCKADE AROUND DIAMONDS

IN THE latter days of May, 1906, and indeed, for some time thereafter, the odd spectacle could have been witnessed, at any time during business hours, of salesmen dealing in diamonds, high-class jewelry and watches behind an eight-foot stockade, on the ground floor of a great, ruined structure on the northwest corner of Post street and Grant avenue. From all sides of this building the plate glass windows had disappeared. From the highest story to the lowest the wind blew bleakly and at will through its ruins.

It was behind this stockade that Shreve & Company resumed business. On the morning of April 18, Mr. Shreve was in San Mateo County. He hastened to San Francisco as fast as possible by train and automobile.

"I arrived in San Francisco," said he, relating his experience, "and went to the store as soon as possible. Two hours later, or about 10 A.M., we had our vaults filled and closed and locked. We had two floors and the basement of the building at Grant avenue and Post street. The jewels and the watches were locked up in the vault the night before. The silverware was outside. We hastened to put that in safety. The art department, china and clocks we had to leave standing to be burned. There was property in the vaults that was worth three-quarters of a million dollars—there was nothing to do but trust to the vault.

"When the fires were out there was work to do. The first in importance was to construct a stockade, eight feet high, around the vault and to have a sufficient guard to protect the contents. Sometimes the soldiers patroled. When

they were called away our own people acted as
sentries. About the stockade, after the vaults
had cooled, we placed rough board counters
and so resumed business. There was necessity
for a temporary office and we used my home on
Pacific avenue. There our mail was opened and
from there we got in touch with the outside
world. Meantime we established a temporary
repair shop and factory in Oakland. Our
business was satisfactory from the time we

opened the vaults and found the contents to be
in good condition.

"In five months from the time we were
burned out, we were in business in a new location, in a new building we had constructed and
with an adequate plant.

"The people have been purchasing as high
cost articles and as numerously as ever. We
have been sorry that we did not have larger
salesrooms."

Van Ness Avenue became the center of the business district

Lumbermen and the Crisis

THE flames had scarcely died away, the ashes were not yet cooled, the cinders had but just escaped from the wafting breezes of those eventful April days which witnessed the burning of San Francisco when the demand commenced for building material. The great fire had swept away almost all the large lumber yards of San Francisco. It is true that some were saved through the capricious efforts of the shifting winds of those three days and through the efforts of man, but the stocks they held were as nothing when the filling of even the orders came to be considered. Early estimates, made by those most closely in touch with the current lumber situation, placed the amount to be needed in the rebuilding of the burnt district in the near neighborhood of two billion feet.

Grotesque curb-stone kitchens served the hungry

Later developments tended to fortify this conservative opinion. How could the paltry fifty million feet saved in the twenty local lumber yards satisfy the demand!

Then it was that the lumbermen, retail and wholesale, came forward with stupendous efforts to furnish the desired material. Three days after the fire, the retail interests met on the outskirts of the burnt district and decided upon a proper course to pursue.

"Prices shall not be advanced," was the first determination of the lumber merchants. The fifty million feet on hand was soon exhausted by the immediate demand for temporary structures for business purposes or for those that must house the refugees. The yards were soon cleared of their stocks. There was no lumber in the limits of the great city. Oakland and the surrounding communities were called upon to contribute what they could. Enormous was the current demand but infinitely small was the stock on hand. Then came the exodus of the yards' representatives who set their faces northward where the large and small mills pursued their operations. Lumber must be secured and secured with all haste. Never before in the history of American lumbering operations had a demand of such magnitude come in the passing of a brief moment. The fir, the redwood, the spruce and the cedar mills, prior even to the 18th day of April, were rushed to their utmost capacity to fill the coastwise, foreign and eastern orders, and added to this, now came the tremendous call for lumber to rebuild San Francisco.

To secure the necessary lumber, to surmount prevailing trade obstacles, the San Francisco merchants were compelled to offer the mills an adequate premium so that eastern and other demands might be transferred to the fire-swept metropolis and San Francisco secure the preference. To obtain the logs necessary to maintain the high ratio of the mill plants, the latters' owners offered higher prices to the timberland owners; vessels were greatly in need for transportation purposes and the metropolitan lumber merchants were compelled to offer better rates in order that the manufactured timber products might reach the San Francisco market in more rapid transit. Labor, worked to its limit, called for more remunerative wages as an incentive to greater efforts; all the lumber

dealers, anxious to get the material to the demanding customer, were forced to meet the demands which were encountered from the stump to the receiving dock. The cost of the manufacture of lumber was forced upward, and in right and justice, the lumber dealers were compelled to cause their customers to pay the increased quotations. The unthinking citizens raised the hue and cry of the "Lumber Gouger," little realizing the economic forces which compelled the many concurrent advances over anti-fire prices.

Before the fire, common fir lumber ruled at a base of $20.00 with redwood ranging at $23.00. To-day, one year later, the former holds at a $31.00 base with the latter selling on a basis of $29.00, while redwood shingles sold before the fire at $2.50 per thousand, sell to-day at $3.00. Cedar shingles then carried a prevailing price per thousand of $3.50, and now bring a return of $4.00.

The figures, as compiled for *Wood and Iron,* show that San Francisco, in 1906, used 55,000,000 feet more redwood than in the year 1905, while fir and spruce came into San Francisco 202,414,101 feet stronger last year than in 1905. These statistics display the enormous amount of lumber utilized in the partial up-building of the city. The total annual receipts of fir and spruce in San Francisco during 1906 amounted to over 685,825,997 feet of which amount 136,383,386 feet arrived prior to May, so that the great balance for the remainder of the last year footed up a grand total of 549,442,611 feet. The great redwood roofing product, shingles, in 1906, from Humboldt County, arrived in San Francisco to the extent of 254,700,500 pieces, of which total 89,429,750 reached this port prior to May with the balance coming in 254,700,500 strong in the following eight months.

The Postmaster's Figures

"ESTIMATING the population of San Francisco by the postoffice receipts, the figures show that the city is again back to where it was a year before the fire or to an estimated population of four hundred and seventy thousand," writes Postmaster Arthur G. Fisk. "This estimate is based upon two significant facts: First, the actual business of the office at this time; and, Second, that the receipts hold up notwithstanding that many sources of income were done away with immediately after the fire, and have been only partially restored.

"For the first days after the fire there was practically no postage paid in San Francisco. Letters and scraps of newspapers, shingles and bits of board and pieces of cardboard boxes —anything in fact that had an address and a message on it—were forwarded without postage, and the revenue that would otherwise have been brought to the postoffice was lost. Not a pound of newspapers was deposited in the postoffice until well along in May, and not a daily statement or a circular was sent out until well into the fall. Were an estimate of the revenue from these sources of income added to the figure of a million and a half—the total receipts for 1906—the figures of the postoffice would run well up to those for 1905, and the population, thus based, would be back to where it was."

STATUS OF LAND TITLE

THE fire which destroyed the business portion of San Francisco also destroyed the places where the public records were kept. A few scattering records were saved here and there. The Recorder saved a few miscellaneous volumes which were removed from the Hall of Records, but the extent of the destruction will appear from the fact that in the Recorder's office there were 1,465 volumes of mortgages, all of which were destroyed except one volume; sixty-nine volumes of homesteads, all of which were saved; ninety-six volumes of liens, all of which were saved; eighty volumes of attachments, of which six were saved; 2,212 volumes of deeds, of which 653 were saved, and many volumes of miscellaneous records, all of which were destroyed.

As will be seen from the foregoing, the vast majority of the records were a total loss. The few that remained were so scattered that there was not left enough to enable one to say of a single foot of ground that the title to it could be deducible of record. Fortunately, however, there was a solution of the difficulty at hand. Providentially the records of some of the title insurance companies were spared. In the case of the California Title Insurance and Trust Company, its records were in the only building

in the heart of the burned district which was not entirely consumed by the flames. This building was known as the Kohl Building, and was fireproof even to the windows and doors, which was an exception in the so-called fireproof buildings of San Francisco.

The Title Insurance and Guaranty Company removed its records on the day of the earthquake from the Mills Building in which they were situated and had them hauled out toward the ocean. The Mills Building was practically a total loss, and with it went the only volumes which this company had not removed, namely, its books of accounts.

Immediately following the resumption of business the public proceeded with its own solution of the situation by taking advantage of the title insurance companies' records, and their policies were generally accepted as evidence of title in the policyholder. The transfer of real estate has gone on with the full public confidence in the validity and security of the title insurance policies, and with a general faith in the ability of the companies to make their claims good. #

Mr. and Mrs. London on board the "Snark," in the Estuary, Oakland, California

The Sailing of Jack London's "Snark"

By ALLAN DUNN

May 1907

THE planning of the *Snark,* the building, and the general idea of the voyage, all came about easily enough. The project was not a new one; Robert Louis Stevenson's idea was similar although the proposed London voyage is much more elaborate in detail. Stevenson was after health, primarily, while Jack London looks more for travel and adventure.

The proposed voyage is adventurous enough to please the most romantic of writers or readers. The *Snark* is a sturdy boat; much smaller craft have sailed successfully on trips as long, but here start out six people: Jack London, with some deep sea experience but little knowledge of navigation; Mrs. London, wife and comrade of the novelist; two young men just out of college, gritty and athletic enough, but no sailors, not even amateurs; a Japanese, and Captain Eames, the last named the only practical mariner as far as navigation goes. Of course the others undoubtedly can and will, master the mysteries of sextant and chronometer, compass and dead reckoning, but they will not do it before they start. "I am going to cram on navigation and gas engines after we get started," said Mr. London in speaking of his plans. And so off they go, their itinerary the globe, their only premeditated destination Hawaii, with the Marquesas, Samoa, Polynesia in general, and then the China Sea as a vague prospect.

The planning and building of the *Snark* was a long labor. London wanted a vessel staunch enough to survive the fury of the gales and the possible bumpings of a shoal or reef. He wanted a boat that would steer with comfort, and of a rig to ride out a gale in easy fashion. He wanted power to stem adverse currents and winds, and bid defiance to calms. So the *Snark* was made a ketch rig, little known in Pacific waters, the popular rig of North Sea fishermen. She carries mainsail and mizzen, differing from the yawl rig in the mizzen being larger and shipped farther inboard. She has staysail and jib, with flying jib, a big spinnaker that can be swung around for a balloon jib, a gaff topsail with a sprit, and a storm trysail. Dirty weather proves the comfort of the ketch. As with a yawl, the mainsail can come down in a storm, and under a small head sail and the mizzen, she will ride out a gale in comfort and need little attention at the helm. The staysail is fitted with a boom and will swing over freely at change of tack.

For cruising up rivers, for stemming unfavorable currents, running through calms, perhaps in escape from canoes of cannibal islanders or from junks of piratical Chinese, for riding out typhoons and all purposes where auxiliary power is needed, the *Snark* carries a seventy-five horse-power engine, that can send her along at ten miles an hour or better. There have been criticisms made as to the unnecessary size of the engine and its consumption of gasoline, but Mr. London feels that he need not run full power all the time and when he wants the engine badly he wants a powerful one. About a pint per horse-power is her gasoline consumption at full power, and behind a water, gas and air tight bulkhead aft, the craft will carry one thousand gallons of gasoline, meaning one thousand miles of power radius at full speed. Going up still waters of river travel, extra gasoline can be carried on deck. Besides this, there is a dynamo and a smaller five horse-power engine, supplying the lights, for the boat boasts electric bulbs and a powerful search light, and power for the winch, this last named arrangement, a most valuable one, as all who have broken out a heavy anchor by hand from deep water will testify.

The "Snark" at anchor in Oakland Harbor

The *Snark* is built to stay. Her knees are ten inches apart, of natural bends; she is copper riveted everywhere, coppered from keelson to waterline, her outside planking two inches thick divided into three watertight compartments by bulkheads, rigged with chain plates, running rigging, stays, blocks and general tackle that would fit a craft twice her size. Expense has been lavished to make her staunch. There are no butts, every plank runs from stem to stern and it will take years of buffeting to make much impression on her sturdy mould. Her cost will probably run close to $25,000 before she sails out through the Golden Gate. She is fifty-seven feet over all, with a draft of seven feet, a free-board of four, and a rail of eighteen inches. She is flush decked, with a beam of 15 feet, and is a roomy craft. Her clipper bow with its ample flare means freedom from going head under, and should keep her nose well in air. Beneath the water line her lines

are better than those that appear above. To the yachtsman she would look better were she a foot or two longer, but she must prove an excellent sea boat.

On deck, in davits, she carries a fourteen-foot power launch, and a double ender whaleboat eighteen feet long, which should prove invaluable for surf landings and bar work. On deck, too, are carried shear poles for unstepping the masts when the exploration of Chinese rivers or other low bridged waters is planned. Upon her deck also will be carried many other things, for despite her bulk, the craft has little room for stowage.

The big engine, the other machinery with the shaft, takes up much of the space. Aft the gasoline monopolizes the usual lazarette storeroom. Mr. London purposes carrying a library of some two thousand books; there is much stationery to go aboard, a phonograph, typewriters and two saddles all of which will take much of the room usually devoted to stores. Just where the water tanks and the provisions are going when everything else is aboard is a puzzle that will doubtless be solved satisfactorily by those who sail. Certain it is that dunnage will be condensed for everyone. The forepeak will carry the chains and spare gear. It is to be hoped her high freeboard will keep her free from seas as it seems imperative to utilize much of the deck for larder stores.

Her trial trip proved the *Snark* seaworthy and her engine powerful. She ran gaily ten miles out to sea and came as briskly back on the flood in a dead calm, while craft that had only sail power, stayed outside all night. She steers with a weather helm and points up closely under sail. A ketch rig is not a fast one, but on the run to Hawaii,—her first anchorage,—the engine should need only a perfunctory turning over and before the steady trades, from fourteen to seventeen days should find the voyagers safe at Hilo.

As the diagram shows, the Londons have their cabins forward. The main cabin has bunk room for four more while Captain Eames has his dormitory aft of the engine. The galley is roomy and the bathroom a luxury. Both London and his wife are expert swimmers but they will be wary of sharks and keep their natatory pleasures for guarded waters. Both, too, revel in horseback riding and the two saddles carried with them will be in frequent use ashore.

The vessel has an armament of shotguns. Winchesters and revolvers, for protection as well as sport, and this will be added to later by a small rapid firing gun. Cruising in the South Seas and Oriental waters is not entirely free from excitement even nowadays and the weapons may well prove needful. The seven years of the cruise spell the Seven Seas also for Mr. London, who has in mind the Amazon, the Congo, the Zambesi, and the Nile before he again sees his home ranch at Glen Ellen.

Mr. London works systematically two and a half hours every day, his wife acting as his amanuensis. The rest of the time not occupied by seamanship will be given up to the pleasures of the trip. Everyone aboard stands watch and has a trick at the wheel, including Mrs. London who shares all of her husband's work and pastime, from athletics to revising manuscript. The voyage can not be considered a continuous one. Mr. London calls the *Snark* his combination workshop, hotel and means of conveyance. He says they will probably be ashore three months to every one month afloat. #

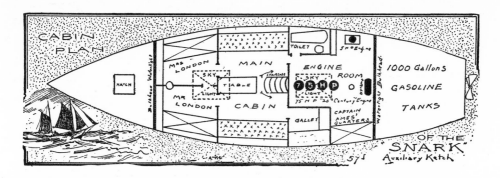

The plan for the vessel had many unusual features

Man's Greatest Pleasure

His truest gratification, everywhere in the civilized world, is in the use of

PEARS' SOAP

Cleansing—soothing—invigorating, it gives a freshness and beauty to the skin, a glow of health to the body—satisfying beyond expression.

Matchless for the Complexion

That Spot

By JACK LONDON

February 1903

WE started for the Klondike in the fall rush of 1897, and we started too late to get over Chilcoot Pass before the freezeup. We packed our outfit on our backs part way over, when the snow began to fly, and then we had to buy dogs in order to sled it the rest of the way. That was how we came to get that Spot. Dogs were high and we paid one hundred and ten dollars for him. He looked worth it. I say looked, because he was one of the finest appearing dogs I ever saw. He weighed sixty pounds, and he had all the lines of a good sled animal. We never could make out his breed. He wasn't husky, nor Malemute, nor Hudson Bay; he looked like all of them and he didn't look like any of them, and on top of it all he had some of the white man's dog in him, for on one side, in the thick of the mixed yellow-brown-red-and-dirty-white that was his prevailing color, there was a spot of coal black as big as a water bucket. That was why we called him Spot.

He was a good-looker, all right. When he was in condition his muscles stood out in bunches all over him, and he was the strongest-looking brute I ever saw in Alaska, also, the most intelligent looking. To run your eyes over him, you'd think he could out pull three dogs of his own weight. Maybe he could, but I never saw it. His intelligence didn't run that way. He could steal and forage to perfection; he had an instinct that was positively grewsome for divining when work was to be done and for making a sneak accordingly, and for getting lost and not staying lost he was nothing short of inspired. But when it came to work, the way that intelligence dribbled out of him and left him a mere clot of wobbling, stupid jelly would make your heart bleed.

There are times when I think it wasn't stupidity. Maybe, like some men I know, he was too wise to work. I shouldn't wonder if he put it all over us with that intelligence of his. Maybe he figured it all out and decided that a licking now and again and no work was a whole lot better than work all the time and no licking. He was intelligent enough for such a computation. I tell you, I've sat and looked into that dog's eyes till the shivers ran up and down my spine and the marrow crawled like yeast. What of the intelligence I saw shining out? I can't express myself about that intelligence. It is beyond mere words; I saw it, that's all. At times it was like gazing into a human soul to look into his eyes, and what I saw there frightened me and started all sorts of ideas in my own mind of reincarnation and all the rest. I tell you I sensed something big in that brute's eyes; there was a message there, but I wasn't big enough myself to catch it. Whatever it was (I know I'm making a fool of myself)—whatever it was, it baffled me. I can't give an inkling of what I saw in that brute's eyes; it wasn't light, it wasn't color; it was something that moved away back when the eyes themselves weren't moving. And I guess I didn't see it move, either; I only sensed that it moved. It was an expression—that's what it was—and I got an impression of it. No, it was different from a mere expression, it was more than that. I don't know what it was, but it gave me a feeling of kinship just the same. Oh, no, not sentimental kinship. It was, rather, a kinship of equality. Those eyes never pleaded like a deer's eyes. They challenged. No, it wasn't defiance. It was just a calm assumption of equality, and I don't think it was deliberate. My belief is that it was unconscious on his part. It was there because it was there, and it couldn't help shining out. No, I don't mean shine. It didn't shine, it moved.

I know I'm talking rot, but if you'd looked into that animal's eyes the way I have, you'd understand. Steve was affected the same way I was. Why, I tried to kill that Spot, once—he was no good for anything—and I fell down on it. I led him out into the brush, and he came along slowly and unwillingly. He knew what was going on. I stopped in a likely place, put my foot on the rope, pulled my big Colt's, and that dog sat down and looked at me. I tell you he didn't plead. He just looked, and I saw all kinds of incomprehensible things moving, yes, moving in those eyes of his. I didn't really see them move; I thought I saw them, for, as I said before, I guess I only sensed them, and I want to tell you right now that it got beyond me. It was like killing a man, a conscious, brave man who looked calmly into your gun as much as to say, "Who's afraid?" Then, too, the message seemed so near that, instead of pulling the trigger quick, I stopped to see if I could catch the message. There it was right before me, glimmering all around in those eyes of his. And then it was too late. I got scared. I was trembly all over, and my stomach generated a nervous palpitation that made me seasick. I just sat down and looked at that dog and he looked at me, till I thought I was going crazy. Do you want to know what I did? I threw down the gun and ran back to camp with the fear of God in my heart. Steve laughed at me, but I noticed that he led Spot into the woods a week later for the same purpose and that he came back alone, while a little later Spot drifted back, too.

At any rate, Spot wouldn't work. We paid a hundred and ten dollars for him from the bottom of our sack and he wouldn't work; he wouldn't even tighten the traces. Steve spoke to him, the first time we put him in harness, and he sort of shivered, that was all—not an ounce on the traces. He just stood still and wobbled like so much jelly. Steve touched him with the whip. He yelped, but not an ounce. Steve touched him again a bit harder and he howled—the regular long, wolf howl, then Steve got mad and gave him half a dozen and I came on the run from the tent.

I told Steve he was brutal with the animal, and we had some words—the first we'd ever had. He threw the whip down in the snow and walked away mad. I picked it up and went to it. That Spot trembled and wobbled and cowered before ever I swung the lash and with the first bite of it he howled like a lost soul, next he lay down in the snow. I started the rest of the dogs and they dragged him along while I threw the whip into him. He rolled over on his back and bumped along, his four legs waving in the air, himself howling as though he were going through a sausage machine. Steve came back and laughed at me and I apologized for what I'd said.

There was no getting any work out of that Spot, and to make up for it, he was the biggest pig-glutton of a dog I ever saw. On top of that, he was the cleverest thief. There was no circumventing him—many a breakfast we went without our bacon because Spot had been there first, and it was because of him that we nearly starved to death up the Stewart. He figured out the way to break into our meat cache, and what he didn't eat, the rest of the team did, but he was impartial—he stole from everybody. He was a restless dog, always very busy snooping around or going somewhere, and there was never a camp within five miles that he didn't raid. The worst of it was that they always came back on us to pay his board bill, which was just, being the law of the land; but it was mighty hard on us, especially that first winter on the Chilcoot when we were busted, paying for whole hams and sides of bacon that we never ate. He could fight, too, that Spot. He could do everything but work. He never pulled a pound, but he was the boss of the whole team. The way he made those dogs stand around was an education. He bullied them, and there was always one or more of them fresh-marked with his fangs, but he was more than a bully. He wasn't afraid of anything that walked on four legs, and I've seen him march single-handed into a strange team without any provocation whatever, and put the "kibosh" on the whole outfit. Did I say he could eat? I caught him eating the whip, once. That's straight. He started in at the lash and when I caught him he was down to the handle and still going.

But he was a good-looker. At the end of the first week we sold him for seventy-five dollars to the mounted police. They had experienced dog drivers, and we knew that by the time he'd covered the six hundred miles to Dawson he'd be a good sled dog. I say we knew, for we were just getting acquainted with that Spot. A little later we were not brash enough to know

Fruit Basket
Made with
NABISCO
SUGAR WAFERS

With luncheon or dinner
With a sherbet or ice,
With beverage or fruit
Or served alone

NABISCO

SUGAR WAFERS.

add the final and crowning touch
to afternoon tea or formal banquet.

RECIPE

Arrange NABISCO Sugar Wafers on a pretty
dish to resemble a fruit basket. Fill the center
with strawberries (or any seasonable fruit),
piling them high. Serve the NABISCO Sugar
Wafers and berries with sugar and cream, or
as fancy may dictate.

In ten cent tins.
Also in twenty-five cent tins.

GOLF
AND OTHER SPORTS AT
DEL MONTE

CALIFORNIA

Hotel Del Monte
is a homelike
and delightful
resort where
every facility
for the
enjoyment of
out-door
sports
**EVERY DAY
IN THE
YEAR**
is provided

A copy of the new
Book of Sports,
of which the
engraving
is the cover, will
be sent free on
request

H. R. WARNER
Manager
Hotel Del Monte
DEL MONTE, CALIFORNIA

anything where he was concerned. A week later we woke up in the morning to the dangdest dog fight we'd ever heard. It was that Spot, come back and knocking the team into shape. We ate a pretty depressing breakfast, I can tell you; but cheered up two hours afterward when we sold him to an official courier, bound in to Dawson with government dispatches. That Spot was only three days in coming back, and as usual, celebrated his arrival with a rough house.

We spent the winter and spring, after our own outfit was across the pass, freighting other people's outfits, and we made a fat stake. Also, we made money out of Spot. If we sold him once, we sold him twenty times. He always came back and no one asked for their money. We didn't want the money; we'd have paid handsomely for any one to take him off our hands for keeps. We had to get rid of him, and we couldn't give him away for that would have been suspicious; but he was such a fine looker that we never had any difficulty in selling him. "Unbroke," we'd say, and they'd pay any old price for him. We sold him as low as twenty-five dollars, and once we got a hundred and fifty for him. That particular man returned him in person, refused to take his money back, and the way he abused us was something awful. He said it was cheap at the price to tell us what he thought of us, and we felt he was so justified that we never talked back. But to this day I've never quite regained all the old self-respect that was mine before that man talked to me.

When the ice cleared out of the lakes and river, we put our outfit in a Lake Bennett boat and started for Dawson. We had a good team of dogs and, of course, we piled them on top of the outfit. That Spot was along—there was no losing him, and a dozen times the first day, he knocked one or another of the dogs overboard in the course of fighting with them. It was close quarters, and he didn't like being jostled.

"What that dog needs is space," Steve said the second day. "Let's maroon him." We did, running the boat in at Caribou Crossing for him to jump ashore. Two of the other dogs, good dogs, followed him, and we lost two whole days trying to find them. We never saw those two dogs again, but the quietness and relief we enjoyed made us decide, like the man who refused his hundred and fifty, that it was cheap at the price. For the first time in months

Steve and I laughed and whistled and sang. We were as happy as clams; the dark days were over; the nightmare had been lifted—that Spot was gone.

Three weeks later, one morning, Steve and I were standing on the river bank at Dawson. A small boat was just arriving from Lake Bennett. I saw Steve give a start and heard him say something that was not nice and that was not under his breath. Then I looked, and there, in the bow of the boat, with ears pricked up, sat Spot. Steve and I sneaked immediately, like beaten curs, like cowards, like absconders from justice. It was this last that the lieutenant of police thought when he saw us sneaking. He surmised that there were law officers in the boat who were after us. He didn't wait to find out, but kept us in sight and in the M and M saloon got us in a corner. We had a merry time explaining, for we refused to go back to the boat and meet Spot, and finally he held us under guard of another policeman while he went to the boat. After we got clear of him we started for the cabin and when we arrived there was that Spot sitting on the stoop waiting for us. Now, how did he know we lived there? There were forty thousand people in Dawson that summer, and how did he savvy our cabin out of all the cabins? How did he know we were in Dawson, anyway? I leave it to you; but don't forget what I have said about his intelligence and that immortal something I have seen glimmering in his eyes.

There was no getting rid of him any more. There were too many people in Dawson who had bought him up on Chilcoot, and the story got around. Half a dozen times we put him on board steamboats going down the Yukon, but he merely went ashore at the first landing and trotted back up the bank. We couldn't sell him, we couldn't kill him (both Steve and I had tried) and nobody else was able to kill him. He bore a charmed life. I've seen him go down in a dog fight on the main street with fifty dogs on top of him and when they were separated he'd appear on all his four legs, unharmed, while two of the dogs that had been on top of him would be lying dead.

I saw him steal a chunk of moose meat from Major Dinwiddie's cache so heavy that he could just keep one jump ahead of Mrs. Dinwiddie's squaw cook who was after him with an ax. As he went up the hill, after the squaw gave up, Major Dinwiddie himself came out and pumped his Winchester into the landscape. He emptied his magazine twice and never touched that Spot; then a policeman came along and arrested him for discharging firearms inside the city limits. Major Dinwiddie paid his fine and Steve and I paid him for the moose meat at the rate of a dollar a pound, bones and all. That was what he paid for it. Meat was high that year.

I am only telling what I saw with my own eyes. And now I'll tell you something else. I saw that Spot fall through a water-hole. The ice was three and a half feet thick and the current sucked him under like a straw. Three hundred yards below was the big water hole used by the hospital. Spot crawled out of the hospital water hole, licked off the water, bit out the ice that had formed between his toes, trotted up the bank, and whipped a big Newfoundland belonging to the Gold Commissioner.

In the fall of 1898, Steve and I poled up the Yukon on the last water, bound for Stewart river. We took the dogs along, all except Spot. We figured we'd been feeding him long enough. He'd cost us more time and trouble and money and grub than we'd got by selling him on the Chilcoot—especially grub; so Steve and I tied him down in the cabin and pulled our freight. We camped that night at the mouth of Indian river, and were pretty facetious over having shaken him. Steve was a funny cuss, and I was just sitting up in the blankets and laughing when a tornado hit camp. The way that Spot walked into those dogs and gave them what-for was hair-raising. Now how did he get loose? It's up to you—I haven't any theory. And how did he get across the Klondike river? That's another facer. Anyway, how did he know we had gone up the Yukon? You see, we went by water and he couldn't smell our tracks. Steve and I began to get superstitious about that dog; he got on our nerves, too, and between you and me, we were just a mite afraid of him.

The freezeup came on when we were at the mouth of Henderson creek, and we traded him off for two sacks of flour to an outfit that was bound up White river after copper. Now that whole outfit was lost. Never trace nor hide nor hair of men, dogs, sleds, or anything was ever found. They dropped clean out of sight. It became one of the mysteries of the country. Steve and I plugged away up the Stewart and six weeks afterward that Spot crawled into camp. He was a perambulating skeleton and could just drag along, but he got there. And what I want to know is who told him we were up the Stewart? We could have gone a thousand other places. How did he know? You tell me, and I'll tell you.

No losing him. At the Mayo he started a row with an Indian dog. The buck who owned the dog took a swing at Spot with an ax, missed him, and killed his own dog. Talk about magic and turning bullets aside—I, for one, consider it a blamed sight harder to turn an ax aside with a big buck at the other end of it, but I saw him do it with my own eyes. That buck didn't want to kill his own dog. You've got to show me.

I told you about Spot breaking into our meat cache. It was nearly the death of us. There wasn't any more meat to be killed and meat was all we had to live on. The moose had gone back several hundred miles and the Indians with them. There we were—spring was on and we had to wait for the river to break. We got pretty thin before we decided to eat the dogs, and so we decided to eat Spot first. Do you know what that dog did? He sneaked. Now how did he know our minds were made up to eat him? We sat up nights laying for him, but he never came back and we ate the other dogs. We ate the whole team.

And now for the sequel. You know what it is when a big river breaks up and a few billion tons of ice goes out, jamming and milling and grinding. Just in the thick of it, when the Stewart went out, rumbling and roaring, we sighted Spot out in the middle. He'd got caught as he was trying to cross up above somewhere. Steve and I yelled and shouted and ran up and down the bank, tossing our hats in the air. Sometimes we'd stop and hug each other, we were that boisterous, for we saw Spot's finish. He didn't have a chance in a million. He didn't have any chance at all. After the ice-run we got into a canoe and paddled down to the Yukon, and down the Yukon to Dawson, stopping to feed up for a week at the cabins at the mouth of Henderson creek. And as we came in to the bank at Dawson, there sat that Spot, waiting for us, his ears pricked up, his tail wagging, his mouth smiling, extending a hearty welcome to us. Now how did he get out of that ice? How did he know we were coming to Dawson, to the very hour and minute, to be out there on the bank waiting for us?

The more I think of Spot, the more I am convinced that there are things in this world that go beyond science. On no scientific grounds can that Spot be explained. It's psychic phenomena, or mysticism, or something of that sort, I guess, with a lot of theosophy thrown in. The Klondike is a good country. I might have been there yet and become a millionaire if it hadn't been for Spot. He got on my nerves. I stood him for two years altogether, and then I guess my stamina broke. It was the summer of 1899 when I pulled out. I didn't say anything to Steve—I just sneaked; but I fixed it up all right. I wrote Steve a note, and enclosed a package of "rough-on-rats," telling him what to do with it. I was worn down to skin and bone by Spot, and I was that nervous that I'd jump and look around when there wasn't anybody within hailing distance; but it was astonishing the way I recuperated when I got quit of him. I got back twenty pounds before I arrived in San Francisco, and by the time I'd crossed the ferry to Oakland I was my old self again, so that even my wife looked in vain for any change in me.

Steve wrote to me once, and his letter seemed irritated. He took it kind of hard because I'd left him with Spot. Also, he said he'd used the "rough-on-rats," per directions, and that there was nothing doing. A year went by. I was back in the office and prospering in all ways—even getting a bit fat. And then Steve arrived. He didn't look me up. I read his name in the steamer list, and wondered why, but I didn't wonder long. I got up one morning and found Spot chained to the gatepost and holding up the milkman. Steve went north to Seattle, I learned, that very morning. I didn't put on any more weight. My wife made me buy Spot a collar and tag, and within an hour he showed his gratitude by killing her pet Persian cat.

There is no getting rid of Spot. He will be with me until I die for he'll never die. My appetite is not so good since he arrived and my wife says I am looking peaked. Last night that Spot got into Mr. Harvey's hen house—Harvey is my next door neighbor—and killed nineteen of his fancy bred chickens. I shall have to pay for them. My neighbors on the other side quarreled with my wife and then moved out. Spot was the cause of it, and that is why I am disappointed in Stephen Mackaye. I had no idea he was so mean a man. #

Open-Air Sleeping

By ELIZABETH FARWELL

August 1909

SLEEPING in the open air is a most commendable fad. It does seem strange, but people have a mortal dread of two things—fresh air and soap and water—and our knowledge of hygiene has taught us that these mean health, longevity. Houses cause consumption, yet no trust has cornered fresh air; it can be had for less than the asking. Dr. Tanner lived forty days without food, and it has been proved that people have lived seven days without water on deserts and in shipwrecks, but no one can live five minutes without air. When we camp in tents in the woods, we know that within six weeks we have gained in color, appetite, energy. The plan of out-of-door sleeping is sound—wonderfully so.

According to a throat specialist, it is especially good for people liable to colds, for colds are infections, and it is one of the greatest strengtheners for weak throats known. I have often ordered children with weak throats to sleep out, and the results have been most gratifying. They take to it with amusing zest —probably because the novelty of it appeals to them, and because they are not fear-ridden like most of their elders. Not until grown people realize that colds cannot be contracted in the open air do they lose their horror of it. In the New York hospitals many diseases of children are now treated in the open air with surprising success. I would say that a person liable to neuralgia should be protected from the wind, and one liable to rheumatism should be protected from dew by overhead covering. #

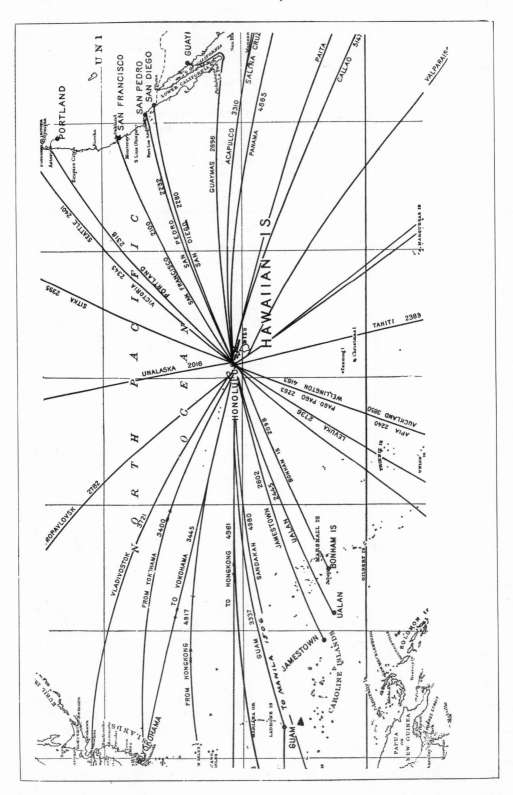

Section of chart showing how the Hawaiian Islands are at the cross-roads of the Pacific, and, incidentally, how Pearl Harbor, the proposed naval station, must be of tremendous value to this government in controlling the commerce of the world's greatest ocean.

Pearl Harbor—
The Key to the Pacific

By H. A. EVANS

August 1908

THE House of Representatives on April 6, 1908, by a vote of two hundred and forty-six to one passed a bill appropriating $2,500,000 to establish a naval station at Pearl Harbor, Hawaii. Not since the days immediately preceding the Spanish war has there been shown in Congress so much interest and patriotic enthusiasm as was displayed in the House regarding the passage of this act. Members from all sections of the country and of all political parties enthusiastically supported the bill, and there could be no clearer indication of the desires and intentions of the people of this country regarding the future control of the Pacific. The action of the House, which will undoubtedly be confirmed by the Senate, is an unequivocal notification to the world that the importance of the Pacific Coast and the Pacific ocean is fully recognized, and that the United States will in the future exert in that ocean the influence that its interests demand.

Hawaii has long been known as "the key to the Pacific," and those who have made any study of the military situation realize that no country can control the Pacific without the possession of Hawaii. The importance of holding these islands is paramount in the defense of the Pacific Coast. No country except England could at the present time carry out an effective attack against the Pacific Coast without first taking Hawaii, while the possession of these islands will be one of our most important defenses in repelling an attack and will be of the greatest importance in carrying out an offensive campaign against any foe in the Pacific.

It does not require any military knowledge to realize the commercial and strategic importance of Hawaii—a glance at the map of the Pacific gives all the information necessary. Situated almost in the center of the Pacific, the Hawaiian Islands possess the only safe ports within forty-five hundred miles of the western coast of America. The distances from the Pacific Coast to Japan, China, Australia, and other countries in the far East, are so great that successful military operations against the Pacific Coast are almost impossible without first securing Hawaii as a base for recoaling. There is hardly a battleship in the world to-day that can cross the Pacific without coaling here. There are no warships of the world to-day that could cross the ocean and still have sufficient fuel to return to a home port if driven away from our coast. This is the natural and only stopping place in the voyage across the Pacific, not only for war vessels but also for merchant vessels as well.

Hawaii possesses the only safe harbor on the route between England's greatest colonies, Canada and Australia. The distance between these two—six thousand miles—is so great that no warship and very few merchant ships can make this trip without recoaling at these islands. These conditions make Hawaii without question the most important strategic point on the Pacific.

What would be the value of these islands to the enemy in case of war between this country and any country in the Pacific? The military value of possession of Honolulu and Pearl Harbor to any enemy in the Pacific is so great that words fail in attempting to express it. With these harbors as a base of operations against our coast we are defenseless. Without them the enemy could do nothing until a port on our coast had been secured as a base, and this could never be accomplished until our fleet had been defeated. England is the one world power that could hope to make a successful attack on our Pacific Coast without first taking Hawaii. Any

A view of Pearl Harbor, looking seaward, showing sugar plantations in foreground

other power would have to be overwhelmingly strong on the seas, and even then a great risk would be incurred in attempting an attack of our coast without first securing a base. With Hawaii in the possession of the enemy the defense of the Pacific Coast is almost impossible without the presence on that coast of a naval force of overwhelming strength.

With these islands in our possession the tremendous advantage of their possession to the enemy is removed and the enemy is without a base of operation until one is secured either by taking the islands or by securing one on the mainland. It is easy to defend Honolulu and Pearl Harbor, and with these secure it will be exceedingly difficult for the enemy to secure a base on the mainland as long as we have a fleet in the Pacific. *Without such a fleet any defense of the Pacific Coast is impossible.* With the ports of Honolulu and Pearl Harbor properly fortified and with a great repair station and coaling plant at Pearl Harbor, Hawaii will not only be our outpost—our sentinel in mid-Pacific—but will be a base from which we can send a fleet to attack in the rear any fleet of the enemy that is attempting to make a demonstration against our home coast, or the fleet from Hawaii could cut off the communications between the attacking fleet and its home ports, or in case the

attacking fleet is driven from our coast the retreat could be cut off.

These ports will also be of the greatest benefit in an offensive campaign against any country in the Pacific. With a strong naval base at Hawaii and another in the Philippines we are in a position to take the offensive on the seas against any foe in the Pacific. Without these bases an offensive campaign is impossible. The history of the world proves that in nearly all cases an offensive campaign is the best defense, and the people of this country will never be satisfied with any other.

Undefended, both Hawaii and the Philippines are sources of weakness. Both countries are of such great value that, lying defenseless as they are, they invite an attack from a foreign power. The majority of the population of Hawaii is alien. It is reported on good authority that many of these aliens are trained soldiers. Under the present conditions these aliens could at any time take Hawaii. It is also recognized that in three weeks' time a foreign power could land a hundred thousand men in the Philippines and another hundred thousand in Hawaii. *Without the presence of a powerful fleet in the Pacific we are powerless to prevent this.*

As far back as 1852 Admiral Dupont, by direction of the Navy Department, made a report on the value of Hawaii in connection with the defense of the Pacific Coast in which he stated:

"It is impossible to estimate too highly the value and importance of the Sandwich islands, whether in a commercial or military point of view. Should circumstances ever place them in our hands they would prove the most important acquisition we could make in the whole Pacific ocean—an acquisition intimately connected with our commercial and naval supremacy in those seas."

In 1872 General Schofield and General Alexander of the army made a report on the great military value to this country of the ports of Honolulu and Pearl Harbor. From 1852 to this date all naval and military authorities have confirmed the views expressed by Admiral Dupont and Generals Schofield and Alexander.

With few exceptions the warships of the world burn coal. Practically no battleships carry sufficient coal to cross the Pacific; none can cross this ocean and have sufficient coal left to carry out operations against the enemy; all would be compelled to coal either in some port near mid-Pacific or in some port at the journey's end. Honolulu and Pearl Harbor are the only ports in the mid-Pacific where ships can safely be coaled, and a port at the journey's end in time of war could only be obtained by capture. The capture of such a port with ships without coal is an impossibility.

Both Honolulu and Pearl Harbor must be made impregnable against occupation by an enemy, and Pearl Harbor, if a naval base, must be made secure against bombardment. The two places are so close together and will in time of war be so dependent on each other that the defense of the two must be considered together. Honolulu can readily be made secure against a landing force attempting to occupy the city. Pearl Harbor, unlike Honolulu, can be made secure from bombardment *as well as* safe from occupation by a landing force. Owing to the distance from the ocean, batteries placed at the entrance of the channel could easily keep the enemy's ships beyond striking distance of the harbor, and these batteries, together with mines and torpedoes, would absolutely prevent any attempt on the part of the enemy's ships to enter the harbor.

England has long recognized the importance of a great naval base in the Mediterranean and has spent millions in making such a base at Malta, and no one will question the wisdom of this expenditure. A naval base in the Pacific is of far more importance to this country than Malta is to England. Let the people of this country immediately recognize this and make for this country, with the greatest possible speed, a second but greater Malta at Pearl Harbor. #

Not War, But Peace

By Judge Edward A. Belcher

January 1908

WHY do the newspapers so persistently prophesy war between Japan and the United States? What reason is there for such a war? In the nature and logic of contemporaneous history a war between the two nations would seem in the highest degree improbable. Continuously since the United States opened Japan to the civilization in which she has made such remarkable progress the relations between the two countries have been cordial. Japan's bright young men are graduated from our colleges of letters and of arms, her merchants have come to reside with us, our merchants have established permanent houses of business there and commerce between the two countries has increased enormously—that of the United States with Japan from about five millions to upward of fifty, and that of Japan with the United States from a few millions to upward of fifty millions of dollars annually, and that increase has largely been accomplished within the last ten years.

The United States has ever been the friend of Japan. Just at the right moment President Roosevelt interceded to terminate by diplomatic methods a great war in which that country had reached the limit of its financial resources and our sympathies throughout that war had been so pronouncedly for the Japanese as to excite protest upon the part of her adversary. What is there to fight about? Do the hoodlum incidents at San Francisco constitute *causus belli?* Assuredly not. They were merely local, and casual, and, at the worst view, of a nature to be fully and satisfactorily adjusted in our own courts—a familiar instance being the Chinese riots of 1876, in which judgments for damages against San Francisco to the extent of thirty thousand dollars, approximately, were recovered by the spoliated Chinese. We have nothing that Japan can want, the Philippines possibly excepted, and those she might be able to acquire from us more cheaply by diplomatic methods than by war; beside, if the Philippines were to be taken from us by force, national prestige, all other considerations apart, would compel us to retake them. Hawaii is strategically too far removed, for Japan can never have any occasion to colonize on this side of the Pacific, and propinquity not alone of blood but of territory is essential to Japanese growth and prosperity. Japan would recognize also that, with our long seaboard to guard—the Hawaiian islands being the strategic key of the northern Pacific—we could not part with these islands under any circumstances. But, all this apart, even though Japan had sound reason to feel bellicose, her statesmen would not fail to perceive that there would be grave difficulties in the way of financing a war against us. It is doubtful if Japan would be able to negotiate a loan for such a war. Great Britain, France and Germany would discern danger to the continuity of their interests in China in the event of Japanese success, for if Japan were to become the sea power of the Pacific, it would not require much effort upon her part to stir the slumbering masses of China and India to such a state of hostility as might eventuate in the ouster of all non-Asiatics from the continent of Asia.

There is another reason why Japan, save for the gravest reasons, would hesitate to declare war against us—if she were to lose one great sea fight with us her loss would be immeasurable, almost irreparable, as it would destroy her prestige, and to a large extent, her power to interpose a sufficient defense against another foe, implacable and ever menacing. No, Japan desires not war with us, but peace! #

A Record-Breaking Motor Run

July 1908

NO event during the past few seasons has emphasized so strongly the rapid improvement in automobile construction as did the recent thousand-mile trip of Fernando Nelson in his White steamer. As the owner of a thoroughbred is proud of the equine so is Nelson proud of his motor car, and he considers the fact that the White secured the blue-ribbon record of the Pacific Coast a great tribute, not only to his machine, but to the usefulness of the "twentieth century vehicle" in general.

On a Tuesday morning in April at three minutes past three with William Wagner at the wheel, Nelson next to him, and two occupants in the tonneau, the big auto left San Francisco (Guerrero and Market streets) for Los Angeles via the Coast route. When the machine was halted in front of the Times building in Los Angeles, seventeen hours and seventeen minutes had elapsed, this being the fastest automobile trip ever made between San Francisco and the southern California metropolis.

Only three years ago automobiles of any kind that could run one hundred miles without stopping for adjustments or repairs were the exception; yet Nelson wasn't content with his remarkable performance and the car was immediately turned around and driven over the same course in nineteen hours and forty-three minutes—though a twenty-four hour schedule had been planned—and the car arrived in San Francisco in perfect condition, the only stops on the entire journey being for water and gasoline, and a single puncture.

There are some persons who claim that road racing of this kind does not mean a great deal because it is merely a matter of luck or ill-luck whether the record sought is broken or not. To a certain extent luck undoubtedly enters into such contests—puncturing of tires may be termed a matter of ill-luck, and there are a score of small mishaps that may be termed ill-luck, but on the other hand the defenders of such records claim that the absence of the small mishaps is a fair proof of the mechanical perfection and the endurance of the car. #

During the spring floods, the Merced Rever cuts away great portions of its gravelly banks

Yosemite—Past and Present

By GALEN CLARK

April 1907

THE Yosemite valley was first discovered and made known to the public by Major James D. Savage and Captain John Boling, who with a strong detachment of mounted troops from what was known as the Mariposa Battalion of Volunteers went with friendly Indian guides to the Valley in March, 1851, to capture and take the resident tribe of Indians out and put them on the Fresno Indian reservation.

The first improved trail for saddle animals to Yosemite was made by a livery stable firm in Mariposa, the Mann Brothers, in 1856, from Mariposa by way of the South Fork of the Merced river, crossing the stream at a point now known as Wawona. In 1857 the regular tourist travel to Yosemite may be said to have commenced, although a few persons had gone there in the previous years. All parties at that time went with camping outfits. The first house in Yosemite was built in the fall of 1856 and

Editor's Note: The writer, who is over ninety years old, has resided in the great Sierra valley for over a half century and was for many years its guardian.

was opened up the next spring as a saloon for the entertainment of that class of visitors who loved whisky and gambling. The next year it was fitted up and used as a restaurant. Several years later it was enlarged and known as Black's hotel. The first building for a hotel was built in 1859, and is now a part of the Sentinel hotel premises known as the Cedar cottage.

Most of the early visitors to Yosemite were Californians, and the number did not amount to one thousand in any one season until the completion of the Union and Central Pacific railroads. Soon after that the number increased to many thousands annually.

All the necessary supplies for the hotels and other purposes were taken into the Valley by pack mule trains from Coulterville and Mariposa, a distance of fifty miles, until the completion of the first wagonroads into Yosemite in 1874.

The grand features and great variety of Yosemite scenery were early and widely made known throughout the civilized world, by pen and press, public speech, paint brush, camera and kodak. But no painting or photograph gives its vivid, thrilling life expression. I have seen persons of emotional temperament stand with tearful eyes, spellbound and dumb with awe, as they got their first view of the Valley from Inspiration point, overwhelmed in the sudden presence of the unspeakable, stupendous grandeur.

Since the completion of the Yosemite valley railroad up the Merced river to El Portal, near the western boundary of the Yosemite national park, the Government is having some excellent work done on the road leading up into the Valley, and if ample means are appropriated by the present congress the good work will continue on up to the hotel, public camps and around the Valley on the interesting carriage drives. It is to be hoped that the California delegation in congress may be successful in getting liberal appropriations for continuing, not only this good work, but all other important work for the protection and preservation of the scenic beauty of the Valley.

A great change has taken place in here since it was taken from the control of the native Indians. In the early years, when first visited by white people, three-fourths of the Valley was open ground, meadows with grasses waist high, and flowering plants. On the dryer parts were scattering forest trees, pines, cedars and oaks, too widely separated to be called groves, clear of underbrush, leaving clear, open, extensive vision up and down and across the Valley from wall to wall on either side. The Indians had kept the Valley clear of thickets of young trees and brushwood shrubbery so they could not be waylaid, ambushed or surprised by enemies from outside and to afford no hiding places for bears or other predatory animals, and also to clear the ground for gathering acorns, which constituted one of their main articles of food.

At the present time there is not more than one-fourth of the floor of the Valley clear, open ground as it was fifty years ago; nearly all the open ground between the large scattering trees is covered with a dense growth of young trees which also extend out over hundreds of acres of the dryest portion of the meadow land. Every pine tree on the floor of the Valley, less than seventy-five feet high, has grown from the seed within the last fifty years.

During recent years considerable work has been done in clearing up the young growth of trees and brushwood to afford better views of the distant scenery and to be better able to control fires, which accidentally get started during the dry season. In many localities where the work of thinning out and trimming up the young growth has been done, are desirable clean, shady groves for camping parties. There are still hundreds of acres where this reclaiming work needs to be continued to make the greater portion of the Valley accessible to visitors, and to break up the hidden retreats of bears which have taken up their permanent residence at several points. This last season an old female bear with two cubs has had a free pass throughout the Valley and has given ferocious chase to every photo artist who has attempted to get a picture of herself and family.

As this work of clearing up and reclaiming a large portion of Yosemite valley is one of great importance and national interest it should be done in accordance with plans submitted by the best landscape engineers, after a careful survey and study of the whole field, so as to show all scenery, local and surrounding, to the best advantage from the carriage roads, private walks and local resting places. Much of this work can be done at very little expense; all the larger growth to be cleared away can be cut into firewood and readily sold to residents for the cost of the cutting.

Another matter of paramount importance is the protection of the banks of the Merced river, as it runs its winding, crooked course through the length of the Valley. In the spring, when the flood waters from the melting snow on the surrounding heights pour over the great falls and fill the river channel to overflowing in many places, the strong current impinging against the gravelly substratum cuts it away and undermines the top surface grass sod, leaving it a loose deathtrap for man or beast that goes near its edge, until it breaks down of its own weight. A space several feet in width is cut away annually. During the past thirty years the river channel in many places has changed sidewise three times its original width, leaving a wide, barren waste of sand and gravel on the opposite side, thus destroying its original beauty.

It may be interesting to the public to know the cause of there being in recent years so much more activity in the river currents than during the earlier known history of Yosemite. When the El Capitan iron bridge was built in 1879 it was located across the narrow channel of the river between the two points of what remains of an old glacial terminal moraine. The river channel at this place was filled with large boulders, which greatly obstructed the free outflow of the flood waters in the spring, causing extensive overflow of the low meadow land above, and greatly interfering with travel, especially to Yosemite falls and Mirror lake. In order to remedy this matter the large boulders in the channel were blasted and the fragments leveled down so as to give a free outflow of the flood waters. This increased the force of the river current, which now commenced its greater eroding work on the river banks, and as the winding turns become more abrupt the destructive force annually increases. Some thorough system of protection should be promptly used to save the river banks from further damage. #

Girls — Two Types

By EUNICE JANES GOODEN

May 1908

Thinks the Cross-saddle Girl of the Side-saddle
    Girl,
  "A century back are you,
With your habit stiff and your modest ways
  And your notions not a few.
You can't take the trails or have any fun,
  And as for your horse, Miss Prim,
If he could but speak, he'd soon let you know
  Which method is kindest to him.

We're in for fun and a jolly good time,
  So we're off and away like the wind;
You, with your modesty, primness and all—
  We leave you far behind.
Ah, Side-saddle Girl, poor Side-saddle Girl,
  I'm sorry for you, you see;
I guess you can't help being as you are,
  So you have but pity from me!"

Thinks the Side-saddle Girl of the Cross-saddle
    Girl,
  "Can't mirrors or friends or books
Once open her eyes, the poor thing,
  To show her how she looks?
Let her climb the trails, the steepest,
  Tearing on with all her might,
If joy that be—but excuse me
  From looking such a fright!

Why, where's that 'girl's sweet modesty'
  The poets used to praise,
And must a girl turn cowboy, to
  Have fun these modern days?
Yet, Cross-saddle Girl, poor Cross-saddle Girl,
  I'm sorry for you, you see;
I guess you can't help being as you are,
  So you have but pity from me."

So the Cross-saddle Girl and the Side-saddle Girl,
  Each continues her pity to waste,
Each pained in the heart beyond all words,
  That the other should show such poor taste!

Safe Advertising

We stand for safe advertising.

Any other kind is unnecessary.

The day when advertising was speculation is over for the man who knows.

A newspaper campaign can be proved out in six towns just as well as in six hundred.

A magazine campaign can be proved in six mediums just as well as in sixty.

Before one spreads out he can know to a certainty what the results will be.

Our question is never, What are you going to spend?

Though our revenue, as with all agents, is a commission, paid largely to us by magazines and newspapers, on the expenditure.

We ask ourselves, rather, What are the possibilities?

And we accept or refuse an account on our judgment of them.

We can do this because we command the ability to make a success of anything possible.

We are willing to abide by results.

The largest accounts we have were started with small expenditures.

On many, we spent ten times our commission in working out the first campaign.

Each dollar spent came back with a profit. We proved it beyond any question.

Then the advertiser, naturally, spent all the dollars he could.

We are ready to do the same with you, if your line has possibilities.

We have spent 35 years in advertising.

Yet every week we learn something new of what it can do.

Note how advertising has multiplied in the past few years.

Note the vast variety of little and big things now being made to pay.

Ten years ago, most of these things seemed impossible.

Hundreds of these new accounts, in unexplored fields, are due to our development.

We have done so many things, never done before, that we have come to believe that almost anything can now be done by advertising.

But it cannot be done, in these days, without experience and ability.

There is too much good advertising to leave any chance for the amateur.

We Pay One Ad-Writer $1,000 per Week

Mr. Claude C. Hopkins, now permanently at the head of our copy department, receives a salary of $1,000 per week.

The highest salary ever paid in advertising.

But Mr. Hopkins, as a salesman in print, is unrivaled.

He has made more money for advertisers, in more different lines, than any other man who ever wrote copy.

Many of the greatest successes of the past twenty years have been due to his copy and schemes.

And he is safe. Experienced enough to avoid the impossible. Able enough to make the possible pay.

We have in our copy department, under Mr. Hopkins, the ablest men we know.

Men whom we pick out, without regard to expense, by the brilliant results that we see them accomplish.

We are seeking everywhere, all the time, for the men who make the exceptional records.

In this vortex of advertising—in this school of experience—such men multiply their powers.

All of these writers advise with Mr. Hopkins. All copy must meet his approval.

Our Advisory Board

Our Advisory Board consists of sixteen men, all masters of advertising.

Each is a man of proved ability, and of vast experience.

Mr. Hopkins is at the head of it.

Before this whole Board comes every large problem of present or possible clients.

Here we discuss the advice to be given to any concern that consults us. And this advice is free.

These sixteen men decide what is possible and what is impossible. They decide on means and schemes and copy.

Thus all the ability, all the experience, at our command is brought to bear on each problem.

That is why we succeed.

Yet this high-priced talent is not an expense to us; not an expense to our clients.

We handle advertising on the usual agent's commission.

These brilliant men all earn their way by developing the small account into the large one.

By making advertising so profitable that it expands, while minor men would kill it.

It is far cheaper for us to keep advertisers, and to develop them, than to constantly solicit new.

To New Advertisers

If your article has possibilities, tell us about it. We will gladly give you our judgment.

If the thing is impossible, we won't undertake it. We cannot afford the time.

If the thing has a future, we will tell you how to safely prove it out.

We have made hundreds of fortunes in this way.

To Old Advertisers

Give us a limited territory—a limited number of mediums.

Do this, if you wish, without disturbing present relations.

Let us prove our claims. Learn what new ideas our able men may work out for you — what new view-point they can bring to bear.

Then compare the results.

Don't let us argue. Let us leave the question of who gets your advertising to some proved results.

Can you, Mr. Business-Man, neglect such an offer as that?

Please cut out this coupon—now while you think of it. Send it to get our book "Safe Advertising"—a brilliant example of our advertising powers.

Then form your own judgment of what we can do.

LORD & THOMAS
NEWSPAPER, MAGAZINE AND OUTDOOR
ADVERTISING

AMERICAN TRACT SOC. BLDG.   TRUDE BUILDING

NEW YORK   CHICAGO

The Hetch-Hetchy Problem

By JOHN P. YOUNG

June 1909

NOTE: The recent action of the citizens of San Francisco in voting for the issuance of bonds to the amount of $600,000 for the preliminary development of an adequate city water supply, and the subsequent steps to secure the supply from the high Sierra in the Hetch-Hetchy valley region has attracted widespread attention to this notable natural wonder and caused much controversy concerning the results of the undertaking. In the following article the writer describes in detail from personal observation the wonders of Hetch-Hetchy and contends that the ultimate utilization of a portion of the floor of the valley as a reservoir site would enhance, rather than detract, from its scenic value:

CALIFORNIA possesses a scenic gem whose name is almost unknown outside of the state, and is chiefly familiar to its inhabitants at present because the future demands of San Francisco for a supply of potable drinking water has attracted attention to its possibilities as a site for a great reservoir. It is about two hundred miles distant from the city by the Golden Gate and is known as the Hetch-Hetchy valley, which, in the language of the Indians of the Sierra, signifies "mighty wind." Since the occupation of California the valley has probably been visited by less than 3000 persons all told. During the season of 1908, it was penetrated by about three hundred, including the soldiers who are policing the Yosemite Forest Reservation, members of the Sierra Club, investigators of water possibilities and a few lovers of nature who do not shrink from encountering the discomforts of the rudest of mountain trails in their quest of beautiful scenery. To the tourist it is a terra incognita.

As the crow flies Hetch-Hetchy is about twenty miles northwest of the Yosemite valley. Its proximity to this great scenic wonder naturally suggests that the increasing number of tourists visiting the valley, celebrated throughout the world for its grandeur and beauty, would interest themselves in a comparatively nearby attraction, but it will not exceed the bounds of truth to assert that of the nearly 10,000 persons who entered Yosemite in 1908, probably not one hundred knew anything of Hetch-Hetchy.

To the adventuresome ready to separate themselves from the enervating luxuries of modern civilization and willing to get close to nature, with all that such closeness implies, Hetch-Hetchy extends an invitation which is well worth acceptance. At present, however, it is not a valley which one may enter without making his plans in advance, for it is absolutely deficient in places of entertainment. The visitor to Hetch-Hetchy must be his own host; he has no other resource than to become a camper, for throughout its length and breadth there exists but one tumble-down cabin, long since deserted, which no self-respecting lover of out-of-doors life would occupy.

The party that I had the good fortune to accompany on its visit of inspection was the largest, with the exception of one sent out by the Sierra Club, that ever entered Hetch-Hetchy in a body. It was composed of the members of the board of supervisors of San Francisco, the engineer of the city and other municipal officials and representatives of the press. Preparations were made in advance by establishing a camp in the valley, as several days were to be spent in examining its watershed and that of Lake Eleanor, which lies a few miles northwest of Hetch-Hetchy, at a higher elevation that can only be reached by an extremely precipitous trail.

The road from the Yosemite to Sequoia, or to Crocker's, as it is more familiarly known, is wholly within the Yosemite National Park. It was formerly used in approaching the Yosemite valley by way of Stockton, but since the completion of the railroad to El Portal it has been abandoned by the stages, and the only traffic over it is of an extremely localized character. In the drive of twenty-six miles

The falls of the Hetch-Hetchy

between the Sentinel hotel in the Yosemite and Crocker's, we encountered a single vehicle and saw but three of four persons. But while evidence of human life and activity are scarce enough along the road to be regarded as a negligible quantity, travel over it is unceasingly interesting.

The floor of the Hetch-Hetchy valley lies at an elevation of 3600 feet above sea level, but the contours of the map of the Geological Survey show that it is inclosed by ridges and peaks which rise to a height of 7000 feet. Before the sightseer's eyes rest upon the object of his quest he is treated to a view of the Poopenaut valley, a narrow bit of emerald, in a rugged setting, through which the Tuolumne flows. It is first seen from the trail at a point, perhaps, 1500 feet above its floor, and provides that delicious sensation which water in combination with green meadows offers to the weary and dust-laden traveler.

Poopenaut performs the double function of relieving the monotony of a zig-zag, up-and-down trail, which is scarcely interrupted by an occasional slip of the mule you are riding, and which has the effect of raising a doubt in your mind regarding his sure-footedness, and it serves as an annunciator of more scenic delights to come, for the glimpse of the narrow vale is very shortly followed by the revelation of the glories of Hetch-Hetchy. They burst upon you suddenly as you make a turn in the trail and come to the bench which has been aptly named Surprise Point.

Perhaps it would be well to at once concede that a description of the impression produced by the view from Surprise Point cannot do justice to the subject. Applause which does not attempt to formulate itself, and is a practical admission of inability to command more definitely expressive language is undoubtedly the best vehicle to unburden oneself of the emotion excited by a great natural spectacle.

Hetch-Hetchy, as already stated, is a depression in the Sierra, lying 3660 feet above the sea level. It is about five miles in length between the points where the river enters the valley from the Grand cañon of the Tuolumne to its outlet through a gorge at its western extremity, and varies in width from a mile where it is broadest to less than 300 yards in its narrowest part. Its floor is nearly level, a fact which explains the slowness of the current of the stream during the dry season, and is broken in but few places by slight elevations, which except in one instance, do not deserve to be described as hills. Except at the places where the river enters and makes its exit the valley is inclosed by ridges, bold walls and peaks which rise to a height of 6000 feet above the level of the sea, or more than 2000 feet above the floor of the valley.

The Tuolumne finds its way into the valley through a gorge at its eastern end, which has been well called a "grand cañon." Grand is a greatly overworked word, but its application in this instance is deserved. The cañon furnishes a marvelous exhibition of the erosive force of water, and differs utterly in appearance from the wonderful gorges of the Colorado and the Yellowstone. The river at the point where it enters Hetch-Hetchy takes a tumble over rocks thirty or forty feet high into a basin nearly circular, in which trout in abundance may be seen disporting themselves. The cañon itself is rugged beyond description and can only be penetrated with great difficulty.

The Tuolumne by no means loses its beauty when it emerges from its rocky gorge to continue its course through the valley. If possible it adds to its charms. In the summer time it meanders peacefully through the verdant meadows, hugging the base of the walls which inclose Hetch-Hetchy on the north, reflecting its peaks and rocks in innumerable places. Mirror lake of the Yosemite is repeated a hundred times in the reaches of this wonderful stream, whose tree-fringed banks are pictured on its glossy surface.

The Tuolumne of August is the one whose praises I sing; of the other Tuolumne there is a different story to tell, one that may be learned without visiting Hetch-Hetchy in the winter to hear it roar its song of power and might, for it is eloquently told in the marks along its banks, which indicate the high-water stage, and in the huge bowlders which strew its bed, many of them worn to a smoothness and roundness that make them fitting playthings for the river when

in its torrential mood. This latter aspect of the Tuolumne is the one which had the most attention bestowed upon it by the supervisorial party, for it presented unequivocal evidence of the capacity of the watershed to fill any reservoir which may be created by damming the outlet of the valley. The most superficial examination of the markings I have spoken of indicates that in normal years a dam at the outlet of the valley 250 feet in height would store 65,000,000,000 gallons, and the impoundment of this vast quantity of water would not interfere in the slightest degree with the irrigation operations of that portion of the great San Joaquin valley dependent upon the Tuolumne.

The creation of this reservoir is not an affair of the immediate future. Before any attempt is made to dam the outlet of Hetch-Hetchy in order to create a water supply for San Francisco, other sources must be exhausted.

But those controlling the destinies of the city by the Golden Gate project themselves well into the future, and predict that before the half-way mark of the present century has been reached it may contain over a million inhabitants, and there are some sanguine enough to dream of still greater numbers. If these optimistic views are realized considerations of estheticism will be swept aside by more imperative demands. While the contest is not imminent, the question has already been raised whether the preservation of a scenic gem is of more consequence than the needs of a great and growing community.

It is probable that when the crucial time comes the protestants will be wholly silent, for the ultimate conclusion of all who will attentively study the results of transforming Hetch-Hetchy into a great lake must be that the transformation will convert it into a greater scenic wonder than it is at present.

It is true that the meadows and trees of the valley would be submerged, but the immense reservoir created would substitute in their place a vastly more attractive feature, which would prove a far more powerful attraction to persons in search of inspiring scenery than the eliminated beauties have in the past. The lake would still be inclosed by towering peaks and massive walls, and the falls of the Hetch-Hetchy, which rival that of Yosemite in volume

*It is hoped to divert a good part of this flow of sparkling
water—The Tuolumne River—to supply San Francisco's daily needs*

of water and height, would still continue to tumble over the depression into which the drainage of an extensive watershed, 2000 or 3000 feet above the floor of the valley converges before taking its sheer leap of nearly 1300 feet to mingle with the Tuolumne—a feat it does not achieve until it takes a second drop of about 800 feet. The magnificent Kulahnah dome, over 2000 feet in height, would mirror itself in the waters of the new creation, as would the massive walls which inclose the valley on its north side, and the Grand cañon would retain its attractions unimpaired, for even with a 250-foot dam at its western end the waters of the reservoir would not back far up the gorge, which would probably be made more accessible than it is at present.

Engineers who have investigated the problem express the opinion that no difficulty which the expenditure of money cannot overcome will be encountered in encircling the reservoir with a road which would permit the inspection of its beauties and that of the surrounding peaks and rocky walls, and which would open to exploration spots now unknown to the most venturesome Sierra climber. Such a roadway would be called into existence by the necessities of construction and maintenance, and would be passable for people whose love of grand scenery is as ardent as that of the hardier admirer of nature who sometimes selfishly urges that none but the robust deserve to be gratified. If the conversion of Hetch-Hetchy into a great and beautiful lake will make its surroundings more accessible, the nature lover will have no cause for complaint. It will not be an exchange of old lamps for new; some of its present adornments will disappear, but in their place will be substituted that which will make Hetch-Hetchy incomparable and cause it to rank as one of the world's scenic wonders. #

Two famous nature lovers in a California garden—
John Muir (by the fern) and John Burroughs, from a photograph taken by King, in Pasadena, on the occasion of
the recent meeting of these great apostles of the out of doors

The Gospel for July

WANDER A WHOLE SUMMER, IF
YOU CAN. THOUSANDS OF GOD'S
WILD BLESSINGS WILL SEARCH YOU
AND SOAK YOU AS IF YOU WERE A
SPONGE AND THE BIG DAYS WILL GO
BY UNCOUNTED. IF YOU ARE BUSI-
NESS TANGLED AND SO BURDENED
BY DUTY THAT ONLY WEEKS CAN BE
GOT OUT OF THE HEAVY LADEN YEAR,
GIVE A MONTH AT LEAST. THE TIME
WILL NOT BE TAKEN FROM YOUR SUM
OF LIFE. INSTEAD OF SHORTENING
IT WILL INDEFINITELY LENGTHEN IT
AND MAKE YOU TRULY IMMORTAL.
NEVERMORE WILL TIME SEEM SHORT
OR LONG AND CARES WILL NEVER
AGAIN FALL HEAVILY ON YOU, BUT
GENTLY AND KINDLY AS GIFTS FROM
HEAVEN.

JOHN MUIR.

July 1909

Down the Sierra by Gravity Car

By RUFUS STEELE

April 1908

"**Z** U-U-U-UT!" It is not easy to spell out the music of a gravity car cut loose from the summit of the Sierra. You cling to the flat platform whose greatest dimension is its width as it streaks along above four shimmering wheels. The whole contrivance weighs less than one hundred pounds—weighs so little that two men can leap from its deck and snatch it from the rails when the Overland, emerging from a curve in the shed, swoops down like a visible bolt of thunder. And, too, it is well to have it light so that when the men have only time to save their lives the ponderous engine, unable even to slacken its speed in so short a space, can pitch the gravity car through the wall or the roof of the shed with no disaster to itself.

"Zu-u-u-u-ut!" The thrill of the ride wakes up your bones before you have rounded the first curve, which is never more than a few hundred feet away. You hurtle along with a smoothness such as no engine-drawn car can ever know. It is most like coasting down a perfect hill in an auto with the gasoline shut off. Five miles of it and your heart has sunk from your throat back into your breast and you know you would never trade this automatic for any auto in the land. They do not weight the flying platform even with a brake!

Crouched upon the swaying deck, you are conscious of the trained man who engineers your special towering above you, braced only by the muscles of his rigid legs. You may feel that he carries his own life as well as yours in one hand; he is remembering merely that in his other he holds poised a rough strip of board. When his fixed gaze catches a shadow in the turn ahead or when his cocked ears gather a faint sound from behind—it can't be far behind or it would never penetrate above the din of your own flight—he shoots the board down against the forward wheel over a projecting bolt which serves as a fulcrum and pulls back with all his strength. Under pressure of the crude brake the spinning wheel shrieks as if it were being ripped out of its skin—if there be a nail in the board the sparks streak out like a fuse—and you halt with a promptness that stirs you to solemn thankfulness.

In a jiffy you are off, the car is off and tilted against the wall of the snowshed. Something big and black and terrible at such close quarters goes by with a string of cars in its wake, and while you are still deaf from the groaning and pounding and still blinded and choked by the smoke, you are free to drop your private train back upon the rails and resume your flight.

After all, in spite of the big engines, greedy for the space you occupy, this is much the safest form of flying. In the splendid exhilaration of whizzing down the sheds, with the car seeming to stand still and the mountain to fly past as we plunged through the inky tunnels, around innumerable curves, now flashing past a fire gap and now out into the broad sunlight to find ourselves shot along the tresseled skyline of a saw-toothed divide, conscious of a mighty backache upon remembering that the Limited, traveling at double our speed, was behind us and due, I almost forgot those more prosaic things which I had come far to see. #

Exploring Oregon's Marble Caves

By JOAQUIN MILLER

September 1909

THE wondrous marble halls of Oregon lie close against the northern line of California, and it is not unreasonable to believe it will be found finally that they pierce entirely through the marble summits of the Siskiyou mountains and have an opening on the California side. As one garrulous old miner told me, "When Joaquin Murietta infested Californy he used to drive his horses through them to Oregon and sell 'em to your web-feet."

As yet the caves are only partly explored. They are not newly discovered, by any means. But they have been left almost entirely alone since 1875, when Elijah Davidson, a hunter trailing a white-faced bear, found the little doorway in the face of a marble cliff, and only

recently has attention been attracted to what will some day be known as one of the wonder places of the world.

A geologist and an all-round learned man of Ashland, Oregon, one C. B. Watson, came to me here in California one summer and said:

"Look here! that thing over there under the line between the two states is not a cave at all; it is a succession of marble grottoes; grotto on top of grotto, four or five stories high and from five to ten miles deep. I have been there twice and know more about this wondrous place than anyone else, and yet I know next to nothing about it, as yet. Come, let us go together and look into it."

Casting about to make up a party, we picked on a native son of Oregon, Jefferson Myers, the founder and real practical father of the recent triumphant Lewis and Clark exposition, and I persuaded him to go with us, to "look into the thing." After nearly two months' delay we three met at a pretty town on the banks of the Rogue River, fully equipped with compass, lines of measurement and instruments of all sorts, blankets, books, maps and so on. We added two local guides to the party—one a sort of sawed-off John Muir, the other a mountain dairyman—and headed for the far-away caves.

We climbed and climbed as if to over-take the evening star, until finally we reached the mouth of the marble cavern, deep in the enveloping woods.

We entered at once, fronting a continuous wind that at first put out our candles. We had a railroad lantern and this served to guide us up the beautiful little stream that flows uniform all the year from the far interior, fresh, sweet and cold, cold as Klondike. We walked erect for a time, almost to our knees in the sparkling stream; then we had to lean very low. Soon, however, we stood erect again. Then we climbed a ladder and were quite away from the swift water on the floor. We stood on the second flat or second story of the piled up tiers of marble-built grottoes.

Then another ladder, then a long descent where one leans low, stumbles, slides, falls, bumps the knees, stubs the toes and, to be frank, cusses. After about two hours of this sort of exploring we found our way out, not far from camp, but about two hundred feet higher than the main entrance. And two, or at most three hours of this constant climbing, creeping, clinging and the inevitable exclamations, is all you want in one instalment. For you must know the strain is constant, almost terrible. It is not the physical torment or the wear and tear of flesh and raiment, but the continuous tax on your mental make-up, as you pass from room to room, from grotto to grotto, each one a museum, a marvel, a miracle, each one utterly indescribable, each one utterly unlike the rest and yet all monotonously alike. But it is the imperial monotony of the stars!

Danger there is in these tortuous interiors, and plenty. For example: there is the Bottomless Pit and Nick's Slide. Then there is Roosevelt's Ride. This is simply a high, sharp marble ridge on which you hitch yourself along with a leg dangling down each side while your head knocks the sharp pendant stalactites at nearly every hitch. But you must keep your seat! For either side of the hog's back or ridge seems bottomless, although you hear the water far below. The only really safe way, to my mind, is to keep away from these places. "Paradise Lost" is a creepy place. Keep out of it. We got in there by accident, or, to be frank about it, we got lost, and so it was that we put up the sign "Paradise Lost."

As we had stayed over time inside, one of the guides seemed to be in great haste to get out and so took us by a cutoff way that had no outlet. He first tried this way and that, but at last sat down exhausted and said we would have to go back. As this native son, too venturesome all the time, by half, had just saved himself from a fall of two hundred feet, simply by being tall enough to reach the roof above with his hand, and as I had "cooned" under a cliff at the risk of my life and felt sure I could not now turn around without slipping off into the chasm below, I began to think of a few of the many bad things I had done and to wish the whole marble show in sheol.

Just then, the little bear dog that we had left in camp came bounding up to join his master, barking at every jump and shaking his dripping hide with delight. Here was a revelation! This dog could not climb the ladders. He had kept on right up the stream and then had found his way to us by unknown passages. The dog brought a full battery of fresh courage to the whole tired and distracted party. We followed his wet tracks back and scrambled out.

After lots of discussion that night the geologist insisted that we must see what possible connection there might be between the Bottomless Pit and the place of entrance by which the dog had come; so he and the whole party, with a lot of Roman candles, pushed away back to the pit, while I remained at the entrance to listen and look. I heard no sound, nothing at all. But by and by powder smoke began to pour out as if they were having a fourth of July. And the smoke must have followed the little brook as straight as a string, for they explained that it did not rise in their faces or cause them any inconvenience whatever.

That night a mountain storm struck us in all the splendor and glory of lightning and thunder. Skeins of fire threaded through the trees and ribbons of flame tied the swaying tree tops together, as a cunning gardener might tie a bouquet of flowers.

The next morning, a dozen wet, draggled and dripping, worn and weary human beings, mostly beautiful Oregon girls, the most beautiful on earth, rode down the precipitous hillside and literally rolled off their horses. They had spent the night of thunder and flame on the mountain top! And never were such glad waiters in all this world as we all were to give them coffee and crackers and bacon and bacon and crackers and coffee. And then we sent them with our guides on a trip of three hours through the less dangerous chambers of the marble halls. And then more bacon and coffee and coffee and bacon; and their faces were set the other way with one of our guides, while we with the other set off in the rain at a run down the plunging creek for the nearest habitation, a miner's cabin five miles distant in the depth of the woods. We had no fish, no hope of fish, nor had we even so much as a bacon rind left. But even though empty of food we were filled with exultation and delight up to the top hoop. #

Eucalyptus—Hickory's Younger Brother

By F. D. CORNELL

March and September 1909

NOTE: Still the eucalyptus fever spreads. Over fifty thousand acres have been planted to these useful trees during the past twelve months in California. In the Santa Clara valley a million trees are being propagated for next season's planting. The Sacramento valley boasts of the largest eucalyptus grove in the world. This state-wide planting of hardwood forests, under conditions favorable to their growth, is one of the notable examples of intelligent provision for the future. An expert in eucalyptus culture points out in the following article the basis of utility upon which this new industry rests.

CALIFORNIANS have a slight acquaintance with the eucalyptus tree, commonly called the "gum" tree, but few possess knowledge of it or have given thought to its commercial value, or the production on an enormous scale to supply hardwood timber.

The tree is a native of Australia and the adjacent islands. It belongs to the family *Myrtaceae,* and to the tribe *Leptospermae,* of which tribe it is the principal genus, numbering over one hundred and fifty distinct species. The genus was first discovered by the French botanist, L. Heritier, in 1788, and was named by him *eucalyptus,* meaning "well concealed," the name being prompted by the closely covered and well concealed flower buds. Baron von Mueller, who was perhaps the greatest authority on the subject of eucalyptus, and to which he devoted a long life of loving labor, suggested the general term "eucalypts," which name has been almost universally adopted.

Through the efforts of von Mueller and several French scientists the genus was introduced into Europe about the middle of the last century. Appreciation of the tree was so great that all sections of Europe, where climatic conditions permit, are now graced with forests—beautiful, profitable, inspiring, and in many instances furnishing a sole source of timber and fuel supply. All countries bordering on the Mediterranean owe a deep debt to the tree. They are planted also in Asia and on an unbelievable scale in the Soudan and in the Transvaal. The British government maintains a bureau for the gathering and distribution of the seed to parts of its African possessions not favored with native forests. The Transvaal is already reaping benefit in many directions from the trees—in timber, fuel, climatic betterment, soil and moisture improvement, and a conservation of the water supply.

The tree was introduced into California in 1856. In 1870, Elwood Cooper, of Santa Barbara, commenced large planting operations to test many species. The success of his experiments was marked and he continued his planting until to-day he has a large forest, comprising many species. They are planted on steep, rocky hillsides, for forest cover, for windbreaks and hedgerows and as a source of fuel, posts and piling. His plantings would be classed as utility plantings, and not as a commercial timber enterprise.

Abbot Kinney, as chairman of the California Board of Forestry from 1886 to 1888, gave the planting of the trees a great impetus, and distributing many species that might otherwise still be unknown to us. He published in 1895 the most complete work on the eucalypts ever produced in America, but the first American work was published by Mr. Cooper in 1875.

The genus comprises a wonderful array of trees, including species which produce specimens so gigantic as to rival the sky-piercing *sequoia;* others are mere bushes; others thrive in swamp land; others in coastal situations or on high plateaus, hillsides, rocky lands and deserts. There seems no limit to the adaptability of some one of the trees to any given

A Fortune for You

IN EUCALYPTUS

Eucalyptus, 1 year old
Willows, California

Eucalyptus, 20 years old
Willows, California

The above is a graphic illustration of the growth of Eucalyptus in Glenn County, California. The year-old tree is 2 inches in diameter. The 20-year-old tree is 36 inches in diameter.

We have 640 acres planted—680 trees to the acre—in Glenn County, California. Our plantations (comprising over 3000 acres) lie on both sides of the Southern Pacific Railway and 7 miles from the Sacramento River, navigable for 50 miles north of our landing. The soil is a rich valley loam and will produce any crop grown in California.

We expect an average diameter growth of 1½ inches per year. A 7-year-old tree averaging 10 inches in diameter is conservatively worth $6.00. Five acres growing 2500 trees would then be worth $15,000.00. Cut one-seventh each year and your annual income will be $2000.00.

The sprout growth from the stump produces another tree in one-fifth less time than the original growth.

We offer you a warranty deed to five acres of this land growing 2500 trees for $250.00 per acre, less 10% for cash. You may buy on easy monthly payments if you wish.

All deeds are held and delivered by the Bank of Willows, Willows, Cal.

Should you die after one-half has been paid the Bank will deliver the deed to your heirs without further payment.

Write us for Bulletins from the Forestry Society of California and our literature, maps, etc., proving the value of Eucalyptus in California.

THE FOREST SYNDICATE

DEPT. S, 963-5-6 PACIFIC BUILDING, SAN FRANCISCO, CALIFORNIA

SUNSET MAGAZINE has investigated The Forest Syndicate through the Commercial Agencies and other sources and all reports received are favorable.

soil and moisture conditions, but the entire genus is intolerant of cold, and therefore is confined to those sections of the globe where favorable climatic conditions obtain.

The eucalyptus most widely known is the *E. globulus,* or blue gum. This has been introduced to most foreign lands where conditions will permit and is found in California from San Diego to Shasta. It is a rapid grower, possibly the most rapid of all, producing a wood that makes an excellent fuel, hard, tough, and very strong. It is being used for agricultural implements, insulator pins, and other purposes requiring an exceedingly strong wood. It is also used for piling and proves fifty per cent more durable and lasting than any wood thus far used on this Coast. The blue gum does not last well in the ground, and cannot be used for posts and poles. It is principally prized for piling, some manufactures, for fuel, and as a windbreak and forest cover.

E. corynocalyx, commonly known as sugar gum, is a species that is certain to be largely grown. The timber is very durable, very strong, tough, resistant. The tree grows tall, slender and very straight, putting out but few branches and dropping these when planted in forest form, as the trees reach skyward. It is a very hardy species, and when treated fairly makes a rapid growth. It will prove of unusual value for poles, and for implement and vehicle work. Like most eucalypts the sugar gum will endure

Hundreds of eucalyptus axe handles, ready for cutting of thousands of eucalyptus trees

Popular forms of mission furniture are being made of eucalyptus wood

almost anything except cold; but also thoroughly appreciates best conditions. As a forest cover on barren hillsides, and for arid desert-like regions the sugar gum will render a magnificent service to the Southwest. It furnishes wood most nearly equaling American hickory. In my judgment *E. corynocalyx* and *E. globulus* will replace oak, hickory and ash in the manufacture of implements, vehicles, and kindred products.

A few short years ago the commercial culture of eucalyptus trees was not numbered among the great opportunities offered by California climate, soil and sunshine, nor was this industry for a moment considered a candidate for first place among industries of the state. To-day commercial eucalyptus, meaning the culture of the eucalyptus tree on a tremendous scale for the production of hardwood timber for the manufactures, industries and arts, is such a candidate. Today there are perhaps ten thousand acres of California soil planted to timber eucalypts, part of this intensely commercial, part more designed for soil reclamation, water conservation, afforestation and fuel. In another twelve months probably fifteen thousand acres of strictly commercial forests will be planted. Another year and the planting will perhaps be doubled or trebled.

The physical characteristics of the timber and its adaptability to a multitude of uses are truly remarkable. The possible uses rise from plow beams to intricate parquetry; from railroad ties to magnificent veneers; from cord wood to the highest type of the craftsman's art. The list of purposes to which the timber of the many species has been found particularly adapted includes the following:

Fuel, posts and piling; for ship building, masts and spars; for decking, sheathing, wharf and pier construction, and all marine architecture; for railroad ties, bridge timbers, car construction and myriad uses of transportation industries; for furniture, fine interior finish, fixtures, carved and parquetry work; barrels, kegs and all cooperage work, tight and loose; tool handles, spokes, felloes, hubs, plow beams, singletrees, tongues, and all implement and vehicle work; bowling alleys, and finest flooring; cross trees, insulator pins, pulley blocks; musical instruments, pianos, organs, violins—in short, the timber eucalypts will supply a satisfactory material for every purpose to which any hardwood is put. For all the purposes named the timber of the eucalypts *has* been used, and will be increasingly used, and, finally, for a vast majority of purposes, exclusively used. #

$\mathcal{C}he$ EDISON PHONOGRAPH

is the only sound-reproducing instrument with Edison's latest improvements. It has the clearest, strongest Records, the most durable reproducing point and the correctly shaped horn.

THE Edison Phonograph also offers a form of amusement which cannot be obtained in any other similar instrument, and that is the fun of making your own records. For a small additional expense you can obtain from your dealer a recorder and blank records, by which you can make your own records, and listen to the sound of your own voice and that of your friends. Many an evening's novel entertainment may be had in this way.

TRADE MARK

Thomas A. Edison

Ten Edison Records made by Mr. William Jennings Bryan

We have pleasure in announcing ten Edison Records made by Mr. Bryan at his home in Lincoln, Nebraska, consisting of the best passages from his favorite speeches. Ready at all Edison stores this month. Ask your dealer. Besides the twenty-four Records in the regular list, the July Records contain five new Grand Opera selections by famous operatic stars. Hear them at the nearest Edison store on June 25th.

Ask your dealer or write to us for the new catalogue of Edison Phonographs, THE PHONOGRAM, describing each July Record in detail; and the COMPLETE CATALOGUE, listing all Edison Records now in existence.

NATIONAL PHONOGRAPH COMPANY, 31 Lakeside Avenue, Orange, New Jersey

Mystics, Babies, and Bloom

Point Loma's Raja Yoga, Where People Live in Sunshine, and Grow in Joy and Wisdom

By KARL HEINRICH VON WIEGAND

August 1909

EMERGING from the past with its history, psychical, occult and spiritualistic phenomena, stories of masters and mahatmas in the Himalayas who projected themselves through space, and charges and counter charges of various kinds tenaciously clinging to it, Madame Katherine Tingley's, theosophical movement at Point Loma has been successfully placed upon a plane as intensely practical as others have appeared mysterious, vague and unreal, by blending ideality with extreme practicability and combining humanitarianism, education and an oriental system of philosophy.

A launch conveyed me across the placid waters of the bay of San Diego to Roseville, a straggling village on the opposite side. From there a ten minutes' walk through a romantic little cañon, or a carriage ride along the winding road up the beautiful slope, brings the visitor to the Point Loma bungalow and Tent village, a summer and winter resort established by Madame Tingley. Here you register, and for ten cents buy a ticket which admits you to the grounds farther up the ridge. A short walk brought me to the entrance, which is through an Egyptian gate. A soldierly appearing young man, clad in a military uniform of olive-tan, stepped from a sentry-box almost hidden in the shrubbery, and took my ticket as well as my kodak, courteously informing me that cameras were not allowed on the grounds.

A watch tower on the ridge to the left; Old Glory floating in the breeze from a tall flagstaff near by, marking the site of the proposed school for the revival of the lost mysteries of antiquity; the military-like figures armed with sprinkling cans, among the shrubbery and flowers; the sentry-box at the gate and a bugle signal by the sentinel announcing that visitors were coming, created the feeling that I was entering a military reservation. This impression, however, quickly left me as I walked up the avenue lined with graceful palms and beautiful trees. The air was redolent with the perfume of flowers. The sweet music of children's voices singing floated down upon the soft, balmy atmosphere from one of the white buildings on the summit, whose immense domes reflected the dazzling sun. Arrived at the top, another khaki-clad figure appeared and took the visitors in charge, who, with the exception of myself, were restricted to a general view of the buildings from the outside and a small part of the grounds. As the place has become a scenic point of considerable interest to tourists, the piloting through of the visitors interrupted the scholastic, artistic and general work of the various departments, distracted the attention of students and interfered with studies.

In every direction a magnificent and different panorama was unfolded. In the center of the picture, amid extensive grounds artistically laid out and set with many varieties of flowers, trees and semi-tropical plants, are the white brotherhood buildings—the Aryan memorial temple and Girls' dormitory and Raja Yoga academy—of striking architecture and graceful lines, o'ertopped with double domes, one of aqua marine and the other of heliotrope or purplish color, which reflect the sun by day and are illuminated by night. Just to the north of the main buildings is a cottage of unique architecture, built upon a geometrical pattern, something like an octagon, with much glass, wide verandas and a small dome, the home of A. G. Spalding, the millionaire

Domes of the Aryan Temple and Raja Yoga Academy, rising amid luxuriant gardens, are visible for miles from Point Loma

manufacturer of sporting goods, who is a prominent member of the organization.

The general architecture of the main buildings, their decoration and general arrangement is strange to the West, but is along a well defined plan and after the style peculiar to ancient Greece, Egypt and Assyria.

It required little effort of the imagination to place oneself on the shores of the Aegean sea or looking down upon the Mediterranean from some of the beautiful villas in Italy or Capri, while the presence of several Hindus with their brightly colored turbans, working among the flowers, lent a dash of oriental color that with the mosque-like domes of the buildings might lead one easily to believe he was in some garden overlooking the sacred Ganges in India.

The property of the organization, which stands in the name of Madame Tingley, stretches for several miles along the ocean front; it has greatly increased in value since it was acquired by her and it is said to be valued now at more than a million dollars. At the northern end is a farm where the milk, butter, eggs and vegetables used on the homestead are raised, and on the right, overlooking the ocean,

is the refectory, the community kitchen and diningroom where the five hundred members of the organization, about three-fourths of whom are children, take their meals. There is no servant question in Madame Tingley's domain. The work is distributed among all the members and there is a rotation of service.

All service, from the simplest of daily duties to the training of the children in an extensive and varied curriculum, to the highest offices and those engaged in intellectual research, I was told, is voluntary and unpaid.

Set in the midst of this semi-tropic garden are a score or more of other buildings, large and small. Among them the industrial buildings of the Women's exchange and mart, machine shops, photographic and art studios; chemical research laboratories, printing and engraving works, where the highest class of printing and engraving is done and a number of magazines and other publications are turned out; unique students' homes, the international headquarters and other office buildings.

Over the whole there brooded a peculiar serenity, quiet and calm quite in keeping with the surroundings. In such an atmosphere I expected to see at least a few members walking about in dreamy meditation and reverential abstraction, their mind intent upon things far beyond this earthly sphere. On the contrary, everybody seemed to be exceedingly busy, to have some task or duty. Every building, the general arrangements and activity, bespoke of system and method. Strict order and discipline prevailed. Every one we met saluted in military style.

The activity of the Universal Brotherhood, of which Madame Tingley is the dominant figure, might be said to consist of the teaching of an amplified evolutionary philosophy, in some respects similar to that of Spencer and Darwin, with the addition thereto that the law of evolution and progressive development works the same in the invisible realms of spiritual existence as it does on the physical plane; to this is joined a system of child training, humanitarian work and practical business methods. To the uninitiated it would appear that the latter is by no means the least and that to the unquestioned administrative genius, capacity for organization and shrewd, sane, practical business methods of Madame Tingley, everywhere apparent, is due the success of the institution at Point Loma more than to the tenets and principles of theosophy.

Did you ever see babies go to school? Babies that are not much more than able to toddle about and whose vocabulary is limited to "papa," "mamma," "doggie," "kittie," etc. At Point Loma the babies first enter the schoolroom when about 18 months old, to watch the older children. It is then that the first lessons by suggestion in watching others are imparted, and the impulse to imitate is aroused in the little minds. At three, they must spend half an hour a day with lessons, and already are being taught to rely upon themselves in the way of dressing and undressing, and to delight in helping to make their beds and care for their rooms. In the training of children, as in many other things, one finds a radical departure in Loma-land from custom and from accepted methods. Contrary to theories of some of the foremost educators that the education of a child should not begin at too tender an age, it is the theory of Madame Tingley that it cannot begin too young, in order that there may be

nothing to unlearn, no harmful thought to eradicate.

Near the sand pile for the children is the nursery building. By a clever arrangement of the interior the blue and white beds are constantly under the watchful eye of a nurse. In an adjoining room was the food for each child, labeled with its name and prepared under the direction of the physician in charge. In the sand were several little tots at play; their cleanliness and apparent happy disposition excited the admiration of a lady with me.

"Whose babies are they?" she asked.

"Most of them belong to the members of the organization," was the reply.

"Kept here during the day, I suppose?"

"And at night, too," was the surprising reply.

"But where are their mothers?"

"They are here, engaged in their chosen work."

"You don't mean to say that the mothers give up their babies, allow their little ones to be separated from them and cared for on a community plan?" asked my companion, her eyes wide with astonishment.

"Give them up? Oh, no. At first they see them once a day, when they grow a little older, once a week, the children usually spending a part of one day every week with their parents."

"I cannot conceive of the mother's heart that would willingly separate herself from her babies. That part of your philosophy does not appeal to me," said the young woman with me.

"It is for the child's good and it enables the parents to work for the good of humanity. What is better for the individual is better for the race," was the reply.

"Can there be a higher duty than that of mother to child?" was asked.

"No. Not if that duty be wisely performed, which it rarely is."

From that moment the place lost some of its beauty to my companion. She thought only of the "homesick" babies. It must be said, however, they did not look it. A happier, brighter and healthier rollicking lot of babies would be hard to find.

The usual school studies are not neglected in any respect under this system. There is an extensive curriculum and on the list given me were the names of sixty-five teachers and instructors to about three hundred and fifty

"Let me have a child from the time of birth until it is seven years old," says Mrs. Tingley, "and all the temptation in the world will not move it"

children in the various departments. This large number of teachers would be impossible because of the vast outlay for salaries but for the fact that all serve without compensation.

There were American children, Cubans, Germans, Swedes, English and one or two East Indians. The tuition paid by three children, I was informed, enabled the organization to educate and train a fourth which could not pay. There were children of wealthy parents and children who were orphans. The latter, I was told, were given the same care and attention that the former received. They lived together in the same dormitory or group homes and were attired alike—the girls in a simple brownish-gray and the boys in natty uniforms.

The indoor study hours are short, and even for the older children do not exceed about half the number of hours of public schools. Practically an outdoor life is led, made possible by the genial climate. Physical culture and manual training, both for boys and girls, are important parts in the daily curriculum, while a forestry and agricultural department, under a former officer of the United States forestry department, is a feature of the outdoor work in which much interest is taken by the children. There is also a meteorological station and weather bureau where careful observations are taken.

Music and drama rank high at Point Loma.

Music, instead of being regarded as an amusement, is taught to be one of those subtle forces of nature which, properly applied, tend toward higher aspirations and higher ideals. There are not many hours in the day that music is not heard from some part of the grounds. Unusual facilities for dramatic work are afforded. In a cañon, with the blue expanse of the Pacific for a background, is a large open-air Greek theater with a seating capacity of 3000, which, it is claimed, was the first to be built in the United States. Here and in the Isis opera house at San Diego, owned by Madame Tingley, are given representations of Greek plays and symposiums by the students of the school. Only plays of the highest standard are produced, among them "Eumenides" of Aeschylus, and Shakespeare's "Midsummer Night's Dream." While not the originator of theosophy Madame Tingley has placed upon it a new interpretation and given it an expression and new application that has stamped it with her own dominant personality and that practically makes it new.

Madame Tingley has a strong antipathy to hypnotism, spiritualism, occult phenomena and psychic practices with which early theosophical history is replete and which first attracted public attention to theosophy. Madame Tingley strictly forbids psychic practices so far as members of the Universal Brotherhood are concerned. She does not deny the existence of psychic forces; in fact, admits that they are all too real, but declares them to be too dangerous to be meddled with. Psychic research is not encouraged by her.

The Universal Brotherhood is a self-perpetuating autocracy. Madame Tingley has the power to appoint her successor and is surrounded by a "cabinet" of advisers, which she selects, not unlike the cabinet of the President, and she directly controls the administrative as well as the executive departments. She can remove any or all officers at her discretion and has sole and unlimited power in all the affairs of the organization. The stranger who may visit Point Loma, knowing nothing about the movement, is not long left in doubt as to who is at the head. He hears: it was planned by Madame Tingley; that was designed by Madame T.; Madame T. conceived the idea; it was laid out in accordance with the directions of Madame T.; it is Madame T.'s wish, etc. The various publications put out fairly teem with her name. Beside reigning supreme in her beautiful principality on Point Loma, her influence extends to other parts of the world: Santiago de Cuba, Newburyport, Massachusetts, England and Sweden. She also purchased San Juan hill, including Kettle hill, where the Spaniards made their last stand against Roosevelt's Rough Riders. This is to become a second Point Loma. Both the Cuban Government and the United States Government attempted to get the property but for some reason failed. The latter has asked per-mission of Katherine Tingley to erect on Kettle hill a monument commemorative of the A-merican and Cuban soldiers who fell there. This has been granted.

It was sought to impress upon me that the Point Loma institution was not a "settlement," "community," "co-operative colony," nor an "experiment."

"What is it, then," I asked.

"It is an exposition and a practical demonstration of theosophy," was the reply.

If the theory of Luther Burbank, the plant wizard, that with children as with plants, environment is the most important factor in their training, growth and development, be a correct one, then Point Loma should produce some wonderful human plants. But after all, it is a question whether such an environment and such ideal surroundings, with the elimination of the temptations of an ordinary existence, is best for building a strong character and bringing out the highest and best qualities in the race. Goethe said: *Es bildet ein Talent sich in der Stille, doch ein Charakter in dem Strome der Welt* (Talent is developed in solitude, character in the rush of the world).

Will children reared within such protective walls, with all that is good, noble and ideal constantly held up before them as worthy of acquisition and emulation, be stronger than those who daily meet the temptations in the turmoil and strife of human experience even in their little life? Time alone will demonstrate the truth or falsity of the theories of Madame Tingley and the Point Loma brotherhood. #

The Raja Yoga system includes daily exercise
in the open air for both boys and girls

The Wit of Porportuk

By JACK LONDON

February 1910

EL-SOO had been a Mission girl. Her mother had died when she was very small, and Sister Alberta had plucked El-Soo as a brand from the burning, one summer day, and carried her away to Holy Cross Mission and dedicated her to God. Never had a more promising dedication been made on the Yukon. El-Soo was a full-blooded Indian, yet she exceeded all the half-breed and quarter-breed girls. She was a treasure. Never had the good Sisters dealt with a girl that was so adaptable and at the same time so spirited.

El-Soo was quick, and deft, and intelligent; but above all, she was fire—the living flame of life, a blaze of personality that was compounded of will, sweetness and daring. Her father was a chief, and his blood ran in her veins. Not a drop of it was slave-blood. Sister Alberta ruled her by compromise. Obedience on the part of El-Soo was a matter of terms and arrangement. She had a passion for equity, and perhaps it was because of this that she excelled in mathematics.

But she excelled in other things. She learned to read and write English as no girl had ever learned in the Mission. Her voice, for an Indian girl, was remarkable for its sweetness and range. She led the girls in singing, and into song she carried her sense of equity. She knew, as by divination, time, and rhythm, and the values of tones. She played the organ, and improved upon the printed music till the Sisters were aghast and delighted. She was an artist and the fire of her flowed toward creation. Had she from birth enjoyed a more favorable environment, she would inevitably have made literature or music, or have worked in colors or marble.

Instead, she was El-Soo, daughter of Kla-kee-Nah, a chief, and she lived in the Holy Cross Mission, where were no artists, but only pure-souled Sisters who were interested in cleanliness and righteousness and the welfare of the spirit in the land of immortality that lay beyond the skies. So El-Soo recited school-reader poetry, played the organ, tampered with the printed music, and created fancy needlework.

The years passed. She was eight years old when she entered the Mission; she was sixteen, and the Sisters were corresponding with their superiors in the Order concerning the sending of El-Soo to the United States to complete her education, when a man of her own tribe arrived at Holy Cross and had talk with her. El-Soo was somewhat appalled by him. He was dirty. He was a Caliban-like creature, primitively ugly, with a mop of hair that had never been combed. But she reflected that he was an old man and a slave. He looked at her disapprovingly, and refused to sit down.

"Thy brother is dead," he said shortly.

El-Soo was not particularly shocked. She remembered little of her brother. She had a vague vision of a slim youth who had teased and frightened her, and that was all.

"Thy father is an old man, and alone," the messenger went on. "His house is large and empty, and he would hear thy voice and look upon thee."

Him she remembered—Klakee-Nah, the headman of the village, the friend of the missionaries and the traders—a large man, thewed like a giant, with kindly eyes and masterful ways, and striding with a consciousness of crude royalty in his carriage. Also she remembered the large house, the feasting and the drinking, and the many chiefs and hunters and white men that came and went.

"What word shall I carry to thy father?" the messenger demanded.

"Tell him that I come," was El-Soo's answer.

Much to the despair of the Sisters, the brand plucked from the burning went back to the burning. All pleading with El-Soo was vain. There was much argument, expostulation and weeping. Sister Alberta even revealed to her the project of sending her to the United States. El-Soo stared wide-eyed into the golden vista thus opened up to her and shook her head. In her eyes persisted another vista. It was the mighty curve of the Yukon at Tana-naw station, with the St. George Mission on one side and the trading-post on the other, and midway between, the Indian village and a certain large log-house where lived an old man tended upon by slaves—old slaves, whose servitude had become habit and whose free natures had insensibly been bartered through the long years for the surety of daily pottage.

All dwellers on the Yukon bank, for twice a thousand miles, knew the large log-house, the old man, and the tending slaves; and well did the Sisters know the house, its unending revelry, its feasting, and its fun. So there was weeping at Holy Cross when El-Soo departed up the river in a poling-boat manned by three of the ancient, mop-headed slaves; and Sister Alberta took to her bed for a week, sick at the loss of so bright a soul.

There was a great cleaning-up in the large house when El-Soo arrived. Klakee-Nah, himself masterful, protested at this masterful conduct of his young daughter; but in the end, dreaming barbarically of magnificence, he went forth and borrowed a thousand dollars from old Porportuk, than whom there was no richer Indian on the Yukon. Also, Klakee-Nah ran up a heavy bill at the trading-post. But it was El-Soo who saw to the details of the bill

and determined the nature of the spending of the thousand dollars. El-Soo recreated the large house. She invested it with new splendor, while Klakee-Nah maintained its ancient traditions of hospitality and revelry.

All this was unusual for a Yukon Indian, but Klakee-Nah was an unusual Indian. Not alone did he like to render inordinate hospitality; but, what of being a chief and of acquiring much money, he was able to do it. In the primitive trading days he had been a power over his people, and he had dealt profitably with the white trading companies. Later on, with Porportuk, he had made a strike on the Koyokuk river. Klakee-Nah was by nature and training an aristocrat; Porportuk was bourgeois, and Porportuk bought his partner out of the gold-mine. Porportuk was content to plod and accumulate; Klakee-Nah went back to his large house and proceeded to spend. Porportuk was known as the richest Indian in Alaska; Klakee-Nah was known as the "whitest." Porportuk was a money-lender and a usurer; Klakee-Nah was an anachronism, a medieval ruin, a fighter, and a feaster, happy with wine and song, and of money splendidly disdainful. He was also a man of his word, with a jealous regard for his honor that was ridiculously medieval, and as out of place as he was in the world of trade and business.

El-Soo adapted herself to the large house and its ways as readily as she had adapted herself to Holy Cross Mission and its ways. She did not try to reform her father and direct his footsteps toward God. It is true she reproved him when he drank overmuch and profoundly, but that was for the sake of his health and the direction of his footsteps on the solid earth. The more she saw of her father, the more he impressed her, and the prouder she grew to serve him and to manage the large house for him according to his way of life.

The latchstring to that large house was always out. In the winter-time there were ever strings of frost-rimed dogs lying in the snow before the door. In the summer-time the Yukon bank was always lined with canoes and poling-boats, barges, and the river steamers of the independent traders. What of the coming and the going, the house was never still. The rafters of the great living-room shook with the roar of wassail and of song. At table sat men from all the world, and chiefs from distant tribes—Englishmen and Colonials, lean Yankee traders and rotund officials of the great companies, cowboys from the Western ranges, sailors from the sea, hunters and dog-mushers of a score of nationalities.

El-Soo drew breath in a cosmopolitan atmosphere. She could speak English as well as her native tongue, and she sang English songs and ballads. The passing Indian ceremonials she knew, and the perishing traditions. The tribal dress of the daughter of a chief she knew how to wear upon occasion, but for the most part she dressed as white women dress. Not for nothing was her needlework at the Mission and her innate artistry—she carried her clothes like a white woman, and she made clothes that could be so carried. She created dresses, lacking, it is true, in the austerity that had been impressed upon her at Holy Cross, but gaining in the beauty that marked the dresses of the white women who, at rare intervals, passed up and down the Yukon on the steamboats.

In her way she was as unusual as her father, and the position she occupied was as unique as his. She was the one Indian woman who was a social equal with the several white women at Tana-naw station; she was the one Indian woman to whom white men honorably made proposal of marriage; and she was the one Indian woman whom no white man ever insulted.

And El-Soo had wit—rarely sharp to hurt, yet quick to search out forgivable weakness. The laughter of her mind played like lambent flame over all about her, and from all about her arose answering laughter. Yet she was never the center of things—this she would not permit. The large house, and all of which it was significant, was her father's; and through it to the last, moved his heroic figure—host, master of the revels, and giver of the law. It is true, as the strength oozed from him, that she caught up responsibilities from his failing hands; but in appearance he still ruled, dozing ofttimes at the board, a bacchanalian ruin, yet in all seeming, the ruler of the feast.

And through the large house moved the figure of Porportuk, ominous, with shaking head, coldly disapproving, paying for it all. Not that he really paid, for he compounded interest in weird ways, and year by year absorbed the properties of Klakee-Nah. Porportuk once took it upon himself to chide El-Soo upon the wasteful way of life in the large house—it was when he had about absorbed the last of Klakee-Nah's wealth—but he never ventured so to chide again. El-Soo, like her father, was an aristocrat, as disdainful of money as he, and with an equal sense of honor as finely strung.

Porportuk continued grudgingly to advance money, and ever the money flowed in golden foam away. Upon one thing El-Soo was resolved—her father should die as he had lived. There should be for him no passing from high to low, no diminution of the revels, no lessening of the lavish hospitality. When there was famine, as of old, the Indians came groaning to the large house and went away content; when there was famine and no money, money was borrowed from Porportuk, and the Indians still went away content. El-Soo might well have repeated, after the aristocrats of another time and place, that after her came the deluge. In her case the deluge was old Porportuk. With every advance of money he looked upon her with a more possessive eye, and felt bourgeoning within him ancient fires.

But El-Soo had no eyes for him. Nor had she eyes for the white men who wanted to marry her at the Mission with ring and priest and book; for at Tana-naw station was a young man, Akoon, of her own blood, and tribe, and village. He was strong and beautiful to her eyes, a great hunter, and in that he had wandered far and much, very poor. He had been to all the unknown wastes and places; he had journeyed to Sitka and to the United States; he had crossed the continent to Hudson bay and back again; and as seal-hunter on a ship he had sailed to Siberia and far Japan.

When he returned from the gold strike in Klondike, he came, as was his wont, to the large house to make report to old Klakee-Nah of all the world that he had seen; and there he first saw El-Soo, three years back from the Mission. Thereat Akoon wandered no more. He refused a wage of twenty dollars a day as pilot on the big steamboats—he hunted some, and fished some, but never far from Tana-naw station, and he was at the large house often and long, and El-Soo measured him against many men and still found him good. He sang songs to her, and was ardent and glowed until all Tana-naw station knew he loved her. And Porportuk but

Only a Thousand People Can
Have the Exclusive Car

Some of those who have waited for the perfect electric can now have the car they have longed for—the Rauch & Lang Electric—the handsomest, most efficient electric car ever turned out of a factory.

Three hundred people were disappointed last year because we could not make deliveries, so we have doubled our capacity and will build 1,000 cars this year.

We never have been able to supply the demand for Rauch & Lang Electrics—we will only make as many good cars as we can and will not sacrifice the Rauch & Lang standard of style and efficiency for a large output.

90 Days to Finish a Body

We spend more time on these cars than other makers think necessary. Each body is the art work of a certain craftsman.

Each requires 90 days to reach the style we demand in our work. Each body receives 24 coats of paint and varnish. This detailed, painstaking attention given the body is simply indicative of the work done in all parts of the car.

We have been carriage makers in Cleveland for 57 years. No one knows better what particular people want in cars

The Safest Electric

We use a unique control. You cannot start a Rauch & Lang car until the control is first in the neutral position.

It is not possible to unlock the control except when it is in the neutral position, so there is no possibility of this car starting until you purposely start it.

Yet all power can be shut off instantly with the control in any position. (6)

The Rauch & Lang Carriage Co.
2196 West 25th Street, CLEVELAND, OHIO

The One Perfect Electric Brake

This is another feature. Our electric brake is positive—never fails to work, and in no wise injures the motor.

The foot brake is strong, extra large and durable. The car answers these brakes at once and the weakest woman has plenty of strength to stop the car almost instantly.

We use a Yale key in the control handle for the power connection. No one can steal the car by using a nail or wire.

We use Exide batteries of the latest design that have enormous capacity combined with extreme ruggedness.

You can ride in a Rauch & Lang Car as far as you'll want to go in a day. This is the car that is giving unqualified service in hilly cities like Kansas City and Pittsburg, and wonderful service in Chicago, St. Louis, Detroit and Cleveland, where great mileage is required.

We Have Spared No Expense

In fact we have spared no expense to make this car not only the handsomest, but the strongest and most efficient car manufactured.

Other cars may be cheaper at first, but Rauch & Lang owners spend practically nothing at all for repairs. After a year's use a Rauch & Lang is found to be by far the most economical car you can buy. See the Rauch & Lang agent at once. We have dealers in most of the principal cities.

Cut out the memo below and mail it to us today for the catalog.

grinned and advanced more money for the upkeep of the large house.

Then came the death-table of Klakee-Nah. He sat at feast, with death in his throat that he could not drown with wine. And laughter and joke and song went around, and Akoon told a story that made the rafters echo. There were no tears nor sighs at that table. It was no more than fit that Klakee-Nah should die as he had lived, and none knew this better than El-Soo, with her artist-sympathy. The old, roystering crowd was there; and, as of old, three frost-bitten sailors were there, fresh from the long traverse from the Arctic, survivors of a ship's company of seventy-four. At Klakee-Nah's back were four old men, all that were left him of the slaves of his youth. With rheumy eyes they saw to his needs, with palsied hands filling his glass or striking him on the back between the shoulders when death stirred and he coughed and gasped.

It was a wild night, and as the hours passed and the fun laughed and roared along, death stirred more restlessly in Klakee-Nah's throat. Then it was that he sent for Porportuk. And Porportuk came in from the outside frost to look with disapproving eyes upon the meat and wine on the table for which he had paid. But as he looked down the length of flushed faces to the far end and saw the face of El-Soo, the light in his eyes flared up and for a moment the disapproval vanished.

Place was made for him at Klakee-Nah's side and a glass placed before him. Klakee-Nah with his own hands filled the glass with fervent spirits.

"Drink!" he cried. "Is it not good?"

And Porportuk's eyes watered as he nodded his head and smacked his lips.

"When, in your own house, have you had such drink?" Klakee-Nah demanded.

"I will not deny that the drink is good to this old throat of mine," Porportuk made answer, and hesitated for the speech to complete the thought.

"But it costs overmuch!" Klakee-Nah roared, completing it for him.

Porportuk winced at the laughter that went down the table. His eyes burned malevolently.

"We were boys together, of the same age," he said. "In your throat is death—I am still alive and strong."

An ominous murmur arose from the company. Klakee-Nah coughed and strangled, and the old slaves smote him between the shoulders. He emerged gasping, and waved his hand to still the threatening rumble.

"You have grudged the very fire in your house, because the wood cost overmuch!" he cried. "You have grudged life. To live cost overmuch, and you have refused to pay the price. Your life has been like a cabin where the fire is out and there are no blankets on the floor." He signaled to a slave to fill his glass, which he held aloft. "But I have lived. And I have been warm with life as you have never been warm. It is true, you shall live long; but the longest nights are the cold nights when a man shivers and lies awake. My nights have been short, but I have slept warm."

He drained the glass. The shaking hand of a slave failed to catch it as it crashed to the floor. Klakee-Nah sank back, panting, watching the upturned glasses at the lips of the drinkers, his own lips slightly smiling to the applause. At a sign, two slaves attempted to help him sit upright again. But they were weak, his frame was mighty, and the four old men tottered and shook as they helped him forward.

"But manner of life is neither here nor there," he went on. "We have other business, Porportuk, you and I, to-night. Debts are mischances, and I am in mischance with you. What of my debt, and how great is it?"

Porportuk searched in his pouch and brought forth a memorandum. He sipped at his glass and began.

"There is the note of August, 1889, for three hundred dollars—the interest has never been paid. And the note of the next year for five hundred dollars—this note was included in the note of two months later for a thousand dollars. Then there is the note—"

"Never mind the many notes!" Klakee-Nah cried out impatiently. "They make my head go around, and all the things inside my head. The whole! The round whole! How much is it?"

Porportuk referred to his memorandum.

"Fifteen thousand nine hundred and sixty-seven dollars and seventy-five cents," he read, with careful precision.

"Make it sixteen thousand—Klakee-Nah said grandly. "Odd numbers were ever a worry.

And now—and it is for this that I have sent for you—make me out a new note for sixteen thousand, which I shall sign. I have no thought of the interest—make it as large as you will. And make it payable in the next world, when I shall meet you by the fire of the Great Father of all Indians—then will the note be paid. This I promise you. It is the word of Klakee-Nah."

Porportuk looked perplexed, and loudly the laughter arose and shook the room.

Klakee-Nah raised his hands.

"Nay," he cried, "it is not a joke. I but speak in fairness. It was for this I sent for you, Porportuk. Make out the note."

"I have no dealings with the next world," Porportuk made answer slowly.

"Have you no thought to meet me before the Great Father?" Klakee-Nah demanded. Then he added: "I shall surely be there."

"I have no dealings with the next world," Porportuk repeated sourly.

The dying man regarded him with frank amazement.

"I know naught of the next world," Porportuk explained. "I do business in this world."

Klakee-Nah's face cleared.

"This comes of sleeping cold of nights," he laughed. He pondered for a space, then said: "It is in this world that you must be paid. There remains to me this house; take it, and burn the debt in the candle there."

"It is an old house, and not worth the money," Porportuk made answer.

"There are my mines on the Twisted Salmon."

"They have never paid to work," was the reply.

"There is my share in the steamer *Koyokuk*. I am half-owner."

"She is at the bottom of the Yukon."

Klakee-Nah started.

"True, I forgot. It was last spring, when the ice went out."

He mused for a time, while the glasses remained untasted and all the company waited upon his utterance.

"Then it would seem I owe you a sum of money which I cannot pay—in this world?"

Porportuk nodded and glanced down the table.

"Then it would seem that you, Porportuk, are a poor business man," Klakee-Nah said slyly.

And boldly Porportuk made answer:

"No—there is security yet untouched."

"What!" cried Klakee-Nah. "Have I still property? Name it, and it is yours, and the debt is no more."

"There it is." Porportuk pointed at El-Soo.

Klakee-Nah could not understand. He peered down the table, brushed his eyes, and peered again.

"Your daughter, El-Soo—her will I take and the debt be no more. I will burn the debt there in the candle."

Klakee-Nah's great chest began to heave.

"Hoh! Hoh!—A joke!—Hoh! Hoh! Hoh!" he laughed Homerically. "And you with your cold bed and daughters old enough to be the mother of El-Soo! Hoh! Hoh! Hoh!"

He began to cough and strangle, and the old slaves smote him on the back.

"Hoh! Hoh!" he began again, and went off in another paroxysm.

Porportuk waited patiently, sipping from his glass and studying the double row of intent faces down the board.

"It is no joke," he said finally. "My speech is well meant."

Klakee-Nah sobered and looked at him, then reached for his glass, but could not take it. A slave passed it to him, and glass and liquor he flung into the face of Porportuk.

"Turn him out!" Klakee-Nah thundered to the waiting table, that strained like a pack of hounds in leash. "And roll him in the snow!"

As the mad riot swept past him and out of doors, he signaled to the slaves; and the four tottering old men supported him on his feet as he met the returning revelers, upright, glass in hand, pledging them a toast to the short night when a man sleeps warm.

It did not take long to settle the estate of Klakee-Nah. Tommy, the little Englishman clerk at the trading-post, was called in by El-Soo to help. There was nothing but debts, notes overdue, mortgaged properties, and properties mortgaged but worthless. Notes and mortgages were held by Porportuk. Tommy called him a robber many times as he pondered the compounding of the interest.

"Is it a debt, Tommy?" El-Soo asked.

"It is a robbery," Tommy answered. "Nevertheless, it is a debt."

The winter wore away, and the early spring, and still the claims of Porportuk remained unpaid. He saw El-Soo often, and explained to her at length, as he had explained to her father, the way the debt could be canceled. Also, he brought with him old medicine men, who elaborated to her the everlasting damnation of her father if the debt were not paid. One day, after such an elaboration, El-Soo made final announcement to Porportuk.

"I shall tell you two things," she said. "First, I shall not be your wife; will you remember that? Second, you shall be paid the last cent of the sixteen thousand dollars—"

"Fifteen thousand nine hundred and sixty-seven dollars and seventy-five cents," Porportuk corrected.

"My father said sixteen thousand," was her reply. "You shall be paid."

"How?"

"I know not how, but I shall find out how. Now go, and bother me no more. If you do"—she hesitated to find fitting penalty—"if you do, I shall have you rolled in the snow again as soon as the first snow flies."

This was still in the early spring, and a little later El-Soo surprised the country. Word went up and down the Yukon from Chilkoot to the Delta, and was carried from camp to camp to the farthermost camps, that in June, when the first salmon ran, El-Soo, daughter of Klakee-Nah, would sell herself at public auction to satisfy the claims of Porportuk. Vain were the attempts to dissuade her. The missionary at St. George wrestled with her, but she replied:

"Only the debts to God are settled in the next world. The debts of men are of this world, and in this world are they settled."

Akoon wrestled with her, but she replied:

"I do love thee, Akoon; but honor is greater than love, and who am I that I should blacken my father?"

Sister Alberta journeyed all the way up from Holy Cross on the first steamer, and to no better end.

"My father wanders in the thick and endless forests," said El-Soo. "And there will he wander with the lost souls crying till the debt be paid. Then, and not until then, may he go on to the house of the Great Father."

"And you believe this?" Sister Alberta asked.

"I do not know," El-Soo made answer. "It was my father's belief."

Sister Alberta shrugged her shoulders incredulously.

"Who knows but that the things we believe come true?" El-Soo went on. "Why not? The next world to you may be heaven and harps—because you have believed heaven and harps; to my father the next world may be a large house where he will sit always at table feasting with God."

"And you?" Sister Alberta asked. "What is your next world?"

El-Soo hesitated but for a moment.

"I should like a little of both," she said. "I should like to see your face as well as the face of my father."

The day of the auction came. Tana-naw station was populous. As was their custom, the tribes had gathered to await the salmon-run, and in the meanwhile, spent the time in dancing and frolicking, trading and gossiping. Then there was the ordinary sprinkling of white adventurers, traders and prospectors; and, in addition, a large number of white men who had come because of curiosity or interest in the affair.

It had been a backward spring, and the salmon were late in running; this delay but keyed up the interest. Then, on the day of the auction, the situation was made tense by Akoon. He arose and made public a solemn announcement that whosoever bought El-Soo would forthwith and immediately die. He flourished the Winchester in his hand to indicate the manner of the taking-off. El-Soo was made angry thereat; but he refused to speak with her, and went to the trading-post to lay in extra ammunition.

The first salmon was caught at ten o'clock in the evening, and at midnight the auction began. It took place on top of the high bank alongside the Yukon. The sun was due north, just below the horizon, and the sky was lurid red. A great crowd gathered about the table and the two chairs that stood near the edge of the bank. To the fore were many white men and several chiefs; and most prominently to the fore, rifle in hand, stood Akoon. Tommy, at El-Soo's request, served as auctioneer, but she made the opening speech and described the goods about to be sold. She was in native costume, in the dress of a chief's daughter, splendid and barbaric, and she stood on a chair that she might be seen to advantage.

"Who wants a wife?" she asked. "Look at me. I am twenty years old, and a maid. I will be a good wife to the man who buys me. If he is a white man, I shall dress in the fashion of white women; if he is an Indian, I shall dress as"—she hesitated a moment—"a squaw. I can make my own clothes, and sew, and wash, and mend. I was taught for eight years to do these things at Holy Cross Mission. I can read and write English, and I know how to play the organ. Also I can do arithmetic and some algebra—a little. I shall be sold to the highest bidder, and to him I will make out a bill of sale of myself. I forgot to say that I can sing very well, and that I have never been sick in my life. I weigh one hundred and thirty-two pounds. My father is dead, and I have no relatives. Who wants me?"

She looked over the crowd with flaming audacity, and stepped down. At Tommy's request, she stood upon the chair again, while he mounted the second chair and started the bidding.

The bidding began slowly. The Sitkan, who was a stranger in the land, and who had arrived only half an hour before, offered one hundred dollars in a confident voice, and was surprised when Akoon turned threateningly upon him with the rifle. The bidding dragged. An Indian from Tosikakat, a pilot, bid one hundred and fifty; and after some time a gambler who had been ordered out of the Upper Country raised the bid to two hundred. El-Soo was saddened. Her pride was hurt. But the only effect was that she flamed more audaciously upon the crowd.

There was a disturbance among the onlookers as Porportuk forced his way to the front.

"Five hundred dollars!" he bid, in a loud voice; then looked about him proudly to note the effect.

He was minded to use his great wealth as a bludgeon with which to stun all competition at the start. But one of the voyagers, looking on El-Soo with sparkling eyes, raised the bid a hundred.

"Seven hundred!" Porportuk returned promptly.

And with equal promptness came the "Eight hundred" of the voyager.

Then Porportuk swung his club again.

"Twelve hundred!" he shouted.

With a look of poignant disappointment, the voyager succumbed. There was no further bidding. Tommy worked hard, but could not elicit a bid.

El-Soo spoke to Porportuk.

"It were good, Porportuk, for you to weigh well your bid. Have you forgotten the thing I told you—that I would never marry you?"

"It is a public auction," he retorted. "I shall buy you with a bill of sale. I have offered twelve hundred dollars. You come cheap."

"Too darned cheap!" Tommy cried. "What if I am auctioneer? That does not prevent me from bidding. I'll make it thirteen hundred."

"Fourteen hundred!"—from Porportuk.

"I'll buy you in to be my—my sister," Tommy whispered to El-Soo—then called aloud: "Fifteen hundred!"

At two thousand one of the Eldorado kings took a hand, and Tommy dropped out.

A third time Porportuk swung the club of his wealth, making a clean raise of five hundred dollars. But the Eldorado king's pride was touched. No man could club him—and he swung back another five hundred.

El-Soo stood at three thousand. Porportuk made it thirty-five hundred, and gasped when the Eldorado king raised it a thousand dollars. Porportuk again raised five hundred, and again gasped when the king raised a thousand more.

Porportuk became angry. His pride was touched; his strength was challenged, and with him strength took the form of wealth. He would not be shamed for weakness before the world. El-Soo became incidental. The savings and scrimpings from the cold nights of all his years were ripe to be squandered. El-Soo stood at six thousand. He made it seven thousand. And then, in thousand-dollar bids, as fast as they could be uttered, her price went up. At fourteen thousand the two men stopped for breath.

Then the unexpected happened. A still heavier club was swung. In the pause that ensued, the gambler, who had scented a speculation and formed a syndicate with several of his fellows, bid sixteen thousand dollars.

"Seventeen thousand," Porportuk said weakly.

"Eighteen thousand," said the king.

Porportuk gathered his strength.

"Twenty thousand."

The syndicate dropped out. The Eldorado king raised a thousand, and Porportuk raised back; and as they bid, Akoon turned from one to the other, half-menacingly, half-curiously, as though to see what manner of man it was that he would have to kill. When the king prepared to make his next bid, Akoon having pressed closer, the king first loosed the revolver at his hip, then said:

"Twenty-three thousand."

"Twenty-four thousand," said Porportuk.

He grinned viciously, for the certitude of his bidding at last had shaken the king. The latter moved over close to El-Soo. He studied her carefully for a long while.

"And five hundred," he said at last.

"Twenty-five thousand," came Porportuk's raise.

The king looked for a long space, and shook his head. He looked again, and said reluctantly: "And five hundred."

"Twenty-six thousand," Porportuk snapped.

The king shook his head and refused to meet Tommy's pleading eye. In the meantime, Akoon had edged close to Porportuk. El-Soo's quick eyes noted this, and while Tommy wrestled with the Eldorado king for another bid, she bent and spoke in a low voice in the ear of a slave. And while Tommy's "Going—going—going—" dominated the air, the slave went up to Akoon and spoke in a low voice in his ear. Akoon make no sign that he had heard, though El-Soo watched him anxiously.

"Gone!" Tommy's voice rang out. "To Porportuk, for twenty-six thousand dollars."

Porportuk glanced uneasily at Akoon. All eyes were centered upon Akoon, but he did nothing.

"Let the scales be brought," El-Soo.

"I shall make payment at my house," said Porportuk.

"Let the scales be brought," said El-Soo. "Payment shall be made here, where all can see."

So the gold scales were brought from the trading-post, while Porportuk went away and came back with a man at his heels on whose shoulders was a weight of gold-dust in moose-hide sacks. Also, at Porportuk's back, walked another man with a rifle, who had eyes only for Akoon.

"Here are the notes and mortgages," said Porportuk, "for fifteen thousand nine hundred and sixty-seven dollars and seventy-five cents."

El-Soo received them into her hands and said to Tommy:

"Let them be reckoned as sixteen thousand."

"There remain ten thousand dollars to be paid in gold," Tommy said.

Porportuk nodded, and untied the mouths of the sacks. El-Soo, standing at the edge of the bank, tore the papers to shreds and sent them fluttering out over the Yukon. The weighing began, but halted.

"Of course, at seventeen dollars," Porportuk had said to Tommy, as he adjusted the scales.

"At sixteen dollars," El-Soo said sharply.

"It is the custom of all the land to reckon gold at seventeen dollars for each ounce," Porportuk replied, "and this is a business transaction."

El-Soo laughed.

"It is a new custom," she said; "it began this spring. Last year, and the years before, it was sixteen dollars an ounce. When my father's debt was made it was sixteen dollars. When he spent at the store the money he got from you, for one ounce he was given sixteen dollars' worth of flour, not seventeen. Wherefore shall you pay for me at sixteen, and not at seventeen."

Porportuk grunted, and allowed the weighing to proceed.

"Weigh it in three piles, Tommy," she said. "A thousand dollars here, three thousand here, and here six thousand."

It was slow work, and while the weighing went on Akoon was closely watched by all.

"He but waits till the money is paid," one said, and the word went around and was accepted, and they waited for what Akoon should do when the money was paid. And Porportuk's man with the rifle waited and watched Akoon.

The weighing was finished, and the gold-dust lay on the table in three dark-yellow heaps.

"There is a debt of my father to the company for three thousand dollars," said El-Soo. "Take it, Tommy, for the company. And here are four old men, Tommy. You know them. And here is one thousand dollars. Take it, and see that the old men are never hungry and never without tobacco."

"Here are the notes and mortgages," said old Porportuk

Tommy scooped the gold into separate sacks. Six thousand dollars remained on the table. El-Soo thrust the scoop into the heap, and with a sudden turn whirled the contents out and down to the Yukon in a golden shower. Porportuk seized her wrist as she thrust the scoop a second time into the heap.

"It is mine," she said calmly.

Porportuk released his grip, but he gritted his teeth and scowled darkly as she continued to scoop the gold into the river till none was left.

The crowd had eyes for naught but Akoon, and the rifle of Porportuk's man lay across the hollow of his arm, the muzzle directed at Akoon a yard away, the man's thumb on the hammer. But Akoon did nothing.

"Make out the bill of sale," Porportuk said grimly.

And Tommy made out the bill of sale, wherein all right and title in the woman El-Soo was vested in the man Porportuk. El-Soo signed the document, and Porportuk folded it and put it away in his pouch. Suddenly his eyes flashed, and in sudden speech he addressed El-Soo.

"But it was not your father's debt," he said. "What I paid was the price for you. Your sale is business of to-day, and not of last year and the years before. The ounces paid for you will buy at the post to-day seventeen dollars' worth of flour and not sixteen. I have lost a dollar on each ounce. I have lost six hundred and twenty-five dollars."

El-Soo thought for a moment and saw the error she had made. She smiled, and then she laughed.

"You are right," she laughed. "I made a mistake—but it is too late. You have paid and the gold is gone. You did not think quick—it is your loss. Your wit is slow these days, Porportuk. You are getting old."

He did not answer. He glanced uneasily at Akoon, and was reassured. His lips tightened, and a hint of cruelty came into his face.

"Come," he said, "We will go to my house."

"Do you remember the two things I told you in the spring?" El-Soo asked, making no movement to accompany him.

"My head would be full with the things women say, did I heed them," he answered.

"I told you that you would be paid," El-Soo went on carefully, "and I told you that I would

never be your wife."

"But that was before the bill of sale," Porportuk crackled the paper between his fingers inside the pouch. "I have bought you before all the world. You belong to me. You will not deny that you belong to me."

"I belong to you," El-Soo said steadily.

"I own you."

"You own me."

Porportuk's voice rose slightly and triumphantly.

"As a dog I own you."

"As a dog you own me," El-Soo continued calmly. "But, Porportuk, you forget the thing I told you. Had any other man bought me, I should have been that man's wife. I should have been a good wife to that man. Such was my will. But my will with you was that I should never be your wife. Wherefore I am your dog."

Porportuk knew that he played with fire, and he resolved to play firmly.

"Then I speak to you, not as El-Soo, but as a dog," he said, "and I tell you to come with me."

He half-reached to grip her arm, but with a gesture she held him back.

"Not so fast, Porportuk. You buy a dog. The dog runs away—it is your loss. I am your dog—what if I run away?"

"As the owner of the dog I shall beat you—"

"When you catch me."

"When I catch you."

"Then catch me."

He reached swiftly for her, but she eluded him. She laughed as she circled round the table.

"Catch her!" Porportuk commanded the Indian with the rifle who stood near to her.

"But as the Indian stretched forth his arm to her, the Eldorado king felled him with a fist-blow under the ear. The rifle clattered to the ground. Then was Akoon's chance. His eyes glittered, but he did nothing.

Porportuk was an old man, but his cold nights had retained for him his activity. He did not circle the table. He came across suddenly, over the top of the table. El-Soo was taken off her guard. She sprang back with a sharp cry of alarm, and Porportuk would have caught her had it not been for Tommy. Tommy's leg went out. Porportuk tripped and pitched forward on the ground. El-Soo got her start.

"Then catch me," she laughed over her shoulder as she fled away.

She ran lightly and easily, but Porportuk ran swiftly and savagely. He outran her. In his youth he had been swiftest of all the young men. But El-Soo dodged in a willowy, elusive way. Being in native dress, her feet were not cluttered with skirts, and her pliant body curved a flight that defied the gripping fingers of Porportuk.

With laughter and tumult the great crowd scattered out to see the chase. It led through the Indian encampment; and, ever dodging, circling, and reversing, El-Soo and Porportuk appeared and disappeared among the tents. El-Soo seemed to balance herself against the air with her arms, now on one side, now on the other; and sometimes her body, too, leaned out upon the air far from the perpendicular as she achieved her sharpest curves. And Porportuk, always a leap behind, or a leap this side or that, like a lean hound strained after her.

They crossed the open ground beyond the encampment and disappeared in the forest. Tana-naw station waited their reappearance, and long and vainly it waited.

In the meantime, Akoon ate and slept, and lingered much at the steamboat landing, deaf to the rising resentment of Tana-naw station in that he did nothing. Twenty-four hours later Porportuk returned. He was tired and savage. He spoke to no one but Akoon, and with him tried to pick a quarrel; but Akoon shrugged his shoulders and walked away. Porportuk did not waste time. He outfitted half a dozen of the young men, selecting the best trackers and travelers, and at their head plunged back into the forest.

Next day the steamer *Seattle,* bound up the river, pulled in to the shore and wooded up. When the lines were cast off and she churned out from the bank, Akoon was on board in the pilot-house. Not many hours afterward, when it was his turn at the wheel, he saw a small birch-bark canoe put out from the shore. There was only one person in it. He studied it carefully, put the wheel over, and slowed down.

The captain entered the pilot-house.

"What's the matter?" he demanded. "The water's hood."

Akoon grunted. He saw a larger canoe leaving the bank, and in it were a number of persons. As the *Seattle* lost headway, he put the wheel over some more. The captain fumed.

"It's only a squaw," he protested.

Akoon did not grunt. He was all eyes for the squaw and the pursuing canoe. In the latter, six paddles were flashing, while the squaw paddled slowly.

"You'll be aground!" the captain protested, seizing the wheel.

But Akoon countered his strength on the wheel and looked him in the eyes. The captain slowly released the spokes.

"Queer beggar!" he sniffed to himself.

Akoon held the *Seattle* on the edge of shoal water and waited till he saw the squaw's fingers clutch the forward rail. Then he signaled for full speed ahead and ground the wheel over. The large canoe was very near, but the gap between it and the steamer was widening.

The squaw laughed and leaned out over the rail.

"Then catch me, Porportuk," she cried.

Akoon left the steamer at Fort Yukon. He outfitted a small poling-boat and went up the Porcupine river—and with him went El-Soo. It was a weary journey, and the way led across the backbone of the world—but Akoon had traveled it before. When they came to the headwaters of the Porcupine, they left the boat and went on foot across the Rocky mountains.

Akoon greatly liked to walk behind El-Soo, and to watch the movement of her. There was a music in it that he loved. And especially he loved the well-rounded calves in their sheaths of soft-tanned leather, the slim ankles, and the small moccasined feet that were tireless through the longest days. Once when the sun was hot in the high altitudes, she cooled her feet in a stream of melted snow, and Akoon, stooping, seized and nested the two feet in his hands and kissed the brown ankles.

"You are light as air," he said, looking up at her. "It is no labor for you to walk. You almost float, so lightly do your feet rise and fall. You are like a deer, and your eyes are like deers' eyes sometimes when you look at me, or when you hear quick sound and wonder if it be danger that stirs. Your eyes are like a deer's eyes now, as you look at me."

And El-Soo, luminous and melting, bent and kissed Akoon.

"When we reach the Mackenzie, we will not delay," Akoon said later. "We will go south before the winter catches us. We will go to the sunlands, where there is no snow. But we will return. I have seen much of the world, and there is no land like Alaska, no sun like our sun—and the snow is good after the long summer."

"And you will learn to read," said El-Soo.

And Akoon said:

"I will surely learn to read."

But there was delay when they reached the Mackenzie. They fell in with a band of Mackenzie Indians and, hunting, Akoon was shot by accident. The rifle was in the hands of a youth. The bullet broke Akoon's right arm, and, ranging farther, broke two of his ribs. Akoon knew rough surgery, while El-Soo had learned some refinements at Holy Cross. The bones were finally set, and Akoon lay by the fire for them to knit. Also, he lay by the fire so that the smoke would keep the mosquitos away.

Then it was that Porportuk, with his six young men, arrived. Akoon groaned in his helplessness and made appeal to the Mackenzies. But Porportuk made demand, and the Mackenzies were perplexed. Porportuk was for seizing upon El-Soo, but this they would not permit. Judgment must be given, and, as it was an affair of man and woman, the council of the old men was called—this, that warm judgment might not be given by the young men who were warm of heart.

The old men sat in a circle about the smudge fire. Their faces were lean and wrinkled, and they gasped and panted for air. The smoke was not good for them. Occasionally they struck with withered hands at the mosquitos that braved the smoke. After such exertion they coughed hollowly and painfully. Some spat blood. And one of them sat a bit apart with head bowed forward, and bled slowly and continuously at the mouth. The coughing sickness had gripped them. They were as dead men—their time was short—it was a judgment of the dead.

"And I paid for her a heavy price," Porportuk concluded his complaint. "Such a price you have never seen. Sell all that is yours—sell your spears and arrows and rifles, sell your skins and furs, sell your tents and boats and dogs, sell everything, and you will not have, maybe, a thousand dollars. Yet did I pay for the woman, El-Soo, twenty-six times the price of all your spears and arrows and rifles, your skins and furs, your tents and boats and dogs. It was a heavy price."

The old men nodded gravely, though their weazened eye-slits widened with wonder that any woman should be worth such a price.

The one that bled at the mouth wiped his lips.

"Is it true talk?" he asked each of Porportuk's six young men. And each answered that it was true.

"Is it true talk?" he asked El-Soo.

And she answered:

"It is true."

"But Porportuk has not told that he is an old man," Akoon said, "and that he has daughters older than El-Soo."

"It is true—Porportuk is an old man," said El-Soo.

"It is for Porportuk to measure the strength of his age," said he who bled at the mouth. "We be old men. Behold! Age is never so old as youth would measure it."

And the circle of old men champed their gums and nodded approvingly and coughed.

"I told him that I would never be his wife," said El-Soo.

"Yet you took from him twenty-six times all that we possess?" asked a one-eyed old man.

El-Soo was silent.

"It is true?" And his one eye burned and bored into her like a fiery gimlet.

"It is true," she said. "But I will run away again," she broke out passionately a moment later. "Always will I run away."

"That is for Porportuk to consider," said another of the old men. "It is for us to consider the judgment."

"What price did you pay for her?" was demanded of Akoon.

"No price did I pay for her," he answered. "She was above price. I did not measure her in gold-dust, nor in dogs, and tents, and furs."

The old men debated among themselves and mumbled in undertones.

"These old men are ice," Akoon said, in English. "I will not listen to their judgment, Porportuk. If you take El-Soo, I will surely kill you."

The old men ceased and regarded him suspiciously.

"We do not know the speech you make," one said.

"He but said that he would kill me," Porportuk volunteered. "So it were well to take from him his rifle, and to have some of your young men sit by him that he may not do me hurt. He is a young man, and what are broken bones to youth?"

Akoon, lying helpless, had rifle and knife taken from him, and to either side of his shoulders sat young men of the Mackenzies.

The one-eyed old man arose and stood upright.

"We marvel at the price paid for one mere woman," he began, "but the wisdom of the price is no concern of ours. We are here to give judgment, and judgment we give. We have no doubt. It is known to all that Porportuk paid a heavy price for the woman El-Soo. Wherefore does the woman El-Soo belong to Porportuk and none other."

He sat down heavily, and coughed. The old men nodded and coughed.

"I will kill you," Akoon cried, in English.

Porportuk smiled and stood up.

"You have given true judgment," he said to the council, "and my young men will give to you much tobacco. Now let the woman be brought to me."

Akoon gritted his teeth. The young men took El-Soo by the arms. She did not resist, and was led, her face a sullen flame, to Porportuk.

"Sit there at my feet till I have made my talk," he commanded.

He paused a moment.

"It is true," he said, "I am an old man; yet can I understand the ways of youth. The fire has not all gone out of me. Yet am I no longer young, nor am I minded to run these old legs of mine through all the years that remain to me. El-Soo can run fast and well. She is a deer. This I know, for I have seen and run after her. It is not good that a wife should run so fast. I paid for her a heavy price, yet does she run away from me. Akoon paid no price at all, yet does she run to him.

"When I came among you people of the Mackenzie, I was of one mind. As I listened in the council and thought of the swift legs of El-Soo, I was of many minds. Now am I of one mind again, but it is a different mind from the one I brought to the council. Let me tell you my mind.

"When a dog runs once away from a master, it will run away again. No matter how many times it is brought back, each time will it run away again. When we have such dogs we sell them. El-Soo is like a dog that runs away—I will sell her. Is there any man of the council that will buy?"

The old men coughed and remained silent.

"Akoon would buy," Porportuk went on, "but he has no money. Wherefore I will give El-Soo to him, as he said, without price. Even now will I give her to him."

Reaching down he took El-Soo by the hand and led her across the space to where Akoon lay on his back.

"She has a bad habit, Akoon," he said, seating her at Akoon's feet. "As she has run away from me in the past, in the days to come she may run away from you. But there is no need to fear that she will ever run away, Akoon. I shall see to that. Never will she run away from you—this the word of Porportuk. She has great wit. I know, for often has it bitten into me. Yet am I minded myself to give my wit play for once. And by my wit will I secure her to you, Akoon."

Stooping, Porportuk crossed El-Soo's feet, so that the instep of one lay over that of the other, and then, before his purpose could be divined, he discharged his rifle through the two ankles.

As Akoon struggled to rise against the weight of the young men, there was heard the crunch of the broken bone rebroken.

"It is just," said the old men, one to another.

El-Soo made no sound. She sat and looked at her shattered ankles on which she would never walk again. And Akoon caught a vision of the small feet he nad nestled in his hands, and of the slim brown ankles he had kissed.

"My legs are strong, El-Soo," he said; "but never will they bear me away from you."

El-Soo looked at him, and for the first time in all the time he had known her, Akoon saw tears in her eyes.

"Your eyes are like deers' eyes, El-Soo," he said.

"Is it just?" Porportuk asked, and grinned from the edge of the smoke as he prepared to depart.

"It is just," the old men said.

And they sat on in the silence. #

Looking down upon the beautiful birdlike Bleriot monoplane as it flew above the audience.
Photographed by A. C. Pillsbury from a captive balloon

On the Wings of Today

By CHARLES K. FIELD

March 1910

HAVE you ever dodged an air-ship? It is a very different matter from dodging the usual motor-car. Most of us have become fairly expert at that—it is only a matter of a jump to one side or the other of a street to which the automobile is confined. There is nothing of this definiteness about an air-ship. The aeroplane has all space in which to swerve as sharply as a hawk while it literally bears down upon you. There is only one way to dodge it—lie down flat upon the ground. If the air-ship does not alight at that particular spot, you have dodged it.

One fact will work in your favor—it will be much more serious for the aviator than for you if he should hit you. This is another difference, considering automobiles. Yet, to one who crossed the aviation field at Dominguez during the aviation meet at Los Angeles, the latter part of January, getting hurriedly out of the way of the bewildering air-craft that came humming at his head, it seemed that if this form of travel is to become general some system of refuge, some underground safety station must be invented for the harrassed pedestrian—assuming that the pedestrian is not a species on the way to extinction.

"Have you seen Trixie?" The question came large from a megaphone at the crowded gates of the field. We had not seen her, and if she were lost in that surging mass of people, so much the worse for Trixie. "The fattest girl in the world," explained the megaphone. Joined to the newest wonder, the flying men, were the oldest of the world's wonders, housed in hasty tents along the great white way to the grandstand—Fatima, the Sultan's Delight—"Just arrived, a mother rattle-snake and five little ones." The Secrets of the Egyptian Pyramids ("tell me your birthday and I'll tell you your horrorscope"), and Cora-Etta, a version of the Siamese Twins, and now, in the light of present-day marvels, fitly termed the Human Biplane. In the line with these motley attrac-

tions, so singularly unnecessary and unrelated to the interest that had drawn the eager people to Dominguez, stretched countless lunch-counters with a varied appeal, and none of it very strong. Behind it lay a deep swale which we called Grub Gulch, its nearer slope covered with lunch débris, offering excellent forage for birds that did not feed on gasoline.

At the end of this gauntlet stood the grandstand, with fourteen sections that held each about a thousand closely-seated people. From the spectators' vantage-ground an open prairie, spread with the soft green of California's January, sloped very gently toward the distant city. Half-way across it were three large circus-tents, respectively the headquarters of Glenn H. Curtiss, with Hamilton and Willard; Paulhan, with Miscarol and Masson and Renan; and the local aviators with their varied engines of the air. It was of these last that some wag said: "The local aviators were early on the ground—and never left it."

It has never been authoritatively stated whether Pegasus was kept in a stable or in an aviary. It is equally unsettled as to which of these terms is to be applied to the housing of a flying-machine. Thus the word *hangar* (pronounced quite otherwise as *unger*), is a welcome addition to a vocabulary which was refreshed only yesterday with *garage*. The great worm-like dirigible balloons, fat and brown and pointed at head and tail, were kept down in Grub Gulch—an added reason for the name. These issued forth unexpectedly from behind the grandstand, casting their gigantic shadows on the people as they sailed over the audience and rose and dived with whatever ponderous-ness may be said to apply to lighter-than-air machines. Knabenshue, sailing over six hundred feet above the field on his slender snowshoe rack under the big yellow bag, the Stars and Stripes flying beneath him, was greeted with cheers for his daring. Beachy, less successful, but equally brave, guided his un-wieldy craft along the erratic air-currents. But the crowd, though cordial, was not there for balloons. Interest centers in the heavier-than-air machines. Men have been lifted from the earth by heated air and by gas for many years—the world has been waiting for them to rise on wings.

As though obedient to this call for wings, Prof. Zerbe's multiplane came on the field with many of them—a queer, lumbering affair that looked like a ship under full sail, or a flock of great white geese, or a stand for potted plants, or some fossil vertebrate out of the enormous past, according to one's point of view. There was a noble spurt along the ground, some steam, and then the great creature with a laborious sigh lay over upon its side. The audience laughed—a cruel thumbs-down laugh—careless of the eager thought that had failed to rise from the ground. Men had flown at Rheims—they must not do less at Domin-guez.

The tents of the aviators, each holding several of the winged engines, looked like cir-cus-tents in which the characteristic wagons had somehow been stripped to their slender frames. When an engine was tested the tent became a machine-shop and the side-flaps stood out straight in the draught from the whirring propeller. In the Curtiss tent the machines were khaki-colored, as though in an-ticipation of military service—frames of bam-boo and ash, and coverings of rubberized silk.

The Farman and Bleriot machines which the Frenchmen operated were grayish-white, taking the sun like silver when in swerving flight; among the other machines there was one of a dawnlike pink—seemingly born to blush unseen.

In the tent of the Frenchmen, apparently deserted, a San Francisco visitor, aflame with the desire for wings, climbed into a Bleriot cross-channel monoplane and sat there imagining the grandstand cheering far below him. This eaglet dream was shattered by a hailstorm of French expletives. A *mecanicien,* his hair and mustaches bristling with rage, fumed beside the machine. With a calm that should some day carry him through aerial difficulties the San Franciscan regarded the irate bird-hostler in astonished hauteur; draw-ing aside his coat-lapel he exhibited the circular button of the Panama Exposition boosters. The *mecanicien* bowed, said *"Pardon,"* and faded away in true European reverence for authority.

Glenn Curtiss is a slender, sober-faced man —a blending of the practical engineer and the young college professor. He appears to have been born deaf and blind to the grandstand. His performance has about as much sensa-tional atmosphere to it as that of a busy man

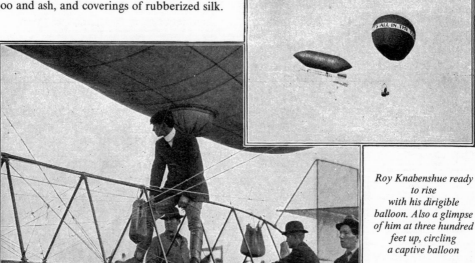

*Roy Knabenshue ready
to rise
with his dirigible
balloon. Also a glimpse
of him at three hundred
feet up, circling
a captive balloon*

"The local aviators were early on the ground—and never left it"

leaving home in his auto for his office. He has an air of quiet authority, of intimate knowledge of his machine, a serious intentness upon the business in hand. He is strictly in the business of selling flying-machines, among other motor vehicles, of which business the winning of the world's speed record is but an incident on advertising account. His demonstration seems to be, not the rivalry of the eagle or the carrier-pigeon—both of whom Paulhan, the Frenchman, has put to shame—but the present-day utility of these novel equipages. And, indeed, as one watches the quiet way in which he takes trips along the air, one understands why to-morrow may see your neighbor practicing over the golf-links with less reason for the family's fear than in the usual auto scorching.

The khaki-colored biplane is drawn along on its pneumatic wheels before the grandstand. Curtiss gives a last look over the machine, climbs into the seat between the engine and the steering wheel, the engine is cranked by its propeller, the men who have been holding the light vehicle against the force of the propeller until Curtiss gives the signal, release it and a new form of automobile, a flimsy double-kite mounted on a tricycle with an unmuffled gas engine, is under way across the grass. Thirty thousand eyes are on those rubber-tired wheels, waiting for the miraculous moment—historical for him who has not experienced it. Suddenly something happens to these whirling wheels—they slacken their speed, yet the vehicle advances more rapidly. It is the moment of miracle. The wheels are on the tops of the grass. Then, as though an invisible incline has been spread before him, Curtiss runs up the air along a gentle slope and soon is coursing along a plane a hundred feet above the earth. It has all happened suddenly, yet how much it signifies! It is the moment for which the faith of a world grown used to material conquests has waited, apparently baffled—it is the dream of centuries come true.

Across the field, attenuated by distance to the lines of a gigantic insect, Curtiss is sailing through the air. On he comes, turning the pylons at the corners of the course with a motion less of the bird than of the machine. As he passes the starting line, drawn in sawdust on the black adobe of Dominguez, his hands fast to the wheel, his gaze intent upon the ground, he shuts off his engine, and with a couple of gentle swoops he alights as delicately upon the green as a gull settles upon a bay, and he becomes for a little way an automobile again. This rising in flight and alighting is really a complete demonstration—the birds have been matched for all the needs of argument.

With eyes fixed upon Curtiss at the finish, few have noticed another biplane rising from the far side of the field and following in the American's wake. It is Paulhan, the Frenchman, in a Farman machine, distinguished from the Curtiss biplane by its color and by its single elevating plane in front and its wide box tail. Paulhan flies far up the field and is gone beyond the horizon of the hilltop. Then, when he has been forgotten in other movement upon the field, there comes the humming of an engine far aloft—the sound the sailors heard that memorable dawn off the Dover coast—and seemingly out of a great black cloud that hangs far above the grandstand bursts the flying creature with his parallel wings. When opposite the audience the intrepid little Frenchman waves his hand for an instant at the gaping people. Then on he goes round the course; passing in review again he waves his woolen cap and the crowd responds, cheering with the breath it has just held; round he goes again and, coming the third time, he stops his engine and coasting down the air he raises both arms to the grandstand and alights like a dove while the crowd goes mad at the performance. Ah, he is a theatrical artist, this Paulhan! He knows the value of an entrance and of cumulative gesture. And he possesses that intangible magnetism that of itself wakes an audience before performance so that the performance is a foregone triumph. He is a born player to the grandstand. Rumor has it that he was once a tight-rope walker. He is an interesting little figure in his thick woolens and his sweater, with heavy-ribbed stockings. He has a face of rose and olive and the smile that won't come off, even in danger. He looks like a debonair Alpine guide,

but his are the unseen mountain slopes, the uncharted glaciers of the air.

Thrilling as is Paulhan's flight, the spectator is aware that Willard, in a Curtiss biplane, has performed a marvelous feat when, after rising from a twenty-foot square of sawdust in front of the grandstand, he circles the field and comes to a stop within that starting-square as true as a bird seeks its nest. Hamilton, the third American aviator, flies his Curtiss machine to heights of seven hundred feet and more, and even when his crank-shaft breaks in mid-air, he comes to the ground with the sweep and the precision that marks these airships as cousins to the birds. Nothing at the Los Angeles meet was more lovely than a flight that Paulhan made toward evening, early in the week. The great

Louis Paulhan, ready to start in a Farman biplane for one of his spectacular cross-country flights

valley, spread before the grandstand like a scene in a vast theater, was already bathed in the lavender of evening, but the wall of snow-covered mountains was brilliant with rosy light. Athwart this background flew the wonderful, wingéd thing of man's invention, so birdlike that man was forgotten in its flight. Turning on the line of the course the wings tipped and were turned by the setting sun into gleaming bronze.

Toward the middle of one afternoon a golden balloon that had been hanging above the valley between the field and Los Angeles, drew nearer and soon came floating gracefully over the field, drawn by a horse. While yet it hung several hundred feet above the field, Paulhan, winged with a Farman biplane, soared into the air and circling the slow-moving newcomer, gave greetings to the party in the basket, which included Mme. Paulhan, chubby, petite, and vivacious, and no small factor in the theatrical element that added so keenly to the enjoyment of the Frenchman's performances.

Both Curtiss and Paulhan took the biplane out of the class of solo performances by taking passengers for short flights, and Paulhan thrilled by flying with his pretty wife nestled close to him in those frail wings, a thousand feet above us and miles away cross-country and over the blue Pacific. Such performances cannot be written of lightly—they are the beginnings of a new era in the history of men.

Stirring as were all these flights to those who thought as they watched them, there was one transcendent afternoon in that calendar of thrills. Paulhan rose lightly into the still air of late afternoon. As he climbed above the landscape the megaphone announced that "Mister Lewis Pollen" would try for altitude. Round and round the course the biplane sailed steadily, ever higher in ever widening circles.

From instruments by the judges' stand an estimate of altitude was made as the bird-man climbed the sky, and as the figures mounted the excitement of the grandstand climbed with them. Now Paulhan was so high that man and engine had merged into one body beyond which the planes, lighted underneath by the setting sun, stretched like the blood-filled membranes of a bat. Icarus, in Greek legend, flew too near the sun and his wings of wax were melted to his undoing. Paulhan, choosing the sunset hour, had flown above the sun and now climbed fearlessly toward the stars. Presently on the blackboard the world's record was written, three thousand and two hundred feet; the hoarse voice of the megaphone called to the throng of listeners: "two thousand and nine hundred feet, and still going up."

The the world's record was passed and the instruments and the cameras lost track of the flying man, and still this new wonder of our strenuous life swept higher into the heavens. As the birdlike figure lessened in the sky until it was but a dark cross against the darkening blue, the crowd of fascinated groundlings grew silent. This man who had flown away before our eyes had become a thing apart, a creature utterly lonely, almost a mile above us in a realm where we did not belong. To the memory of many must have come the speech of Bryant to the waterfowl—in the desert and illimitable air above us, one of our own kind, yet different, was lone wandering yet not lost. It was the realization, there in that early dusk of an enchanted winter-day, of Shelley's soaring skylark that "soaring ever singest." There, lonely and cold as he was, that man-bird must irresistibly have sung aloud as he dared the condor's "roads between the thunder and the sun." #

World's Records made at Los Angeles

1. *Height—Louis Paulhan (former world's record, 3200 feet) 4165 feet*
2. *Quick Start—Glenn Curtiss (former world's record, 8 seconds) 6⅗ seconds*
3. *Short Start—Glenn Curtiss (former world's record, 115 feet) 98 feet*
4. *Accuracy—Charles F. Willard; rising from a square of twenty feet on an edge, he made a complete circle and brought his machine to a full stop on the same square*
5. *Cross-Country with passenger—Paulhan and Mme. Paulhan, 21¼ miles*
6. *Cross-Country alone—Paulhan, 45.1 miles in 1 hr., 2 min., 42⅘ sec.*

The Planes that Fly Straight Up

By Pitt B. Hand

March 1910

WHEN you were a child you often amused yourself by twisting a piece of spirally-cut cardboard about one end of a lead pencil, rapidly revolving the pencil thus equipped by dragging it through the hands, each moving in an opposite direction, quickly releasing the thing and watching it soar upward as it continued to turn from the momentum imparted. When you did that you were experimenting with the principle which governs the present-day heliocopter, probably the most scientific of the flying-machines of the present.

Having the resistance of the aeroplane in its lift and the direct assistance of the heliocopter principle in combination, it is believed it will be more steady and more sure in the air than any other form of flying-machine that has, as yet, occurred to the mind of man.

The heliocopter, or top-principle lifter, has a number of devotees among the California inventors. In fact, the costliest of all the machines constructed in California have been built upon this principle.

Peter and W. P. English, father and son, have constructed in guarded secrecy at Sather station, Fruitvale, near Oakland, a heliocopter so mammoth and elaborate that they have already expended upon it nearly $10,000. This token of confidence in success of the idea follows one year of experiments which have amply proved the lifting-power of the apparatus. The Englishes, who are practical machinists, have incorporated a million-dollar company to handle their heliocopter.

The English has at its top two gigantic adjustable-disk propellers, lying horizontally at each end of an upper truss, each of which by forced spinning is capable of lifting nearly one thousand pounds. The propellers are twenty feet in diameter and are driven by a seventy-five horsepower, eight cylinder, water-cooling gasoline engine. Two curved planes with eight hundred square feet of supporting surface for soaring extend over the top of the machine. This auxiliary aeroplane canopy is of finest prepared silk. The framework, which is of nickel tubing and brass, provides an operating platform at the bottom, which bears seventy-five per cent of the weight and gives equilibrium. As the total weight of the machine is six hundred and fifty pounds, the great and powerful propellers are figured to provide such a tremendous surplus lifting-power, that the completed heliocopter will easily carry four or five persons.

The idea of the machine is to make a straight ascent by the horizontal whirling of the propeller-wheels, then travel at will both by soaring on gravity and by propulsion. Upon reaching the height desired, the propellers can be deflected by levers on the operating platform to vertical positions and utilized for driving the ship horizontally through the air while it rides on the sustaining power of the planes. Before commencing the construction of the large machine, the lifting-power of the arrangement was thoroughly tested by means of small models. The men have been at work on their large machine for six months past and expect to make a public flight over San Francisco bay before the close of the year. The English machine is kept under close watch in a large, specially-constructed shop at Fruitvale. Few persons have been permitted to inspect it and no photographs or drawings of the detail of its construction have been permitted.

Another most interesting air-ship of the heliocopter type under construction on an elaborate scale in San Francisco is that of Leonard H. Lane, of 1158 Francisco street, West Berkeley. Lane, who is a mechanical engineer, has spent several years in study and experiment, from which he has evolved what he terms an "automatous heliocoptic aeroplane" that is remarkable in its detail. His machine, which will cost slightly in excess of

$5,000 for construction, is more than half completed, and it also is being handled by a stock company controlled by the inventor.

This inventor kept his secret ambition to solve air-travel so well that the first information his wife had of the reason for his prolonged absences from home and considerable expenditures was when he came sailing down from the skies into the front yard one evening. Now his wife has developed into his most enthusiastic and intelligent helper in perfecting the great machine with which they both count on winning fame and fortune.

Lane's "automatous heliocoptic aeroplane" possesses several distinctive and entirely original features not included in any other California air-ship. Firstly, its propelling power is the expansion of compressed air, and this fundamental departure Lane has guarded zealously as to its detail. Secondly, the aeroplane feature is composed of automatically-opening and closing shutters or valves of aluminum. Thirdly, its lifting propellers all revolve around one central shaft, making the equilibrium as absolute and certain as that of a spinning-top.

The aeroplane portion of Lane's machine which covers the top like an enormous umbrella, is twenty feet wide by thirty feet long. In traveling this will present its broad side forward. The entire plane is composed of a series of thin sheets or plates of aluminum, similar to the scales of a fish. When the machine, in response to the whirling horizontal propellers, shoots upward, these plates hang downward, permitting the air to pass through without hindrance to the rise. When the desired height is attained horizontal progress may be begun either by tilting the machine slightly downward and soaring or by the use of a secondary propeller at the front of the ship. The sideward motion automatically closes the valvelike flaps, and when descent is begun they are slammed shut by the air-current, and form a perfect parachute for safe and slow descent. Supplementary to the main aeroplane are two side gliders or wings, which aid in sustaining the ship in flight or descent. For steering there is a two-way tail or rudder.

It is in his motive power of compressed air that Lane has his most radical departure and claims his greatest exclusive merit. Lane, in simple, proposes to create a gale beneath the sustaining surfaces of his ship, devoting a portion of this energy to driving his lifting propellers. The mechanism of the ship looks like two gigantic bicycles, laid sidewise, one on the top of the other. There is concentration of power for lifting by double whirling circles about the central shaft. The propeller-disks whirl about their own axes, and the wheels themselves revolve on their carriages around the big central shaft. The two sets of wheels go in opposite directions, compelling an even balance. The motors which generate the compressed-air power are placed with the operator's seat in the hanging carriage below. The machine complete weighs four hundred pounds.

Lane made five flights by means of compressed air last September and created a sensation with a cheap and primitive device designed simply to demonstrate the practicability of his theory. With a crude machine operated by hand and foot-power, surmounted by a small balloon and meager spread of wings, he rose from an open field in West Berkeley to a height of seventy-five feet and floated about over the tops of the trees and houses to the amazement of the townspeople. He remained aloft for seven minutes on one occasion, pumping desperately with hands and feet to continue the explosive expansion of air beneath the wings. Finally, exhausted by his terrible exertions at the pump-handles, he descended slowly, the wind by a peculiar chance wafting him and his strange device down to his own dooryard, where his astounded wife greeted him as he floated through the treetops and for the first time learned of his long-cherished ambition. On this and successive flights, Lane lifted a total of one hundred and sixty-two pounds dead weight with the compressed-air power. #

The Lady Ada, one of the crack yachts on San Francisco Bay. These birds of pleasure spread their wings when April brings the trade-winds through the Golden Gate

A San Francisco Pleasure Cure

Being Echoes of the New
City's Laughter

By SINCLAIR LEWIS

April 1910

THE Master Builder had wielded men, while the men wielded steel and cement, for the four years "since." Then the doctor had his say: "My dear man, you've been working too hard and you're going pot unless you get your nerves tuned up. Try Tahiti."

"I will not," answered the Master Builder. "I won't leave my brand-new six-foot bath-tub for all your surf-boards. If I must be a child again, I'll stay right here in San Francisco and see if they've made any new playthings since the fire."

He told The Wife, and ended, gloomily, "Now lead us to the rejuvenating merriment."

"Very well. I've been wondering how long it would be before you'd stop being a crab—walking backward through life. We'll start with the theaters."

As they were whirled to their show, in a taxicab, the Master Builder exclaimed, still resentful, "Now here you are, in spite of all the doctor-men say about working too hard. Where'd you play-folks be if we hadn't been building—building theaters and garages and taxicab companies. Doesn't look much like fire and disaster, does it, to ride in one of these rigamajigs?"

"Odious term!"

"—does it? Why, there's so many taxicabs and private cars in town, a dealer was telling me, that the chauffeurs have an association, with about five hundred members. Oh, we've been building in lots of things besides stone."

"Yes, in cafés, and Spanish dancers, for instance. We'll see La Castillaña tonight, after the show."

They did. They wandered along the New White Way, from the Portolá to Techau Tavern—Tait's—the Bismarck—the Odeon—the St. Francis—the Palace; peeping in at each; till The Wife reported that careful investigation indicated that another claret lemonade would cause a Central American revolution in the stomatic regions.

With a feeling of infinite luxury, he slept late, next day, Sunday, till afternoon, when they went autoing to the beach. From the terrace of the New Cliff House, they watched the absurdly grave and bearded sea-lions waltz through ethereally blue waves. They looked up the training quarters of a world-famed pugilist, and dropped in at the mild little road-houses along the perfect boulevard, where their auto wheels whirred silkenly, and wandered up into the gardens of Sutro Heights, whose highest rampart overlooked the enormous yellow crescent of hard beach, edged with sunny foam and scattered with colorful picnicking parties —overlooked the vast sweep of sea—from Golden Gate to Far Cathay!

"Great Saints!" cried the Master Builder. "*Is* it good to be out of the office? *Is* this a pleasure city? Look at those people down there in the Seeing San Francisco car. Even such untrained aliens are handed one of the cheerfulest pleasures—sightseeing. We must have some of that, eh? Takes a native not to know his own city."

"But now let's go down and picnic on the beach among the pro-le-tar-i-at!" suggested the Master Builder.

They purchased a lunch-in-er-paper and trotted gaily down to the peopled sands. The air was sweet and the small girls paddling gingerly, were funny and frolicsome. Their lunch was flavored with the Salt of Life as well as the salt of the sea.

"Lord but the people here do enjoy themselves," the builder said, as they rode home, through Golden Gate Park. "Track meet at the Stadium, eh?"

"You, revered sir," smiled The Wife, "had better get your strong young manhood back again. You may just dismiss the chauffeur and take me for a row on Stow Lake."

With sunset among the pines on Strawberry Hill, they slid softly among the lily pads, like the swans about them. They had tea, afterward, in the Japanese Garden.

The Wife announced that they would vary the sport by another glimpse of the night side of town; and they "did" Fillmore street; the avenue of lights and Mardi Gras gaiety; of derelict Mexican restaurants and—nickelodeons! it seemed improper not to have confetti flying, here, under the quadruple arches of lights.

The towers and the scenic railroad's runway at "The Chutes" glowed before them. "Come on!" the builder cried. "I want to get joggled on the Human Roulette Wheel, and look upon the Small Brothers in the hotel de Monk."

The Wife explained to him, with care, that it was not at all decent for a man of his dignity to be seen flying down the Chutes and coasting the Devil's Slide, and gaping at open-air acrobats, but the Master Builder was obdurate. When they left "The Chutes," he was even seized by a notion that it was his duty to attend either an all-night masquerade at the Auditorium or go roller-skating; and she had to wile him home.

At breakfast, next morning, the Master Builder announced himself a confirmed sporting person, now.

"Yes," said The Wife. "But I won't let you become that only. Be a gent., with emphasis on the waistcoat, indeed! Bein' as it's rainy, to-day, you're to do the opposite sort of pleasures with me. See the bookstores and the rest."

The Master Builder was astonished to find just how much the shops of luxuries had been re-built. A picture store, with an Italian courtyard, smacking of dreamy Verona; a half-dozen bookstores; a music shop where they listened to a piano-player concert—with heads turned lest highbrow acquaintances should spy them—these were their rainy-day diversions.

"Now," said the builder, as they sat at hot chocolate in a delightfully rococo little shop

*The air was sweet, and the
small girls, paddling
gingerly,
were funny and frolicsome*

—an echo of Paris—"let's go to one of those continuous - moving - picture - and - vaudeville palaces on Market street."

"Aren't you *ashamed* of yourself."

"Nope. And, if it weren't growing late, I want to emulate the tourists and spend an hour down at the State Board of Trade's exhibits at the Ferry Building; see the mining display and the steropticon views of orange trees. But here's the sunshine again. Cummon!"

As they roamed up Grant avenue, among the smart shops, he glanced up the hill to the glittering pagodas of Chinatown, and remarked, "There's something we've been neglecting."

A jade and teak-wood salon was discovered for their dinner; with a joss house across the street from the balcony where they ate. "B'lieve this *is* better than it was before the fire," mused the builder, as they left a Chinese theater. "Cleaner. Glad those old shacks are gone. These buildings give 'em more chance to tog out in purple and gold. Look at that little Chinese girl. Wish I could wear lavender silk trousers embroidered in silver!"

The Master Builder was so frisky a builder, by now, that The Wife began taking him on

long tramps, after having tested him by the ascent of Telegraph Hill, above Italian town and above studio-land—a real Quartier Latin. From Buena Vista heights, they saw the new city before them, with scarcely a trace of the fire. They climbed the Twin Peaks, and wandered through Richmond, and along Pacific Heights, with its castle homes. Then he was, at last, graduated into the tennis-playing class. In the Golden Gate Park courts, and the grounds of the Alta Plaza, from whose plateau they could see Lone Mountain, with its great, mysterious cross, standing solitary, they played and loafed and played, till the Master Builder was not missing *every* serve.

He took to swimming too, and splashed in the salt-water tanks of the Sutro Baths; and the new Lurline, built in Roman-wise. He had already been renewing habit in his two clubs, and was looking forward to the Bohemian Club jinks, that pageant in an outdoor cathedral whose pillars were redwoods. Now, he edged his way into one of the four golf clubs, and trotted through long afternoons over the Presidio links, in the great Government reservation. Old friendships with army people were renewed there; and he was even seen at post tiffin, and the Presidio hops.

"Why, you'll be teaching your teacher," The Wife laughed, as they cantered through the park together. "You're getting almost too athletic and social for me."

"Well, let's have a quiet day to-morrow, then. I say, do you remember what we used to do in courtin' days, before there were motor-cars? Go buggy-riding! We'll just do that, to-morrow."

Through the Oakland and Berkeley streets of leisurely homes, past the University campus and the dignity of the Greek Theater, they went a-buggy riding; a long, lazy, dreamy ride, with the sun bright on the hard leaves of the eucalypts and soft in the pepper-tree foliage. Finally, they drove to the golden hills beyond, and stood at gaze, looking over to the peaks of the dimly-seen High Sierras, while the Master Builder said:

"Guess I'm ready for a diploma in the course in getting young, now. Weren't the Spaniards chumps to think the Fountain of Youth was in the tropics! For it's by the Golden Gate, and we've found it, eh?" #

A Frenchman Looks at Co-education

By BARON D'ESTOURNELLES DE CONSTANT

November 1912

IN the East the problem of the co-education of the sexes is beginning to be discussed; in the West it appears to be clearly settled in the affirmative. At Stanford University, at Berkeley, and later at Salt Lake City and in Colorado, as also at Seattle and Chicago, I saw young people from eighteen to twenty years old, mingled together, forming an audience very attentive to new ideas. At the University of California, I spent an afternoon and evening and gave one of my principal lectures. One could not wish for a more intelligent, homogeneous, or alert audience. At Stanford, the men students invited me to visit their houses and dormitories. They have the choice between two very different kinds of life; some living in groups of twenty to twenty-five, in houses where they are their own masters; under the direction of one of their number, who has been elected president because of his fitness and merit. They work, play in the open air, exercise in athletic sports, sleep out-of-doors in all kinds of weather, and, in the evening, they assemble in the drawing room, play, sing and amuse themselves. Others lead exactly the same life in a more spacious building, a dormitory, where they number several hundred, but are just as free.

Likewise the young women have their houses with their gardens, in groups, and also their independent dormitory. The houses of the young men and those of the young women are adjoining, intermingled, and one never hears of a scandal. The young girls go out every day, even in the evening, into the gardens, the street, the playgrounds; they play, ride horseback, always astride, and gallop with bare heads, just as they walk, without fearing anything.

After I had given three or four lectures, the young women invited me to dine in one of their lodges. They had donned evening dress, and it was a joy to see them so fresh, with the blonde or dark hair, their blue or black eyes, smiling and confiding.

An extraordinary thing! By the side of the two Japanese students who acted as butlers around this table blooming with youth, a tall young man, very gentle, very simple, an American, was serving also. He was a student serving of his own free will, such as you find everywhere in the universities of the United States, among the young men who have no means to defray the expenses of their education. All this was so simply and naturally done, that one would have been a brute to venture a jest in this company by asking how such a paradox was possible. During the dinner, from time to time, the young women, without rising, sang a chorus, then another, now gay, now sentimental or witty, but above all gay. Then they stopped, chatted, laughed, and sang again. This dinner appeared very short to me.

Afterward I went to see the young men who were waiting for me to the number of several hundred; their good, fresh faces were pleasant to see. All these young people are not thinking of evil. But how much more easily they can be misled, carried away! How necessary it is that they should be put on their guard, as much against their individual errors as against those of the government. Such is the fear that I have often expressed on leaving these young men and young women abandoned, so to speak, to their instincts alone.

In the end, however, I asked myself whether this education is not the surest of safeguards and whether the use of liberty is not the best of precautions and discipline. Our French young people would be wrong in believing that the American education is only good for the muscles and nerves, and that, in all other respects, it forms ingenuous beings, incapable of getting over difficulties outside of their own country. No, it forms men and women who are everywhere at home. They can prove in any case that their independent education, far from separating them, brings them into closer touch with the rest of the world. #

Sculpture Between Tides

By MYRTLE GARRISON

September 1911

THE story of sand modeling on our beaches is comparatively short, yet the few who are developing it are enthusiastic and their work is meeting with success among the artist folk.

At first the work was started at one of the southern beaches by an amateur who made a few busts of famous men. It was crude enough but it started the fad, and then some enterprising and ambitious artist saw a chance to make money out of it and so put it on a commercial basis.

About two years ago one of these artists started the work in Long Beach, and at once his work interested the people to such an extent that it became one of the principal beach attractions. During the summer and winter he worked from morning until evening and against the coming and going of the tide. His studio was but a little square out of the broad white sand, without even an imaginary line drawn around it. He charged nothing, but usually there was a little sign neatly carved in the sand "Remember the Worker" and as a general thing the score or more of people who were always gathered around him were generous. Sometimes the silver came in nickels and dimes, then there were good days when half-dollars and dollars were given. One day there appeared this sign in the sand: "Every little helps toward my aim in life as a sculptor." This did more than anything else to interest the people and make them realize the high ambition of the man.

One of the favorite statues with the people who were daily visitors to the sand pile was, "Cast up by the sea." It pictured a mother with her baby in her arms as they had been cast up by the waves.

There is something pathetic in the carving of these figures when we stop to think of the labor and love worked in each one and know that by night time they will be washed away. #

Los Angeles, Feb. 15, 1914

Dear Folks!

This picture was taken at Old San Gabriel Mission, one of the many interesting places on the great Trolley Trips of Southern California. Write to the railway company for the _complete_ story of our tour, "Trolley Trips through Wonderland". A post-card will bring the booklet.

We may decide to live here
Yours, John

OLD MISSION
TROLLEY TRIP

PACIFIC ELECTRIC RAILWAY
D.W. PONTIUS, TRAFFIC MANAGER, LOS ANGELES, CAL.

Dancing is delightful
to the music of the Victrola

Every one enjoys dancing to music of such splendid volume, such clearness and perfect rhythm—and the Victrola plays as long as any one wants to dance.

The Victrola brings to you all kinds of music and entertainment, superbly rendered by the world's greatest artists who make records exclusively for the Victor.

Any Victor dealer will gladly play the latest dance music or any other music you wish to hear. There are Victors and Victrolas in great variety of styles from $10 to $500.

Victor Talking Machine Co., Camden, N. J., U. S. A.
Berliner Gramophone Co., Montreal, Canadian Distributors

c

New Victor Records demonstrated at all dealers on the 28th of each month

California's First Cubist House

By BERTHA H. SMITH

August 1915

WHEN Mrs. Mary Banning of Los Angeles decided to build a house, she had a lot of definite, original ideas about it. She learned of an architect who had bolted all the customs and traditions that have achieved for the United States the distinction of having the ugliest domestic architecture of any country on the map.

Irving J. Gill, long ago had set himself against the popular taste for gimcrack ornament, cheap and tawdry construction and all the false effort and effect that are the inevitable result of our continued content with being cheap imitators of every other age and country. Gradually, doggedly, against all opposition, he has evolved a type of house that is the beginning of a realization of our perennial vision—a truly American style of architecture.

The Banning house kept everybody in the neighborhood guessing when they saw men day after day wheeling barrow loads of concrete onto a huge table supported at an angle of forty-five degrees by steel walking beams, and still more when they saw a seventy-three-foot wall, smooth finished and complete with window and door openings, projecting window-boxes and small balconies,

raised to perpendicular by means of a single little donkey engine. They kept on guessing as the house took form in simple cubic units, the walls rising sheer and roofless without cornices or trim of any kind, cutting boldly across the blue sky.

The outward form is merely an expression of the spirit within, of absolute simplicity, absolute sincerity, absolute independence. The most radical departure from orthodoxy in the interior is the almost complete absence of wood. There is no moulding for pictures or plates or chairs, no baseboards or paneling or wainscoting, no wooden window or door frames.

The rooms are all free from the distracting, feverish attempt to divert attention by means of excessive ornamentation—false beams, elaborate beadings and mouldings, grotesque mantelpieces, what not?—from essential deficiencies, as one tosses a baby and shakes gay colored things before its eyes to make it forget it has the colic. These walls dare to be plain and unbroken because the man who plastered them is an artist and the plastering in itself is a thing of beauty; because also there is something satisfying in the proportioning of the rooms and of the doors and windows.

The Banning house is not the only example of the Gill style. He has built many houses in San Diego, La Jolla, Pasadena, Hollywood, Los Angeles. He has built churches and schools and railway stations, and a booth in one of the San Francisco Exposition palaces—this last under protest of a director who balked at the boldness and baldness of his design. #

The Roadtown is a line of city projected through the country. It is not a town; not a rural community—it is both.

The Continuous House

By MILO HASTINGS

January 1914

EDGAR Chambless has come to San Francisco. Chambless is the Roadtown man and Roadtown is a machine for making an improved variety of civilization at a reduced cost.

And this man Chambless, seventeen years ago sat on Angel's Flight in Los Angeles and wondered why the ground was bare within a stone's throw of the most expensive land of the city. He was half blind, this inventor, and books for him were closed. But his mind had eyes, and he saw many things that mere light rays cannot convey. He saw, as he sat on Angel's Flight, the relation that exists between transportation and land values. He saw the paradoxical struggle of men to find dwellings accessible to the public mart and yet isolated and hidden for the home nest—for men like birds will not mate and reproduce amid the flutter and chatter of the flock.

And Chambless played with the needs of men and built the blocks of civilization into new playhouses of the mind. When the blocks were arranged at last, the builder breathed deeply and said that it was good. He had invented Roadtown, the new plan of housing that promises to give us quick and easy access to things and to each other, and yet greater privacy for the home nest, and fellowship with the land and the live things—our companions of the ages before bricks were made.

In giving Roadtown a hearing remember that it is not a town and not a rural community. It is both. Compared with our present ideas of either it will have obvious advantages and obvious shortcomings, but take it as a whole and compare it with a modern town plus the surrounding farm territory, and then judge of Roadtown.

The Roadtown is a line of city projected through the country. This line of a city will be in the form of a continuous house. In the basement of the house are to be placed means of transporting passengers, freight, parcels and all utilities which can be carried by pipe or wire.

The first good seen in the continuous house idea is that of economy of construction. The excavating will be done with steam-shovels. The entire structure can be made of cement and part or all of the building will be poured. Mr. Edison figures he can build a seven-room cement house for $1200. In Roadtown this expense will be further reduced, not only by the elimination of one wall and the economics of repetition and continuity of construction, but by the fact that the Roadtown may all be constructed from a railroad track alongside. The great task of shifting steel molds, which is well nigh insurmountable in the individual house pouring scheme, becomes in Roadtown an easy duty for a steam crane on the railroad.

One of the essentials of Roadtown is a noiseless method of transportation. From each house a stairway will lead down into the endless basement, where the trains will run with no more disturbance to the inhabitants than is made by elevators in a hotel. It is just as feasible mechanically to make a noiseless horizontal, as a noiseless vertical car. The electric automobile running on smooth asphalt is sufficiently near the goal of silent efficiency to further prove the point.

Another stairway will lead from the Roadtown dwelling to the endless roofway above. Upon the outer edges of this roof promenade will be paths for bicycles and rubber-tired roller skates.

Another plan is to eliminate the basement, except a central trench for pipes and wires. The supporting walls would then be built well-trussed to carry a roofway sufficiently rigid for light-running motor vehicles.

No streets will be needed in Roadtown. This permits the windows and doors on both sides of the house to open into private gardens with no traffic beyond. With the heavy cement walls between the individual houses and with the traffic ways shut off from sight and sound, the

Public buildings, surrounded by parks instead of farms, will depend upon the service through the endless basement.

Roadtown home, in spite of the actual proximity to neighbors will give more privacy than is now attainable in village or city life.

The continuous passageway underneath the house will contain the pipes and wires which will bring into every home the conveniences that now mark the chief difference between city and country life. The more common of these are sewerage, hot and cold water, gas for cooking, telephone, steam heat (or hot water heat) and electric light.

All of the above list of utilities are now found in prosperous city homes, but every additional pipe laid into a city house means that the pavement in the street must be dug up and replaced, the sidewalk and cellar wall torn open, and the politicians well paid for a new franchise. In the Roadtown the adding of a new utility will cost but the expense of the house length of main pipe and a connection to lead through the floor into the room above.

Hence it will be practical to install in the Roadtown home a brine pipe for refrigeration, eliminating the use of ice; vacuum dusting and sweeping; distilled drinking water; carbon-dioxide gas for putting out local fires and making "fizzy" drinks; a disinfecting gas, the telegraphone or recording telephone, and the dictograph or loud speaking telephone, and electrically conveyed music.

Quite as marvelous as the utilities to be brought into the home by pipes and wires is the change which will be effected in home life by superior transportation. A parcels carrying system, not unlike that used in department stores or to carry books in large libraries, will serve central stores and the individual home. Each car will be set with a key trip which will automatically switch it into the proper house.

One of the most significant features of the Roadtown is that this perfected mechanical system of distributing solids, liquids and gases makes coöperation of all kinds more practical. This will not only apply to the marketing of farm crops and the purchase of raw supplies, but will undoubtedly extend to laundrying and cooking. It will be entirely feasible to send a daily bill of fare into each home from which prepared food may be ordered by telephone, and delivered from a central kitchen in heated or chilled receptacles, as the case may be. In like manner the dishes may be sent back to be washed, hotel fashion.

Previous schemes of coöperative cooking have failed because the common mess halls destroyed family life. In the Roadtown the actual mingling with one's neighbors will be about like that of the suburban or country town.

Mr. Chambless hopes to see Roadtown built and managed by restricted corporations, with provisions for the ownership ultimately passing to the inhabitants. Roadtown bonds paying a moderate rate of interest would be sold to the investing public. The tenant of Roadtown would be required to pay such a rental as would meet running expenses and interest, and pay off the principal in perhaps fifty years.

Is the Roadtown inhabitant to be the owner of his home? That depends on what we call ownership. The savage chief who owns an island owns it absolutely until some one takes it away from him. The man in New York or Sacramento, who owns his house and lot, owns it with the provision that the city may tax him for paving, water, sewerage and police protection; while private corporations charge him for light, heat and transportation. If he does not pay the first his house is taken away from him, and if he refuses to pay the latter, his house is useless. Clearly there are different kinds of ownership. The form of ownership worked out for Roadtown may differ from that with which we are now familiar, but the principle will be the same.

Few of us realize how little land we really use in production. On the basis of 33-foot houses and five to a family, it would take just about three thousand miles of Roadtown to house all the people of California. Parallel to this imaginary "state house" California's magnificent irrigated belt would form a strip extending but three-fifths of a mile on either side of the building. The wheat fields would form a band one-fourth of a mile wide and the alfalfa belt the same. The state's magnificent combined acreage of table, raisin and wine grapes would form a continuous vineyard 57 rods wide. The poultry, with 400 hens to the acre, could be provided for in a yard 37 feet in width. And all of these crops and all others, all improved farm land, in fact, could be placed within less than three miles of this ultra-urban civilization of the endless house. #

The Tin Can's Hideous Leer

December 1913

FILLED, the tin can is the gaudy emblem of modern mass civilization, an efficient labor-saving container of undifferentiated, standardized food. Empty, the tin can becomes the modern curse, a weapon whose ragged edges cut man's esthetic soul to the marrow, a ubiquitous nuisance killing romance and poetry as effectively as the stockyards perfume murders the odor of the violet.

The wilderness, the high places, the aisles of the forest, the mountain meadows and the banks of singing brooks are the front lawn of the West. Nature waters it, sweeps it, keeps it clean, but Nature can no longer cope with the growing piles of tin cans, leering hideously from the center of every inviting spot, with the swirling sheets of greasy paper and pasteboard plates shed in transit by motor campers. Even unto the snow line the curse of the tin can lies over the West.

If those privileged to commune with Nature cannot enjoy her hospitality without defiling the face of the hostess, why not penalize thoughtlessly dirty campers in the National Forests? The man who will scatter tin cans and waste paper will likewise forget to put out the fire before he leaves. #

Can the Panama Canal Be Destroyed from the Air?

By RILEY E. SCOTT

April 1914

THE Panama Canal—the most stupendous engineering feat of an engineering age—is nearing completion. The shriek and hiss of a thousand locomotives, the monotonous purr of compressed-air drills, the boom of blasts and the creak and groan of giant cranes and shovels have almost ceased. Soon the healing hand of Nature will bind up the scars of conflict and the commerce of a world will float between picturesque tropical hills. Naturally, the American people are proud of the job and proud of the men who have consummated this great undertaking without hitch and without taint of graft or scandal, where hundreds of millions have been involved. It is a magnificent achievement and we have reason to be proud.

For the past six years, at least, the problem of fortifying the Panama Canal has engaged the attention of our ablest military authorities and, naturally, every precaution has been taken to insure, as far as possible, its impregnability. But, during this time, a new factor in warfare has gradually been developed—a factor whose vast importance is just beginning to be realized by even the most progressive strategists and tacticians. I refer to what the French call "the Fourth Arm"—the aeroplane.

When we stop to consider it, the progress that aviation has made during the past five years is simply amazing. At the end of 1908, not over half a dozen machines were flying, with a duration record of about an hour and a half, a speed of some forty miles per hour and a height record of 320 feet. At this writing, the duration record is over sixteen hours without landing, a height of three and eight-tenths miles has been attained, a speed record of 126 miles per hour has been made, continents have been crossed, seas have been traversed, mountain ranges and deserts have been flown over and the number of machines is legion. France alone has over 800 military aeroplanes ready for service and is making a desperate effort to maintain the mastery of the air; while Germany, Russia, Great Britain, Austria, Italy and Japan are training aviators and providing machines as fast as possible. In short, military experts are coming to realize that the aeroplane is not only a factor in warfare, but may become a decisive factor.

Over a year ago, in France, the writer demonstrated, beyond doubt, that remarkable accuracy can be attained in dropping bombs from an aeroplane by placing twelve out of fifteen bombs within a square of about 120 feet from a height of over one-half mile and at a speed of nearly a mile a minute. During these experiments, a weight of 225 pounds was dropped at a single time from a light machine, and, at the present time, aeroplanes exist that are capable of carrying and dropping bombs of five hundred pounds without difficulty. It is safe to predict that the next year or two will develop machines capable of carrying one thousand pounds of high explosives.

Without discussing the possibility of destroying our coastal cities—even the capital itself—by aeroplanes from an enemy's fleet, let us consider the vulnerability of the Panama Canal from the air. This discussion assumes that, in the near future, battleships and cruisers will be equipped with aeroplanes, which assumption is supported by the opinions of high naval authorities.

A study of the Canal reveals to us several vital and vulnerable points which, in the writer's opinion, could easily be destroyed from the air. The most vital and probably the most vulnerable of these are the great concrete locks which will lift vessels over the continental divide. They are six in number—three at Gatun,

This is one of the most significant photographs ever published in this country. Below the aeroplane from which the picture was taken lie the Naos islands, in the bay of Panama, on which the United States Government is now mounting batteries of the heaviest artillery in the world, to protect the Pacific approach to the Panama Canal. On the island almost directly under the aeroplane can be seen the emplacement for the most powerful weapon ever constructed, the first 16-inch disappearing gun, which has an effective range of about twelve miles. Here is the significance of this photograph: the aeroplane might have come, in time of war, from a battleship out of range of the big gun, flying at a safe height and carrying five hundred or more pounds of high explosive, instead of a camera. Would not the big gun be helpless against such a foe?

This remarkable photograph was taken by Ray A. Duhem from the hydro-aeroplane of the noted aviator, Robert G. Fowler. Under unusual difficulties Fowler made a daring flight across the Isthmus from the Pacific to the Atlantic, so far the only aviator to make the journey. Shortly afterward, President Wilson issued an executive order forbidding such flights, under heavy penalty. The photographs made on this flight, in themselves a notable achievement in motion photography, are probably the only pictures that will ever be taken of the Canal from the air, except for purposes of war. This page in Sunset Magazine is the first publication of any of the photographic records of that unique flight.

A review of military aeroplanes after the autumn maneuvers in France. Over seventy of these aeroplanes performed arduous scouting duty during a period of two weeks, without a single serious accident, and then assembled near Paris for a grand review by the Minister of War

about eight miles from deep water on the Atlantic side of the Canal, and three at the west end of Culebra Cut, about the same distance from the Pacific.

Supposing that the enemy's fleet arrived during the night and that the first attack is made at daybreak, a single day would be sufficient to attack all vital points as far as the western locks. Culebra Cut would undoubtedly make a good target, providing the enemy had information concerning the points where slides were most likely to occur, which he probably would. By placing several tons of explosives where the walls are weakest, it is quite probable that a serious slide would be produced. If the slide were at all bad, it would stop traffic and take several weeks, or even months, to remove. The administration buildings at Culebra and the headquarters, storehouses and barracks of the troops could be easily destroyed. Even the emplacements of the big guns would offer excellent targets—and who will say that five hundred pounds of high explosive, placed on or near a disappearing gun carriage, would not do serious harm?

It will probably be necessary to fight aeroplanes with aeroplanes. For example, if we should have a preponderating air fleet of fast machines on the Isthmus, lightly armored underneath as a protection against rifle fire and armed with rapid-fire guns, it would be possible to meet and fly above the heavier, more slowly moving bomb-carriers and pick them off, one by one. The aerial battle of the future is not an improbability, and the writer ventures to predict that many a deed of heroism and daring will take place in the blue above contending armies. #

The Terrible Consequences of Clothing

With Women Inside of It

By Miriam Michelson

February 1915

"So-called good women go upon the streets in clothes which serve to ensnare men."
—Police Commissioner,
San Jose, California, A. D. 1914

IT is always enlightening, in this change-ful world, to come upon a constant quantity, one that is not affected by time nor place nor circumstance, that remains fixed and unalter-able, however at variance it be with facts or reason or common sense. Such a constant quality is man's world-old tirade against woman's garments, his perennial disposition to blame her clothing for the sins of him.

For, please note, fashions change. Indeed it's axiomatic that they do little but change; some-. times over night, certainly from season to season, always from century to century. But man's shrewish vituperation of them? Never. That is immutable. Whatsoever woman hap-pens to be wearing at any epoch and at all epochs—let that be anathema. It—whatever it is—is designed "to be a snare to men."

The quotation is from Clement of Alex-andria who, eighteen centuries ago, was fore-most in the discovery and denunciation of things-to-be-shocked-at in woman's clothes.

Alas, these things-to-be-shocked-at! If only *they* would remain constant, how readily might a magnanimous sex make its toilet for the good—not of its own body, but of man's soul. But they don't; they change with the fashions. It is possible for that pitiably frail and volatile thing—masculine virtue—to be imperiled by fashions precisely contrary. The full skirt and the scant skirt and the slit skirt affect it alike disastrously. At different periods man's ap-prehension for his own susceptibility have been awakened by the tight bodice, by the Mother Hubbard, by the Simple Susan. He has

become vocal and vituperative over the dan-ger—to himself—in high heels, no heels, pan-iers, too many petticoats, and too few. One age thunders against corsets; another is shocked at the natural figure.

One shrieks with hysteric fear of veils; another exclaims at the uncovered face. One sounds the alarm at clocked stockings; another pales at the threat to virtue in white spats. One is panic-strick n at the use of starch; another pants with terror of the insidious corruption in silk. And the waist line, as it rises or falls, is the barometer of sex-morals, carrying with it man's uneasy susceptibility; only it always registers the same degree of pressure and whatever it points to, it invariably threatens storm!

And oh, the innocent things these male scolds raise tempests about! Different colors were denounced at different times by the alert watchman over his besieged morals. Four cen-turies ago it was yellow that stampeded him. I don't know why. It may be the prescient male mind anticipated the sensationalism one day to be attached to "yellowness" and strove to dis-suade females from its use ahead of time, thus being modest and virtuous vicariously, as still is the unselfish habit of men. But at an earlier period it was "these stupid and luxurious purples; would it were possible to abolish them!"

Poor busy St. Clement! There was so much he wished to abolish. There were "head-dresses and varieties of head-dress and elaborate braidings and infinite modes of dressing the hair, and costly specimens of mirrors —characteristic of women who have lost all sense of shame"; there were "these su-perfluous and diaphanous materials which are the proof of a weak mind"; there were "gold-plated and jeweled mischievous devices

From Paul to Clement, from the Vatican to the Friends' meeting-house, from
Savanarola to Napoleon and Schopenhauer the weighty word flies,
from century to century, evidence of man's immutable
belief in the tradition of tempatation

of sandals, and Attic and Sicyonian half-boots, and Persian and Tyrrhenian buskins." The head should be veiled and the face covered, he declared, and "it is prohibited to expose the ankle. Nor is it seemly for a woman to wish to make herself conspicuous by using a purple veil. Base in truth are those sandals in which gold ornaments are fastened. Let not women's ears be pierced, contrary to nature. And thrice I say, not once, do they deserve to perish who . . . stain their eyebrows with soot and rub their cheeks with white lead."

It sounds very up-to-date, doesn't it? Not the letter but the spirit of it—the very same spirit which inspires the Saint Clements of today.

Four centuries before Christ, Aristophanes' list of things-to-be-shocked-at included:

"Snoods, fillets, natron and steel,
Pumice-stone, band, back-band,
Back-veil, paint, necklaces,

Paints for the eyes, soft garments, hairnet,
Girdle, shawl, fine purple border,
Long robe, tunic, Barathrum, round tunic,
Ear-pendants, jewelry, ear-rings;
Mallow-colored cluster-shaped anklets,
Buckles, clasps, necklets,
Fetters, seals, chains, rings, powders,
Bosses, bands, olisbi, Sardian stones,
Fans, helicters."

"I am weary and vexed," cries one who quotes him approvingly, "at enumerating the multitude of ornaments."

The esthetic intention of costuming is not always clear, but its effect seems to be to put emphasis now upon one part of woman's body, now another; on the ankle and leg in 1900, on the arms and back in 1800, on the hips in 1700, on the bosom in 1600, on the abdomen in 1400. And though fashions may come and fashions may go, in every instance the bell of male susceptibility rings out an alarm against the perennial offender—in matters of costume, a call to arms to grave students of sociology, men of affairs, clergymen, criminologists, against what the leading religious paper of the twentieth century denominates the "shameless styles."

What is modesty for women, so far as clothes express it? Who invented it—the men who set women's fashions, or the men who cry out against them? It certainly had its origin in the sex that is still devout and decorous and chaste—by proxy.

The court of James I was noted for its indecorousness, according to the old chroniclers. So little sense of decency there was that "no female could pass through any part of the king's palace without being grossly affronted." And yet in those days fashion prescribed, in addition to the full, round skirt, the long,

as was ever done in the long history of dress concealment. Poor, stylish Anne, with her high ruff above her ears, her broad collar over her breast, her long, narrow, rigorous, pointed stomacher, her wide Dutch skirt draped over the flat projection of her farthingale's round-table-like edge, triumphantly keeping sacred that mystery, vital to civilization, of the anatomical connection between woman's feet and her waist line!

I wonder how long we must still make believe to believe in that curious mental and moral obliquity, initiated in the Garden of Eden and made sacred through centuries of precedent, which recognizes masculine frailty as something vicariously to be atoned for by feminine suppression? And will it allay the panic today at feminine provocation to stitch up that terrifying slit skirt and revive the perilous alternatives—the bustle, the panier, the hoopskirt, the corsetless Mother Hubbard denounced by an outraged world, the decolletage that troubled Tartuffe?

After all, isn't all this talk about clothes a reversion to type, the old, old use of one sex as the whipping-boy for the other's offenses; the excuse that Adam handed down, an eternal masculine legacy, to sons as weak and willing as the first great evader of responsibility?

lace-cuffed sleeves and the stomacher, a hood over the hair and three pairs of gloves one on top of the other. Besides this, "the great ladies do go well masked, and indeed it be the only show of their modesty, to conceal their countenance." There has come down to us in the portrait of Anne of Denmark, queen of James, a female figure as successfully distorted

One of our modern Saint Simeons declares the fashions of today to be a direct and conscious protest of the feminine woman against the suffragette type.

"In her natural repugnance to being mistaken for what she is not—a suffragist—the woman feminine is displaying her charms," says he. "The more the woman suffragist asserts herself the more necessary it is for the woman feminine to assert herself. It is woman's silent duel, and dress, or should I say undress, is playing a big part in it."

So, indirectly, it is still the advanced woman who is to blame.

But as a matter of fact, the female radical is as far from the mondaine as a statesman is from a macaroni. The freest woman in America today (freest in the sense of being least dominated by conventions, civil, religious or social) wears no hobbled or slit skirt, no corset to her knees, no transparent silk stockings and French-heeled slippers. She may be seen upon the public platform in every large city of the country discussing civics, religion, sex, with a breathtaking audacity, and presenting a broadhipped, short-waisted, sturdy figure in her wide, round, old-fashioned skirt just clearing the ground upon which her common-sense flat soles and heels stand firm. The tyranny of fashion is not for her; she has broken her pioneer way through too many conventions to become entangled in the Lilliputian undergrowth of style.

As for the adventuress, sex incarnate, femaleness at its deadliest has hitherto been associated with frills and furbelows; above all petticoats, petticoats, petticoats. Yet the domesticity, the femininity of the petticoat has been the rock of inconsistent man's creed for woman, and now that she wears none he is curiously at sea in sartorial morals. But neither is the preying woman an experimenter in hemi-demi-semi-masculine costume. It takes a George Sand, remember, to make dress reform really revolutionary. But seductive?

The truth is so simple that, of course, it is overlooked by those who read in a farfetched significance to clothes. Styles for women have really no more effect upon sex-morals than styles for men, the man who wears the unlovely coat and trousers of today being as attractive to the twentieth century girl, and not a bit more or less so, than was he who dressed with the frank indecency of certain medieval fashions to the lady who wore the hennin and affected Botticelli attitudes—before Boticelli was born! The average woman wears slit skirts, neither as an evidence of emancipation nor as a protest against suffrage and strongmindedness generally, but because "They" are wearing them. And "They" wear them because the ideal of the sex in things sartorial and that of the business men who cater to it, is change.

Yet, granting that the fault-finders are in the right and that all the various appurtenances to and coverings for the bodies of women are of such scandalous and provoking sort as to "serve to ensnare men," what can woman do about it? She may not go unclad, she may not clothe herself in any fashion ever conceived in the brain of milliner or dressmaker in two thousand years and escape criticism. She has tried 'em, each and every one, with the same result—a fearful howl of protest from a hair-trigger masculine susceptibility at woman's inhumanity to man!

Granted that women never did dress decently. (We have it on authority of saints and police commissioners, emperors and clergymen; it has been said in almost every century in almost every country in almost every language.) Perhaps—perhaps—one suggests it with diffidence—they can't dress decently. Perhaps, dress or no dress or any sort of dress, they are designed, as those early Christian fathers believed, by the devil for his work. Yet, can we not outgrow the old superstition? Take heart, ye timid and terrified, Satan's in one's point of view—not in haberdashery. #

New York Fall Styles Brought to You

THIS VALUABLE CATALOG IS FREE

Here is a book full of beautiful new styles for the Fall and Winter season, 1909-10. There are many fashion catalogs offered free, but most of them are not worth the postage it costs to carry them. You must have discovered this as well as we. Our catalog costs us over $200,000.00 every year to print and mail. When we say to you that our catalog is valuable we leave it to you to prove this. Send for it **today**. If this catalog doesn't help you save money, if it doesn't make shopping doubly easy for you, destroy it. It will be **our loss, not yours.**

This latest Fall and Winter Catalog places all the New York shopping advantages right in your own home. In its 265 pages is illustrated and described all that is new, stylish and correct in wearing apparel for women, men and children; all the latest novelties and household supplies. **The prices quoted are lowest in America.** We tell you in our catalog **how to save express and freight charges.** We guarantee the quality of every piece of merchandise we sell. The demand for our catalog is always very great. To avoid disappointment, be sure and write for it today. It is FREE. Address Department 5X.

Here Are Three Typical Siegel Cooper Bargains

No. 70 x 7X Waist $1.00

No. 79 x 7X Skirt $4.95

No. 69 x 7X—This Tailored Suit will be the favorite style this Fall. It is made of good quality broadcloth, in navy blue, black, green and smoke gray; the jacket coat is cut in 40-inch length, in single-breasted style, fastening with large jet buttons; semi-fitting back; the back seams and pockets are trimmed with silk braid loops and small jet buttons; notch collar and close fitting coat sleeves, finished with turn-back cuffs; lined with guaranteed satin lining; the skirt is designed in the very latest style, with cluster plaited panels which terminate in a graceful full flare; sizes 32 to 44 bust; skirt lengths 37 to 43 inches; would be a bargain at $15.00; **our special price $11.75.**

No. 70 x 7X—This Waist of white linene is the latest Fall style; the blouse front is elaborately trimmed with pin tucks, lace insertion in Irish crochet pattern, and is beautifully embroidered in a pretty floral design; cluster tucked back; full length sleeves with tailored cuffs, fastening with button and buttonhole; tucked and lace trimmed collar; fastens in back; sizes 32 to 44 bust; **price only $1.00.**

No. 79 x 7X—New Style Fall Skirt, made of fine quality all wool Panama cloth, in black, blue and brown; it is designed with a panel front, trimmed with twenty-four self-covered buttons; either side of panel and back to below hips made in yoke effect, below which the skirt is closely side plaited, falling in a graceful flare; it is excellently tailored and finished in the best possible manner; lengths 37 to 43 inches; waist measure 23 to 29 inches; **special value, at $4.95.**

Siegel Cooper Co's Liberal Guarantee

is absolute and goes with each article purchased from this advertisement or from our catalog. If your purchase does not prove **satisfactory in every detail,** if it does not prove the best value you ever secured, return it to us at our expense and **your money and all charges will be promptly refunded.** The advantages are all yours—New York's latest styles at bargain prices. The risk all ours.

Don't delay in sending for your copy of this valuable catalog. Write for it just as soon as you've read this advertisement. Remember that in this way over a million American women are shopping regularly in New York and are thus securing better values for less money than they could get anywhere else in the world.

No. 69 x 7X Suit $11.75

The Only Woman Railroad-President

By JAMES P. HOWE

September 1913

"A CHARMING gown, my dear. Those Bulgarian color combinations are fetching, aren't they? .... Yes, as I was saying, my contention is that Nietzsche never would have—the telephone? How annoying!—Hello! Yes. I said seventy-pound rails, and I want them. Not at all: seventy I said, and seventy goes. Tell the superintendent of construction to see me at eight-thirty o'clock tomorrow. Good-by— Nietzsche fully demonstrated" and so forth.

It sounds like the ravings of a rarebit fiend, doesn't it? But it's only the fragment of an afternoon tea conversation with Mrs. Meta J. Erickson. For Mrs. Erickson is the only woman railroad president in the world—and, though a student of philosophy as well, she is all woman, even if a railroad man at the same time.

The Amador Central Railroad is in Amador county, California. It runs from Ione, where it connects with the Southern Pacific, to Martell, a distance of twelve miles. Mrs. Erickson's home is in Oakland. Her office, now that she takes up the presidency of the road in which she is the principal stockholder, is in San Francisco. When this railroad president is at home she is not planning some coup in the world of finance, but instead she is looking into the future, anticipating, and attending to her household duties and doing little things in behalf of her family—three boys and a daughter.

Mrs. Erickson is not a railroad president in name only. She is most practical in every particular, being familiar with the construction work as well as the details of operation. Why, she can run a locomotive and run it well!

Just at present the Amador Central president has under consideration the purchase of several additional locomotives, freight-cars and other equipment made necessary by increased business.

"I shall be at my office nearly every day" says she, "but I have no idea of neglecting my home life. Nor my clubs."

Mrs. Erickson's favorite recreation is reading, especially books on new thought and philosophy, and the works of some of the old masters. She believes in suffrage, but asserts most emphatically that she is not a suffragette. Despite her activities in the business world and as a club woman, she is also a "home-body."

Although Mrs. Erickson is a talented pianist and singer, she is no stranger in the kitchen. When the only woman railroad chief executive feels like meddling in that stronghold—where a Chinese cook holds forth—guess what she does: dons an apron and in less time than it takes to get up steam in a locomotive the table is covered with dainty tempting deliciously browned cookies.

Mrs. Erickson might talk railroad business all day, or for weeks, and would appear as an ordinary business woman—a shrewd, well educated, energetic business woman familiar with all the details of the business of which she is the head. But when she speaks of her family—the boys and the little girl, the baby—it is then that her face lights up and her eyes glisten, and she forgets for the time that she is the world's only woman railroad president— forgets everything but that she is a mother. #

A Secretary and Her Salary

By WILL T. KIRK

August 1913

MISS Fern Hobbs, age twenty-seven, is drawing the highest salary of any woman in public service in the United States. She is private secretary to Governor Oswald West of Oregon and receives $3000 a year. If she had secured her position through the manipulation of politics the telling about it would not be half so interesting; but she secured it because she earned it. She says she won the place because the governor is broad enough to employ a woman as readily as a man when she does the same work. All that he wants is results.

She came to Oregon from Salt Lake City after finishing high school and became governess in a wealthy home in Portland. She was ambitious. She wanted to get out into the commercial world, so she purchased a typewriter and a book on stenography and put in all her spare moments studying. It was not long until she obtained a position as private stenographer to the president of the Title Guarantee & Trust Company. While doing her office work she also kept house for her brother and sister, both of whom she was putting through school. Her ambition urged her toward further achievements, so she began the study of law, grasping the fundamentals so readily that her tutor gave her credit for being one of the brightest students in his class.

While she was thus employed the bank failed, resulting in investigations and prosecutions. As confidante of the president of the bank she was in the thick of the financial storm, and she recalls the experience as one of the most trying of her life. But it was the loyalty and spirited defense of her employer during those turbulent weeks that opened the way for her to obtain her new $3000 position.

As a considerable sum of the state's common school fund was on deposit in the bank when it failed, Governor Chamberlain appointed Ben W. Olcott, now secretary of state, to represent the state in the investigation of the bank's affairs. When Olcott began to probe into the intimate papers and documents of the institution he met the open hostility of Miss Hobbs, who was then employed as stenographer to the bank's receiver. She did not hide her hatred of the men who were endeavoring to uncover illegal transactions on the part of her former employer. This loyalty caused Olcott to take particular notice of her and to make inquiries about her.

When the investigation was over Miss Hobbs was employed by the Ladd Estate Company. A little later Olcott became campaign manager for Oswald West, successful candidate for governor. Shortly before the time for the

governor-elect to be inaugurated Olcott asked him if he had any one in view for his private stenographer. He had not, so Olcott told him he knew of a girl just suited for the position. Olcott sent for Miss Hobbs and on the day the governor took the oath of office she was presented to him. In the two years she served as his stenographer her mettle was put to the test in a number of unusual ways and she proved so capable that when the governor appointed Ralph A. Watson, his private secretary, as corporation commissioner to administer the new "blue sky" law, he chose Miss Hobbs to succeed him. She took her new position on the third of June, being the first woman to serve as secretary to the governor in the history of the state. Then another laurel of success came to her. It was a diploma from the law department of the Willamette University. While at the capitol she had continued to give her law studies the time that most young women give to parties, balls and theaters. Yet she is young and girlish and a jolly companion, as proud of her success as can be, and is determined to "make good." #

From an inside pocket O'Shea brought forth the warrant for Rand's arrest and showed it to his prisoner. "Watch me serve it," and he tossed the fragments into the surf.

At The Top of the Mast

By PETER B. KYNE

January 1914

THE two natural gifts which made of Michael P. O'Shea a great detective were a marvelous memory and a photographic eye. All of the written information on crimes and criminals contained in the upper office filing cabinets was on perennial tap in O'Shea's brain. Crooks he had never seen before in the flesh he recognized at a glance, provided he had once seen their photographs. Courage he had to spare, and bulk and brawn, and Irish cunning, combined with an attractive and winning personality when he desired to forget the argot of his calling and play a part. His were no ham-like hands, no cold, forbidding eyes. His neck was not thick, nor his brow low and receding, nor his lower jaw prognathous and blue, after the popular conception of the great detectives of the regular force. Far from it. For five successive years Michael P. O'Shea had been voted the Adonis of the department and elected to lead the grand march at the policeman's ball for the benefit of the widows and orphans of the department. Indeed, in a rented dress suit and Mrs. O'Shea on his arm he was always worth two sticks of publicity and a picture lay-out in the newspaper accounts of the ball.

Arrayed now in a handsome suit of tweeds, which he had ventured to order on the strength of his prospective share in the $5000 reward and a liberal expense account from the insurance company, and carrying a gold-headed cane which had belonged to his father, Detective Sergeant O'Shea landed at Victoria, B. C., and registered at the best hotel as M. P. O'Shea, of Decatur, Illinois. He lunched with the utmost enjoyment, filled his pockets with twenty-five cent cigars and strolled up town to the real estate office of McDougall & Rand.

In front of the office he paused and displayed great interest in an array of cards advertising bargains in small farms, timber lands and bungalows. He puffed thoughtfully at his cigar for several minutes while he studied the signs, then he glanced casually into the office of McDougall & Rand and saw a man at a desk. This man was watching Michael P. O'Shea, for the window display was a bait to catch the transient investor, and O'Shea was immediately conscious of a feeling which must be greatly akin to those of a deerhound when he picks up a warm trail; for the man at the desk was either John F. Mallory or his double!

O'Shea's glance wandered again to the window display. Once more he read the advertised bargains, scratched his ear in evident indecision, pulled out his watch, started to walk away, paused undecided, looked at his watch again—and stepped into the office of McDougall & Rand. He approached the man at the desk.

"Is Mr. McDougall or Mr. Rand in?"

"I am Mr. Rand, at your service, sir. What can I do for you?"

"Well," replied O'Shea, "I haven't got much time to discuss the matter with you now, Mr. Rand, but I happened to notice that timber land advertisement in your window. I'm in the market for some timber, but that acreage is too small for my purpose. If you have larger tracts I would be interested in looking over your maps and other information with a view to doing business if the land suited me."

"We have larger tracts, Mr. —"

"O'Shea. M. P. O'Shea. I'm from Decatur, Illinois, looking around in your big western country for a timber investment."

"How long do you purpose remaining in Victoria, Mr. O'Shea?"

O'Shea smiled—and a particularly likeable smile had Detective Sergeant O'Shea when he chose to use it. It had its instant effect on Rand. Mentally he labeled M. P. O'Shea as a bluff brisk keen Irish-American gentleman with money to burn.

"I'm flitting around, Mr. Rand, hoping to

light somewhere and grow up with the country. I don't know exactly what I want, but I thought a few hundred thousand put into timber wouldn't be a bad investment."

" 'Buy trees and grow rich' is the motto of this country, Mr. O'Shea. However, if you are pressed for time just now, you might care to have me look over our timber lists and wait upon you later at your hotel, at some hour convenient to you."

He glanced casually into the office and saw a man at a desk.

"That would be bully, if you'll do it, Mr. Rand. I'm staying at the Empress. Suppose you do that. Look over your lists of large tracts and meet me at the hotel at six-thirty this evening. We can dine together and discuss the timber situation. I am a stranger in your country and anxious to glean a little information."

"Delighted" replied Rand. "Thank you, sir. I shall be there at six-thirty. I think we can fix you up. Thinking of erecting a sawmill and engaging in the lumber business?"

"Not I" laughed Detective O'Shea. "I'm going to take it easy. But I have a boy growing up and he can tackle it fifteen years from now if he feels like it. I understand timber values are increasing very rapidly." He glanced again at his watch. "I must be running along, Mr. Rand. See you at six-thirty. So long" and with a friendly wave of his hand he was gone in a great hurry, swinging his father's gold-headed cane.

"Ain't I the great come-on kiddo?" he told himself admiringly, as he turned the corner and slowed down to a leisurely walk. His plans were working out well, for he had had the precaution to investigate the Canadian timber laws. He had learned that one cannot buy timber outright and let it lie idle as an investment. On the contrary the contracts of purchase from the Dominion government specify that milling operations must commence within a certain period and that a royalty on the manufactured product must be paid to the government. It was this knowledge that had led O'Shea to feign an interest in timber lands, for by talking carelessly of an investment of a couple of hundred thousand dollars he knew he would arouse Rand's interest. Then, with that interest aroused, O'Shea planned to discover, regretfully, that an investment in Canadian timber was impossible. He must have his lands in fee simple, and the only place where such timber lands were for sale was the United States.

Rand arrived at the hotel at six o'clock and talked timber lands until six-thirty, when they went in to dinner. By ten o'clock O'Shea, by adroit questioning, had fathomed every angle of the Canadian laws relating to purchases of timber, and with well-simulated regret he played his trump card.

"I'm sorry, Mr. Rand" he said, "but after talking this matter over with you, it seems best that I should abandon the idea of purchasing on this side of the water. I want a tract of timber, but I want to buy it now and forget all about it for ten years, at least. For an operator your propositions are well worthy of consideration, but as an investment—no."

Rand's face plainly showed his disappointment.

"However," continued O'Shea, "you have been to some little trouble to go into this matter with me and if you can find me a suitable tract in Washington or Oregon I shall be very glad to permit your firm to consummate the business for me. I leave for Seattle tomorrow morning, and will be in Portland, Oregon, Wednesday night. Now, if you can line up a tract within the next week or ten days, a wire from you will reach me at the Hotel Portland. Unless I have found what I want by that time I shall leave for California and look into the sugar and white pine country there."

Relief was apparent in Rand's face now. "Thank you, Mr. O'Shea" he said. "I appreciate your courtesy greatly, I assure you. I'll look around and see what I can find for you. Perhaps my partner may know of something."

They shook hands cordially and departed. O'Shea went into the writing room and sent a brief note to Horton, his chief.

"Frederick Rand is John F. Mallory, and John F. Mallory is Henry Price, late Convict No. 23187 at Joliet. He has the mole behind his left ear in the edge of the hair, scar on little finger of the left hand, slight nervous affliction of the right eyelid. As nearly as I can judge, the measurements are the same—height, weight, complexion, everything. I expect him in Portland to see me some day next week. When I wire you he is on his way, send the warrant."

For three days following his arrival in Portland Detective O'Shea gave himself up to seeing the sights of that interesting city while he waited for a telegram from Rand. It came, on the evening of the third day. Rand wired that he had a splendid property down on Coos Bay, Oregon, and was sending his partner, McDougall, to Portland the following day to consult with him. O'Shea wired back immediately:

Would prefer that you come yourself, if possible. Haven't met McDougall and would much prefer to do business with you.

"That will make him uneasy," O'Shea mused, "and he'll be afraid to take chances. So will his partner, and he'll urge Rand to come in person. Rand can't refuse, for his partner will batter down all of his excuses. Guess I'd better wire Horton."

He did. Whereupon Horton swore to a complaint, on information and belief, and a felony warrant was issued for John F. Mallory, alias Frederick Rand, alias Henry Price, and dropped in the mail with a special-delivery stamp on the envelope. That envelope had no sooner been deposited in the San Francisco post-office than Detective O'Shea received a wire from Rand, stating that in deference to the former's wishes he was coming to Portland himself.

Rand arrived at O'Shea's hotel in Portland some eight hours before the warrant for his arrest. He had a map of ten thousand acres of Douglas fir down on Coos Bay, and suggested that they go down there, starting the following morning, for an examination of the property.

O'Shea was on the point of dissenting and playing for delay until the warrant should arrive, whereupon he would place Rand under arrest, until it occurred to him that he was on his vacation! Why not, then, combine business with pleasure? Rand would, without doubt, secure guides, cruisers and horses and take him on a tour of inspection of the property, and the trip would doubtless be most enjoyable. It would take them a week at least to make even a cursory survey of the property.

The prospect of a week's camping trip in the great northern woods decided Detective O'Shea. He would not serve the warrant in Portland, but would hold it in case of emergency. He would look at the land, declare himself willing to purchase it and *induce Rand to accompany him to San Francisco voluntarily for the alleged purpose of closing the deal.* And he would so arrange it with Horton that immediately upon their arrival in San Francisco some other officer would make the actual arrest, and Rand would be none the wiser, for once arrested and charged with a felony he would, of course, naturally abandon any further efforts to close for the timber lands with O'Shea. He would consider that his arrest and impending conviction would frighten his pseudo customer away.

"We'll start in the morning, Mr. Rand" he

informed his victim. "And as I suppose we'll be out in the woods at least a week, I'm going to buy a fishing rod and a rifle and some outing clothes."

"By all means" replied Rand, and he went with Detective O'Shea and helped him select his purchases.

That was without doubt the finest vacation Detective O'Shea had ever had. The manager of the North Bend Lumber Company, which owned the land that O'Shea pretended to be inspecting, furnished them with horses, a guide, an excellent cook and grub for ten days, and they plunged into the wilderness. When they returned they were bearded, ragged and tanned and excessively cheerful. O'Shea professed himself as delighted with the property, and but one obstacle stood in the way of his immediate purchase of it. As a matter of principle he always consulted his wife and advised with her, but this, he assured Rand, was a mere formality. Would Rand accompany him to San Francisco and consummate the deal? It would be necessary for O'Shea to arrange with the bank there for the transfer of funds from his bank in Decatur, Illinois. Moreover, the main office of the North Bend Lumber Company was in San Francisco and it would be necessary to proceed there in order to look over the abstract of title and have the deed drawn up by a reliable attorney. In fact, O'Shea cited a number of reasons why Rand should accompany him to San Francisco, any one of which dwindled into insignificance when compared with the all-important reason—the desire for a tremendous commission to McDougall & Rand.

As O'Shea had figured he would, Rand readily consented to accompany him. As a steamer was sailing from North Bend for San Francisco the following morning, he suggested that they book their passage on her, and O'Shea declared he would go and purchase tickets. When he returned he was secretly amused to discover that as a precautionary measure Rand had shaved his mustache!

"Hello!" O'Shea said bluntly. "Why did you do that? You're an ugly customer without a mustache."

"I know it, Mr. O'Shea. But while shaving I accidently chopped a piece off it. It was lopsided then so I had to sacrifice it entirely."

The coasting steamer *Omega,* carrying miscellaneous freight and passengers (also miscellaneous, for the list included Detective-Sergeant O'Shea and Henry Price, alias John F. Mallory, alias Frederick Rand) proceeded slowly down the winding channel of Coos Bay and breasted the choppy seas that rolled in from the Pacific to lash themselves into a wild smother of foam on Coos Bay bar. To the south and west the sky was dark and lowering, and a southerly breeze, carrying a hint of rain, sang through the rigging of the *Omega.* Detective O'Shea, finding that his head and his stomach were inclined to behave in the open air, left his stateroom a few minutes after the first premonitory wallow of the steamer informed him she was passing out, and climbed to the hurricane deck.

In the lee of the chart-house and just aft the bridge he paused to light a cigar. The captain, enveloped in a heavy watch coat, was striding nervously backward and forward across the bridge, pausing occasionally to stick his head through a little opening from the bridge into the pilot house and address a brief order to the man at the wheel. While O'Shea was standing there Rand came up on deck and joined him.

"I don't like the looks of this bar, O'Shea" he said. "It's breaking very heavily."

"I do wish we'd crossed out earlier in the day. It's getting rougher every minute, and dinner is out of the question until we strike smooth water—*good land of love, Rand, look at that wave!*"

"Hang on!" yelled the captain, and the two passengers sprang for the iron bridge railing and grasped it, just as a huge green sea came in over the port counter, swept the entire length of the hurricane deck and poured off in huge cascades on the starboard side, carrying everything movable with it. O'Shea and Rand were drenched to the skin and a little frightened as the water receded and left them, half blinded and gasping, still clinging to the iron bridge railing. They could feel the *Omega* shiver with the impact of the terrific slap from that sea.

"The helmsman let her fall off that time" sputtered Rand. "She took that sea over her counter. Listen to the skipper roast him."

The skipper was, indeed, reproving the helmsman in no uncertain language. "Hold her head up, you blighter" he roared. "Hold her up. D'ye want to blanket her and sink us like pig lead?"

"She won't hold up, sir" the helmsman

All out-doors invites your Kodak.

No trip too long, no conditions too rough for a Kodak outfit.

You can take, title and finish the negatives on the spot by the Kodak system. You can make sure.

Kodak catalog free at your dealer's, or by mail.

EASTMAN KODAK CO., ROCHESTER, N. Y., *The Kodak City.*

shouted back. "I gave her half a dozen spokes that time, sir, and she wouldn't answer me."

O'Shea saw the captain spring to the speaking-tube that led to the engine room. "Kick her wide open and give her all you have" he called to the chief. He looked up as he turned from the tube and saw his two passengers still clinging to the rail. O'Shea expected the captain would grin at their bedraggled appearance, but instead the sight of him and Rand appeared to deepen the anxious look in the master's eyes, and instinctively O'Shea scented trouble.

"Go below and lock yourselves in your cabin, gentlemen" the captain commanded. "We're in for a bad buffeting on the bar and if you hang around on deck we're extremely liable to lose you—*hard-a-port!*"

The last words were a ringing shout, and through the little aperture leading from the bridge into the pilot house O'Shea could see the spokes flying as the helmsman spun the wheel. But the *Omega* was sluggish and another sea came in over her counter, completely blanketing her. As it receded the captain again took up the speaking-tube and O'Shea pressed nearer to hear what he might say.

"What's the matter down there?" he heard. "Haven't you got any steam? She keeps falling off, Chief. She won't buck into them and ride them out—*leaky tubes!* Oh, damn the owners! Why will they send us to sea in a coffin? . . . Yes, Chief, I know. But pour the fuel into her. I *can't* turn back now. I might lose my rudder. It's safer to go ahead. Maybe we'll weather it."

Slowly the *Omega* crept out over the bar, shipping a sea every few minutes, wallowing frightfully and groaning in all her aged timbers. They were almost over when a succession of monstrous combers came rushing in from sea to meet her. She rose to the first and rode it out, swung a little, despite the helmsman's desperate efforts to hold her head up, and took the second wave over her lower decks. While she was still awash, yawing frightfully, the third sea blanketed her completely.

"What the devil's the matter with her?" shouted O'Shea.

"Leaky, rotten boilers, that's all" replied Rand cooly. "She's a big boat in a frightful sea and she hasn't power enough to buck her way through." He reached for a cork ring that hung on the bridge railing at the starboard end and slipped it over his shoulders.

"Better help yourself, O'Shea" he advised. "We'll be lucky if we aren't kicked back on the bar, smothered and banged to pieces."

At that instant the fourth wave hit her. She heeled far over on the port side and swung broadside on in the trough of that awful sea. An instant later another sea had snatched her rudder out as clean as a dentist extracts a tooth, and O'Shea saw the wreckage whirled by, riding high on the crest of the departing wave. Thirty seconds later another monster wave raked her, and before their very eyes the charthouse tore loose from its anchor bolts and went over the side. The captain, grasping the other cork ring at the port end of the bridge, went with it.

"This is no place for the head of the O'Shea family" gasped Mike O'Shea. "To the top of the mast for me. This is a wet spot," and as the water receded for a brief period he rushed for the mainmast shrouds. Rand followed him and ere the next wave swept the doomed *Omega*, driving her a hundred yards shoreward, hunter and hunted were high in the ratlines above the boiling wash of the decks.

Screams echoed through the dying ship, and beyond, in the smother of foam, O'Shea could make out half a dozen human forms struggling hopelessly. With her rudder gone the *Omega* was helpless, and under a merciless and triphammer buffeting from the ravenous seas she drove rapidly toward shore. A dozen of her crew and passengers had sought safety in the mizzen rigging, but the main rigging remained occupied exclusively by O'Shea and Rand.

Presently, as the battered hull drifted over the darkening water, her house went by the board and tons of water poured into her engine room, exploding her boilers and drowning her engine crew like rats in a hole. With the engines dead the boat drifted more rapidly. She presently entered the long fringe of white spume that marked a sunken reef. Over the first ledge she drove; rose high on the crest of a wave and fell with a horrible crash, impaling herself on a spindle of rock that thrust its cruel nose six feet into her vitals. Her back was broken and her stern tore loose, carrying the poor devils in the mizzen rigging into eternity. Detective O'Shea turned his face away and climbed higher in the rigging, nor paused until he had reached the masthead. Rand followed.

They were alone on the wreck of the *Omega*, and of the Omega all that showed above the water was sixty feet of mainmast, at the top of which the two men clung. Rand still had his cork ring around his body, but O'Shea had nothing but his two sturdy arms and legs to defend his life when the mast should go.

In fifteen years on the San Francisco police force Mike O'Shea had risked his life too often to be afraid now in the face of death. Moreover, he was of the breed that dares to face it smiling, and he smiled now as he glanced down at the man he had been sent to rope! Fate had played Horton and him a colossal joke, and Michael P. O'Shea was human enough to laugh any time the joke was on him. Rand glanced up and met the detective's half-sad, half-whimsical, smile. He did not smile back, for there was no humor in this dreadful predicament for him. Nevertheless he essayed a jest.

"It's pretty tough, losing a nice fat commission, after I've worked so hard to put this land deal over" he complained.

Again O'Shea smiled. He liked Rand for that speech. "I wish you joy of your life preserver" he retorted. "If a fellow could win past these breakers there's fairly smooth water inside the reef. I believe I could make it, but drat the luck, I never learned to swim."

"It will be rather hard on Mrs. O'Shea and the kiddies" said Rand sympathetically. "Still, it isn't half so hard when a man knows he's leaving his family well provided for."

O'Shea winced at that. He thought of his wife and the little girls and his boy Jim awaiting his return in the little mortgaged cottage in the Mission, and the whimsical look died out in his Irish face while his fine eyes filled with tears.

"It's tough" he murmured. "It's awful tough."

· Rand unswung the cork ring from his body and handed it up to Detective Sergeant Michael P. O'Shea. "A wise business man always protects his deals" he said with another faint attempt at humor. "I can swim a little, and we might get through and put this deal over yet. If I don't—well, what matter? You've got a family—you've got responsibilities—the world needs you. Take the life preserver, my friend, and try for the shore before you get chilled

clinging here in your wet clothing."

O'Shea choked up. He could not speak, so filled was he with admiration and gratitude to this hunted man for his simple sacrifice. He wanted that cork ring—not for himself, but for his loved ones at home—for his girls, that he might guard and protect them, for his boy, that he might train him in the same rugged honesty that had brought his father to his death. But under the circumstances Michael P. O'Shea knew he could not accept. He was a roper, and this man who made the offer was a crook. O'Shea shook his head.

"You're a brave man" said Rand simply. He reached out his hand and clasped O'Shea's. "But I'm not afraid to go, either. In fact, I'm a little glad it's coming, friend. It may save me the disgrace of some day blowing out my own light!"

Even in that supreme moment Mike O'Shea was detective enough to be a good listener.

"I have something on my mind, O'Shea" Rand continued quickly. "It's sat on my soul so long I've got to tell it to somebody, and of all the men I've ever met you seem to be the only one that would understand."

He drew a check-book and a fountain pen from his pocket. "Hold me, O'Shea" he continued. "I want to write something."

O'Shea held him and Rand wrote. The detective couldn't help seeing what it was his victim was writing. It was a promissory note for twenty thousand dollars, in favor of the Pacific Life Insurance Company, and Rand signed it "John F. Mallory." Then he blotted it and endorsed the note "Frederick Rand." He handed it to O'Shea.

"We're going to take our chances together on this cork ring, O'Shea" he said. "I want you to take this promissory note. It constitutes a valid claim against my estate, which is able to pay it. If I am drowned and you survive, turn this note over to the Pacific Life Insurance Company at San Francisco. I owe them twenty thousand dollars. Now listen to what I'm going to tell you, O'Shea. It's important, and your testimony is all that will help right a wrong—that is, if you survive. If we both go out—why, the thing ends there. But if one or other of us gets through I want to square myself. I've always intended to but I've procrastinated, and besides nobody knew me and I needed the money to give myself another chance in life—"

Detective Sergeant Michael P. O'Shea tucked the note, written on the back of a blank check, in his inside vest pocket.

"Very well, Henry Price" he said calmly. "I'll do that for you, if I live. And never mind your story. I know all about it—everything except the motives back of it. The fact of the matter is, my friend, I'm not a timber-buyer at all. I'm Michael P. O'Shea, a detective sergeant from the San Francisco police bureau, and I came to Victoria to get you. I'm what we call a roper. I've induced you to put your foot on American soil, and if we had reached San Francisco you would have been arrested and charged with a felony on this insurance deal the moment you came down the gang-plank," and O'Shea unbuttoned his vest and showed his shield pinned to his suspender. From an inside coat pocket he brought forth the warrant for Rand's arrest and showed it to his prisoner.

"There's the warrant for you" he said blithely. "Watch me serve it," and he tore it up and tossed the fragments into the surf.

Rand's face was very white and pitiful. "But I— I—" he stammered—

—"are no crook" supplemented O'Shea. "You're an honest man and the only honest man I ever knew that did time. You forged a check and did three years in Joliet. Why?"

"It was a woman's honor against mine" replied Rand brokenly. "I thought more of hers."

"I believe you" O'Shea answered. "And this insurance deal—that was an accident. I always said so. You paid the premium a year in advance, which was throwing away money, because you pulled the trick in six months. Again, why?"

"I married, you know—and I changed my name and moved to California before that. I didn't tell my wife. I thought perhaps she would never know. I—"

"One of your old friends from Joliet bumped into you and blackmailed you, eh? They usually do—the damned crooks!"

Rand nodded. "My poor wife had social aspirations, O'Shea, and the good Lord hadn't given her a very broad vision. The news hurt. She was ashamed of me, although she stuck by me. But I knew she didn't love me any more, and life was a hell. She was always afraid the neighbors would find it out and she'd be disgraced. You see, O'Shea, I had to leave her, because she wasn't happy with me. I didn't think it was fair to myself to commit suicide. One day I went fishing up the Sacramento and in the bushes at the edge of the railroad embankment where the Shasta road skirts the river, I found a dead tramp. He'd been pitched from a car roof on the curve, I guess; I think his neck was broken. He looked a good deal like me—about my weight and height—"

"I see" interrupted O'Shea. "It was a good idea. You changed clothing and salted the stiff with your watch and pocketbook and shoved him off into the river. Then you disappeared. And you'd done all this before you remembered about the life insurance."

"I never thought about life insurance at all. I just wanted to get away clean and start life all over again. I came to Victoria, got a job as salesman with the McDougall Realty Company, made a few deals and got some money together and bought into a partnership. The insurance policy had been collected before I heard about it, and while I was wondering how I was going to square the company my wife married again. That complicated matters worse and now—what are you going to do with me, O'Shea?" Poor Rand's face was very pitiful as he raised it to the detective.

"Ask you to forgive me, you poor devil" murmured O'Shea and extended one cold hand. "I've played a dirty game, old man, and it wasn't even in the line of duty. I was doing it for money—blood-money. There was $2500 in it for me and I'm a poor man and needed the money. Most crooks do, I guess" he added humbly.

"I understand that pressure—thoroughly" Rand smiled wanly as he took the detective's hand. "Of course I forgive you. I think I like you better in your true role. It's worth losing that commission to know you. But if you reach shore alive you'll have to make a report on me."

"When we reach shore" retorted Mike O'Shea—"and we'll try for it before we get any colder or stiffer—you head north and I'll head south. I won't see you again, and as far as the law is concerned, I'll square this case. Are you ready to swim for the shore, sailor?"

"Ready" responded Rand, and they descended the ratlines until the seas swept them to their knees; then, each with one arm looped into the cork ring between them, they went out into the breakers, paddling desperately with their free arms.

It was an hour before they won to the firm white sand of the beach, and they were too weak to walk. O'Shea found some matches in his pocket in a waterproof safe, and crawled around on his hands and knees collecting driftwood for a fire. When he had the fire blazing well, he dragged his benumbed companion to the flames, undressed him and slapped the life back into him.

At daybreak they parted. "Good-by, Fred" said Detective O'Shea, addressing his prisoner by the first part of his latest alias. "Go your way and sin no more, and God bless you. You're the finest crook I've ever met." #

Chief of Police of "Spotless Town"

September 1913

ACCORDING to the Board of Geographic Names, "Spotless Town" is not on the map. And yet the entire Pacific Coast is applying this pleasing nick-name to the University city of California which preserves the memory of Bishop Berkeley and his prophetic line, "Westward the Star of Empire takes its way." Reference to the Berkeley census of 1910 will show that there were within its gates 40,434 rich men, some poor men, but seldom a beggar or thief. And the reason why the latter undesirables have given Berkeley a wide berth is not due to its estimable doctors, lawyers or merchants, but to its Chief, Gus Vollmer. Through his efforts the municipality has been cleaned up until evil weeds, vegetable and human, have no place in its precincts. In 1905, when the population was 25,000, property to the value of $21,780 was stolen from the good citizens of Berkeley. Now that the population in 1912 has doubled, the average loss through theft is only about $12,000 a year, a proportion of about one-fourth per capita of the former amount. #

The Lotus and the Rose

By NICHOLAS VACHEL LINDSAY

June 1914

The wide Pacific waters
   And the Atlantic meet.
With cries of joy they mingle,
   In tides of love they greet.
Above the drowned ages
   A wind of wooing blows;
The red rose woos the lotus,
   The lotus woos the rose.
The lotus conquered Egypt,
   The rose was loved in Rome,
Great India crowned the lotus,
   (Britain the rose's home),
Old China crowned the lotus,
   They crowned it in Japan.
But Christendom adored the rose
   Ere Christendom began. . . . .
The lotus speaks of slumber,
   The rose is as a dart.
The lotus is Nirvana,
   The rose is Mary's heart.
The rose is deathless, restless,
   The splendor of our pain—
The flush and fire of labor
   That builds, not all in vain.
The genius of the lotus
   Shall heal Earth's too-much fret,
The rose, in blinding glory,
   Shall waken Asia yet.
Hail to their loves, ye peoples!
   Behold, a world-wind blows
That aids the ivory lotus
   To wed the red red rose!

A Poem written on the near-completion of the Panama Canal, showing how the genius of the West, here typified by the Rose, and the genius of the East, here typified by the Lotus, are to be merged and mingled in one through the world-event which is to find its initial celebration in the Panama-Pacific International Exposition.

From Russian Hill

By INA COOLBRITH

July 1915
Night and the hill to me!
   Silence no sound that jars;
Above, of stars a sea;
   Below, a sea of stars!

Trancèd in slumber's sway,
   The city at its feet.
A tang of salty spray
   Blends with the odors sweet

From garden-close and wall,
   Where the madroño stood,
And tangled chaparral,
   In the old solitude.

Here, from the Long Ago,
   Rezánov's sailors sleep;
There the Presidio;
   Beyond the plumèd steep;

The waters, mile on mile,
   Foam-fringed with feathery white;
The beaconed fortress isle,
   And Yerba Buena's light.

O hill of memories!
   Thy scroll so closely writ
With song, that bough and breeze
   And bird should utter it:

Hill of desire and dream,
   Youth's visions manifold,
That still in beauty gleam
   From the sweet days of old!

Ring out thy solemn tone,
   O far off Mission bell!
I keep the tryst, alone
   With one who loved me well.

A voice I may not hear!
   Face that I may not see,
Yet know a Presence near
   To watch the hour with me . . .

How stately and serene
   The moon moves up the sky;
How silverly between
   The shores her footprints lie!

   Peace that no shadow mars!
     Night and the hill to me!
   Below, a sea of stars!
     Above, of stars a sea!

What is Home Without a Garage?

By ALBERT MARPLE

September 1916

SECOND only in importance to the house itself nowadays is the garage. In planning a new home, or remodeling an old one, no feature is given more attention and consideration than the garage. However, this has not always been so, for it is but a year or so since the general opinion was that "anything would do" so long as it has a water-tight roof and four sides. But since the coming of the automobile into general use there has been a tendency toward the better garage and now we see many auto houses that are really a credit to their owners. In fact, the garage has superseded the parlor of ye olden time in importance.

There seems to be a gradual drifting toward the garage that is "different," that is built along lines that are not generally used and that are located at points where other structures of this type have not yet been placed. The practice of placing the garage before the home located upon the hilly lot seems to be growing in favor, this doubtless on account of this type of garage having advantages that are not enjoyed by the owner of the garage at the rear of his lot. These before the home structures, however, call for artistic design. In many instances they are more prominent than the homes themselves, and if they are not properly kept up the home place in general suffers in appearance.

The photographs of garages here shown will give an idea of what a little originality and thought can do toward making this feature of the home place attractive. One illustration shows a pair of cobble-stone garages. These have been termed "Twins." They are 14 x 16 feet in size and have been built in the front of the lots between homes to which they belong. Each garage serves the structure almost immediately behind it, the approaches to the homes running around the sides of the automobile houses. These cost about $175 each.

In another illustration may be seen an elaborate "Clock Tower Garage." This is made

The "Clock Tower" garage cost $2000

entirely of concrete, with the exception of the trimmings. It is three stories high. The first floor is taken up by the machine room, the second contains the rooms of the chauffeur, while on the third is a game and observation room. The clock is located above the game room. Every hour and half hour the chimes of this clock ring out, and its pure tones may be heard from a mile or so down the valley. This garage cost in the neighborhood of $2000.

These neighborly garages are called "The Twins"; each serves the house behind it.

This is a barrel-full of automobile

This unique garage is the invention of a Spokane man. With wrench the garage may be dismantled in fifteen minutes and put on a wagon, the parts being made in units and bolted together, enclosed in four metal bands or hoops. It cost a hundred dollars. Unskilled workmen can put it up in an hour. It has a flat floor and double door, a square window at one end and a round window at the other. The floor is tongue-and-groove lumber, so are the two-inch staves. The structure is very stout, and is not only weather-proof but air-tight, an advantage in cold weather, for a car driven in warm will keep the building at a moderate temperature all night.

The little garage home is a feature which is perhaps peculiar to the southern portion of California. There is probably a greater percentage of people in that locality who own their own homes than in any other section of the country. The new arrival in that section wonders at this home-owning craze, but it is not a great while before he too, has yielded to it, and the desire for a "little ranch" is racing through his veins. Generally he gets it, too. Sometimes it is in the form of a palatial brown-stone; oftener it is a pretty bungalow; again it is merely a small shack on the rear of the lot. The little garage homes are not the least in real value of the rear-of-the-lot dwellings.

Even if the homebuilder has no intention of adding an automobile to his possessions, it is well for him to plan for garage accommodations in the event of selling his property. Many a sale has been prevented by the absence of sufficient space for a garage on a home-site. #

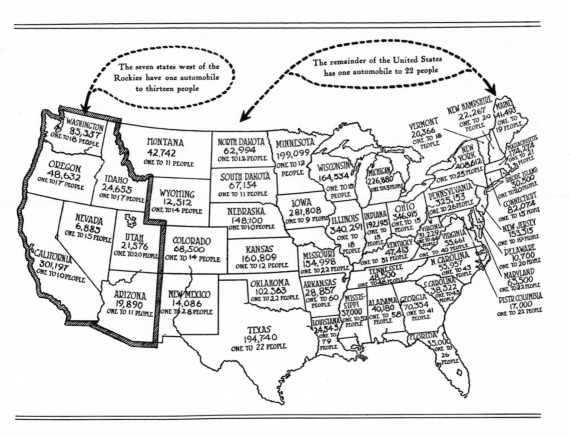

If the roads in the West seem crowded to you, this map tells you why.
March 1918

A WHITE STEAMER FOR $2000!

Not since 1904 have we made a car priced at so low a figure as $2000. The White—"the car in a class by itself"—has thus been brought within the range of a larger number of purchasers than has been the case in recent years.

The new $2000 White car, known as our Model "O," has none of the attributes of the "cheap machine." It is simply a "smaller edition" of our $4000 car. The new Model "O" is rated at 20 steam horse-power, which means that it can do the work of gasoline cars rated at much higher figures. The wheel-base is 104 inches; the tires, both front and rear, are 32x3½ inches. The car is regularly fitted with a straight-line five-passenger body. The frame is of heat-treated pressed steel. The front axle is a one-piece forging of I-beam cross section.

The nature of the steam engine is such that the engine of small power has all the desirable attributes of the engine of high power. In other words, as the weights of our small car and our large car are proportionate to the power of their respective engines, the small car can do anything that our large car can do.

To summarize the features of our new Model "O" car—it is noiseless, odorless, smokeless and absolutely free from vibration. All speeds from zero to maximum are obtained by throttle control alone. The speeds of the car respond instantly to the throttle; the engine can never be stalled. The directions for driving are summed up in the phrase, "Just open the throttle and steer." It starts from the seat—"no cranking." It is the ideal moderate priced machine. It is the best for the man who wishes to drive and take care of his own car. It is the result of our nine years of experience in building the White Steam Car—the only machine which finds a ready market in every portion of the globe.

Write for Circular Giving Full Details of this Car

THE WHITE COMPANY
CLEVELAND, OHIO

New York City: Broadway at 62d Street
Chicago: 240 Michigan Avenue
San Francisco: 1460 Market Street, at Van Ness Ave.
Pittsburg: 138-148 Beatty Street

Philadelphia: 629-33 North Broad Street
Boston: 320 Newbury Street
Cleveland: 407 Rockwell Avenue
Atlanta: 120-122 Marietta Street

The Californiacs

By Inez Haynes Gillmore

February 1916

CALIFORNIA is populated mainly with Californiacs; but the Californiacs are by no means confined to California. They have, indeed, wandered far afield. New York, for instance, has a colony so large that the average New Yorker is well acquainted with the symptoms of *Californoia.* The Californiac is unable to talk about anything but California, except when he interrupts himself to knock every other place on the face of the earth. He looks with pity on anybody born outside of California and he believes that no one who has ever seen California, willingly lives elsewhere. He himself often lives elsewhere, but he never admits that it is from choice. He refers to California always as "God's country" and if you permit him to start his God's country line of talk, it is all up with intelligent conversation for the rest of the day. He will discourse on California scenery, climate, crops, athletes, women, art-sense, etc., *ad libitum, ad infinitum* and *ad nauseam.* He is a walking compendium of those Who's Whosers who were born in California. He can reel off statistics which flatter California, not by the yard but by the mile. And although he is proud enough of the ease and abundance with which things grow in California, he is even more proud of the size to which they attain. Gibes do not stop the Californiac, nor jeers give him pause. He believes that he was appointed to talk about California. And Heaven knows, he does. He has plenty of sense of humor otherwise, but mention California and it is as though he were conducting a revival meeting.

Once a party which included a Californiac were taking an evening stroll. Presently a huge full moon cut loose from the horizon and began a tour of the sky. Admiring comments were made. "I suppose you have them bigger in California," a young woman observed slyly to the Californiac. He did not smile; he only looked serious. Again, a Californiac mentioned

to me that he had married an eastern woman. "Any eastern woman who marries a Californian," I observed in the spirit of badinage, "really takes a very great risk. Her husband must always be comparing her with the beautiful women of his native state." "Yes," he answered, "I often say to my wife, 'Lucy, you're a very pretty woman, but you ought to see some of our San Francisco girls'." "I hope," I replied, "that she boxes your ears." He did not smile; he only looked pained.

Once only have I seen the Californiac silenced. A dinner party which included a globe-trotter were listening to a victim of an advanced stage of Californoia. He had just disposed of the East, South and Middle West with a few caustic phrases and had started on his favorite subject. "You are certainly a wonderful people," the globe-trotter said, when he had finished. "Every large city in Europe has a colony of Californians, all rooting for California as hard as they can and all living as far away as they can possibly get."

Myself, Californoia did not bother me for a long time after I first went to California. I am not only accustomed to an offensive insular patriotism on the part of my countrymen, but, in addition, all my life I have had to apologize to them for being a New Englander. The statement that I was brought up in Boston always produces a sad silence in my listeners and a long look of pity. Soft-hearted strangers do their best to conceal their tears but they rarely succeed. I have reached the point now, however, where I no longer apologize for being a Bostonian; I proffer no explanations. I make the damaging admission the instant I meet people and leave the matter of further recognition to them. If they choose to consider that Boston bringing-up a social bar sinister, so be it. I have discovered recently that the fact that I happened to be born in Rio Janeiro offers some amelioration. But nothing can entirely remove the handicap. So, I reiterate, indurated as I am to pity, the contemptuous attitude of the average Californiac did not at first annoy me. But after a while even I, calloused New Englander that I am, began to resent it.

This, for instance, may happen to you at any time in California—it is the Californiac's way of paying the greatest compliment he knows:

"Do you know," somebody says, "I should never guess that you were an Easterner. You're quite like one of us—cordial and simple and natural."

If you mention the eastern winter to a Californiac, he tells you with great particularity of the dreadful storms he encountered there. Nothing whatever about the beauty of the snow. To a Californiac, snow and ice are more to be dreaded than hell-fire and brimstone. If you mention the eastern summer, he refers in scathing terms to the puny trees we produce, the inadequate fruits and vegetables. Nothing at all about their delicious flavor. To a Californiac, beauty is measured only by size. Nothing that England or France has to offer makes any impression on the Californiac because it's different from California. As for the glory that was Greece and the grandeur that was Rome, he simply never sees it. The Netherlands are dismissed with one adjective—*flat*. For a country to be flat is, in the opinion of the Californiac, to relinquish its final claim to beauty. A Californiac once made the statement to me that Californians considered themselves a little better than the rest of the country. I considered that the prize Californiacism until I heard the following from a woman-Californiac in Europe: *"I saw nothing in all Italy,"* she said, *"to compare with the Italian quarter of San Francisco."*

Remember always that California has virtually no weather to contend with. For three months of the year rain appears; for the remaining nine months it is eliminated entirely. And so, with a country of rare picturesqueness for a background, a people of rare beauty for actors, everybody more or less permeated with the artistic instinct and everybody more or less writing poetry—California has a pageant for breakfast, a fiesta for luncheon, and a carnival for dinner. They are always electing queens. In fact any girl in California who hasn't been a queen of something before she's twenty-one is a poor prune.

In the country—especially in the wine districts where the merrymaking sometimes lasts for days—these festivals are beautiful. In the city—it depends largely, of course, on how much the commercial spirit enters into it; but whether they are beautiful or the reverse they are always entertaining. Single streets, for instance, in San Francisco, are always having carnivals. The street elects a king and queen, plasters itself with bunting, arches itself with electric lights, lines its curbs with temporary booths, fills its corners with shows, sells confetti until the pedestrian swims in it—and then whoops it up for a week. All round, north, south, east, west, every other street is jet-black, sleeping decorously, ignoring utterly that blare of color, that blaze of light, that boom of noise round the corner. They should worry—they're going to have a carnival themselves next week. Apropos, a San Francisco paper opened its story of one of these affairs with the following sentence, "Last night" (shall we call him Hans Schmidt?) "was crowned with great pomp and ceremony king of the _____ Street Carnival and fifteen minutes later, with no pomp and ceremony whatever, he was arrested for petty larceny."

When the deep, cylindrical cisternlike reservoir on Twin Peaks was finished, they opened it with a dance; when the Stockton street tunnel was finished, they opened it with a dance; when the morgue was completed they opened *that* with a reception.

And the climate being of the kind that, for three-quarters of the year you can count on unvarying sunny weather, the women dress on the streets with nothing short of gorgeousness. All the colors that the rainbow knows and a few that it has never seen, appear here. And worn with such *chic*, such *verve!* Not even in Paris, where may appear a more conventional smartness, is sartorial picturesqueness carried off with such an air of authority. For the Californian does not really know what female ugliness is. I have a theory that the Californian men can not quite appreciate the beauty of their women. They take beauty for granted; they have never seen anything else. #

Ishi, the aboriginal hunter, calling game

Ishi, shooting his favorite bow

Learning Archery from Ishi

By SAXTON POPE

October 1917

IT WAS Ishi, the California Indian, the last uncivilized American, that started us on archery. He shot the bow as the Indians did when Cabeza de Vaca explored this continent. He lived by the bow and the salmon spear. With his bow he killed small game, deer and bear. To shoot was a business, not a pastime. So we got started by a master archer, and from him learned the tricks of the trade.

At first we shot Indian fashion; later we adopted the long bow and the old English method of shooting.

We make our bows of Oregon yew, six feet long, and back them with thin rawhide to keep them from breaking.

The arrows we use for hunting are made of birch 11/32 of an inch in diameter, 29 inches long, feathered with pinions of the turkey. They are tipped with steel heads.

Ishi shot a short sinew-backed bow, held diagonally across his body, and pulled his bowstring with his thumb instead of his fingers. He did not approve of our long bows and general style of shooting, but after a few months' practice, when some of his pupils began to beat him at his own game, he was puzzled. However, he never changed his methods to meet competition.

At shooting small game, the Indian was very skilful. He killed rabbits, quail and squirrels at distances ranging from ten to forty yards. I have seen him shoot the head off a squirrel at this latter distance.

In deer hunting, he used the methods of ambush. Hiding behind a boulder or bush, near a deer trail, while others beat the brush up the canyon, he waited until his game came within range. He also used a deer's head as a decoy and thus made his game approach within shooting distance.

He did not run over the hills like a white man, hunting for deer; he studied the habits of his quarry and met him on his own ground. Nor did Ishi use dogs in hunting. If he wounded a deer he did not chase it, but let it run. It soon lay down. Once down, the animal either dies or becomes stiff and unable to rise. Then it may be trailed and found.

Ishi could call small game to him and shoot it at short range. When he told me this I put it down as a bit of romancing. For while he never lied, he often mixed his folk lore with his history. But on one of our hunting trips in Tehama county he proved his ability to do this. Having chosen suitable ground, and put ourselves in hiding, he made the call. It consists of a plaintive squeak, like a rabbit in distress, and is produced by a kissing sound with two fingers held against the lips. He repeated this sound again and again. In less than a minute, a jackrabbit ran out of the brush ninety yards away and came directly up to us, within ten yards. At the same time a wildcat sneaked into the open, listened and advanced cautiously, seating itself on a log fifty yards distant. The cat let me shoot four arrows at him without moving, and only jumped back into the forest when a shaft grazed him between the ears. Twelve times in that same afternoon Ishi repeated this call, and five times we had animals come out of the brush in response. This is more than a coincidence.

Rabbits, squirrels, coyotes, wildcats and bear, all will come for it. The first come because the cry is an imitation of that of their young in distress. The predatory creatures—"varmints" —come in hope of sharing in the feast.

It takes months or years of training to be able to shoot the bow. Accuracy at archery is as difficult to acquire as proficiency at golf. In fact, the two games resemble each other very much, especially in that there are so many technical difficulties to each.

The bow is a very difficult implement to master, and one must use with it those wiles and arts of the chase that demand patience and effort. But to us it seems fairer to the game, better sport, and represents more personal achievement than does the mere pulling of a trigger. #

The Size of Henry Ford

December 1915

THOMAS Edison and Henry Ford came, conquered and departed, fresh laurel wreaths of Far Western growth piled high upon their brows. They were honored by special 'days' at the San Francisco and San Diego expositions; they were banqueted, displayed, bespeeched and committeed, presented with medals and cheered to the echo; schools were dismissed and the children conducted to the stations for a glimpse of the great men. Their triumphal procession across the country added another chapter to the history of hysterical hero-worship peculiar to the United States.

Thomas Edison is a great inventor. Wherever and so long as the incandescent bulb sheds its white radiance, his name will be remembered and honored.

But is Henry Ford really a great man?

He did not invent the internal-combustion motor; he did not originate the automobile; he did not produce the rubber tire, the carburetor or the magneto. He saw the possibilities of manufacturing one type of motor car on so vast a scale that its price could be reduced until a million families could afford to purchase the conveyance. This he did. He organized a vast factory which, through his clear perception of the value of large-scale, standardized production, became immensely profitable. It is to his credit that he paid his workmen exceedingly well, but his own profits did not suffer. He is popularly supposed to have amassed a fortune of a hundred million dollars in ten years.

Edison invented, originated, improved, perfected. Ford merely cheapened. For three or four years his product has not been altered. The same ugly lines that characterized his first machine are still retained. There has been no progressive improvement. His output has not gained in beauty, dignity, strength or utility. Before Ford can lay claim to greatness even in the industrial field he will have to prove that he is a man of more than one idea. #

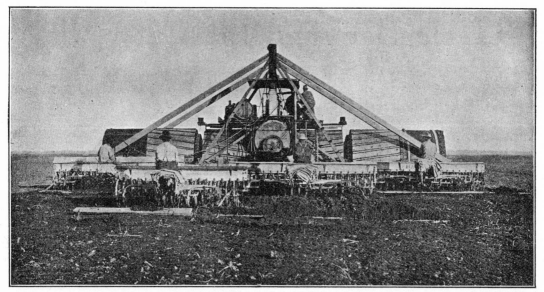

An early Holt outfit, a steam tractor with drive-wheels thirty-six feet wide.

"Uncle Ben" and the Caterpillar

By Carl Crow

January 1917

IT IS necessary to go back to the early days of California agriculture to appreciate all that "Uncle Ben" Holt's endeavors have done for the farmer.

If somebody had started to plow the hundred-thousand-acre California ranch of Joseph Cane with a 2-horse team when Chester A. Arthur was elected president and had kept at it every day since then, plowing five acres a day, he would now be about half through and could look forward to finishing the job about the middle of this century. A plowman might start a furrow at one end of a big Miller & Lux tract and the season would be ended before the furrow reached the other end of the tract. In the great valleys of California originated the story of the ranches so large that those who started out to plow, harvested the crop on their return trip to the ranch house.

To plow and seed such gigantic tracts one needed armies of hired hands at a time when a selective draft would not have netted a skeleton regiment. And the ranchers had to depend on voluntary enlistment. Anyone who could handle a plow was equally able to swing a pick and in those days few wanted to plow when one stroke of the pick might uncover wealth equal to the wages of a season. The rancher might be lucky enough to get men to plant his crop in winter, but there was no certainty that his luck would repeat itself the following summer and give him enough help to harvest it.

In the whole wide world there was no place where devices which would reduce the need of man power in farm work were so much needed as on the Pacific Coast.

Great steam plows were introduced into the fields. But they didn't solve the problem. A story has survived which illustrates one of their weaknesses. The pioneer rancher tells it: "Though there wasn't anything especially to kick about, I had had a couple of very unsatisfactory years. The crops were good and the prices I got for my wheat were fair and each season I looked forward to a good profit. But when I came to balance up the books I always found that with all the horses and men I had to keep to plant the crop and harvest it, the ex-

The caterpillar tractor differs from the old wheel types in that it runs on a track which it lays itself, the track being an endless chain of plates which are picked up and laid down as the machine travels forward. It cares nothing for "the lay of the land"

pense for wages and for food just about ate up all the profit I made. The mortgage on my ranch began to look like a permanent investment for the bank.

"Then I bought a steam plow which was guaranteed to do the work of twenty-four horses. According to my mathematics it was going to cost me only about half as much to run that engine as to keep the twenty-four horses and drivers. I got out to the ranch a few days after the plow was started and I went out and sat on the fence and watched it work, feeling mighty happy and contented. There was that plow chugging away and sure enough doing as much work as a dozen teams and doing the work just as well. I did a little mental arithmetic and came to some very comfortable conclusions, based on the difference in cost of feeding wood and water to an engine as compared to the hay and oats a bunch of horses would eat.

"While I was watching it, a team drove up with a load of wood for the engine and a few minutes later another team came up with a load of water. Then I counted 'em. I had fourteen horses hauling water for that monster and sixteen hauling wood. I did some more mental

arithmetic and then I just headed the old steam plow straight for the nearest deep ditch and went back to my twenty-four horses."

It began to appear that the mortgage would be a permanent guest on the ranch. But in the meantime the Holt family had decided to move to California. The Holt family is an old one in New England and in the middle of last century operated a wagon factory in Concord. There were a number of brothers in the enterprise and one of them, backed by the capital of the others, came to San Francisco in 1860. He started a hardware store and lumber yard and in this business soon saw the need for a wagon wheel factory on the Pacific Coast. Stockton, at the lower end of the San Joaquin valley, was finally selected as the location for the Holt activities. It was believed that wagon wheels made in the damp San Francisco bay district would dry out and fall to pieces in the parched heat of the interior valleys. The wheel factory was so successful that it soon outgrew the New England establishment.

In 1863 Benjamin Holt, the brother who later became the leader in the Holt enterprises, was induced to come out to California to make his home. He has lived there continuously since

Hauling freight in Alaska. On any old road, or no road at all, the little old tractor rambles right along. The Germans surprised the world with the size of the field guns they brought to bear because they had requisitioned the California-made tractors in use in Germany and Austria

that time though he daily betrays his origin by the quaint New England idioms which slip unwittingly through his nose.

Benjamin Holt is the seventh in a family of eleven children, a fact which the superstitious may cherish. California agriculture, operated on a scale which made the farming ventures of his home state puny by comparison, interested him immensely. California was then in its heyday as a wheat producer and the harvester and threshing machine had been introduced to solve one of the problems of the farmer. Holt, with the twofold interest of farmer and mechanic, watched them work. The harvester cut the wheat and bound it in bundles which were hauled to the thresher in some distant part of the field. Often the man and horse power required to haul the wheat to the thresher were as great as the man and horse power required to do the harvesting and threshing. "It should all be done in one operation," said Holt, and he set to work with the result that the Holt Combined Header and Harvester was soon an accomplished fact. This machine harvested the grain, threshed it, and delivered the clean wheat in bags. It was successful from the first and it is estimated that at the present time and

for many years past 90 per cent of the wheat on the Pacific Coast is harvested by this machine.

The Holt Combined Harvester required many more horses than the binder and the old need for a serviceable tractor was increased. Holt first put an engine on the harvester to drive the machinery, thus relieving the horses. Thereafter, the Holts made steam tractors to pull the machine. Like the earlier steam plows, they worked beautifully if conditions were just right. If not, the wheels dug into the earth, and buried themselves deeper with each revolution. In order to avoid this the wheels were made wider and wider until the height of this development was reached with immense wheels eighteen feet wide and twelve feet in diameter.

The mechanical problem all along was to provide a larger gripping surface where the wheels of the tractor came in contact with the ground and many thought Holt had reached the limit of development in this line when he built the machine with the drive wheels eighteen feet wide. Perhaps a good many men would have stopped there. But Holt wasn't satisfied and he continued to experiment. It would be an idle psychological study to attempt to trace the idea, but eventually the now famous caterpillar tractor came to gladden the heart of Mother Necessity. The caterpillar type differs from the old wheel type of tractor in that it runs on a track which it lays itself, the track being an endless chain of plates which are picked up and laid again as the machine travels forward. These plates, corresponding to the cross-ties of the railroad, support inner rails, which in turn support the motor's revolving wheels.

A very little thing sometimes stands in the way of success that is nearly won. The caterpillar idea had been worked out and eventually the first machine was made and given a trial on the street in front of the factory. It did travel over the ground, but in traveling it nearly shook itself to pieces. Now it is a peculiar mechanical fact that when a belt connects two pulleys of exactly equal size, the belt will flop and vibrate violently, but if the pulleys are of different size the belt pursues its course serenely. Why this happens I do not know any more than I know why little pigs curl their tails. In this first caterpillar the wheels which revolved the endless chain of tracks were of the same size and the heavy tracks had caused much of the shaking. Holt sent the tractor back to the machine shops and in a short time it emerged for its second trial trip with one wheel smaller than the other. It moved without the racking and shaking, pulled heavy loads, climbed steep grades and ambled awkwardly but without a pause over muddy and freshly plowed fields.

"I've got it! I've got it!" yelled Holt, jumping up and down like an excited school boy.

And he did have it. There have been changes and improvements since that first trial trip about fifteen years ago, but the principle in the latest tractor is the same. This is the California type of tractor, which is also made by the C. L Best Manufacturing Company at San Leandro and by the Yuba Manufacturing Company at Marysville. Each company calls the tractor by a different copyrighted name, but their locomotion is based on the same principle. This tractor is pulling the world's heaviest loads over the world's roughest roads. It is snaking heavy mahogany logs out of the forests of Africa, hauling sugar cane in Hawaii, dragging sledges over snow and ice in Alaska and moving field guns on the European battle fields, though their principal use is that for which they were originally designed, hauling gang plows and harvesters over the fields of the West.

When the Germans surprised the world with the size of the field guns they were able to bring to bear against the Belgian forts, the feat was made possible only because the German government had requisitioned the few hundred California tractors which had been sold to German and Austrian farmers. Ten years ago tractors made in California were used by the British army in South Africa and during the battle of the Somme a year ago the British introduced the use of the now famous "tanks." It may be remarked here that no "tanks" have been made in California. The Holt factory has shipped to the allies a good many very heavy tractors of the ordinary type, but they are converted into tanks on the other side. At the Holt factory no one pretends to know anything more about the construction of tanks than can be learned through the newspaper accounts of their operation. They were as much surprised as the layman when they learned of the military uses to which their steel Percherons had been put. #

A Wish

By HELEN WILLS

June 1925

I'll set my house on the cliff's edge,
    Though the town lies down by the sea.
And I'll build my wall just high enough
    To shut the town from me.

Oh mine the glory of wave and sky,
    Of clouds and evening star!
White flashing breasts of wheeling gulls,
    And gleam of sails afar!

Oh safe and glad on my cliff's edge!
    And only will I look down,
When the fairy lamps of night are lit,
    Like stars, in the hidden town.

Stop
Stretching

To connect your electric iron and all of your other handy, labor saving electrical devices.

Have a safe, convenient electrical connection put in with Wiremold at just the place you want it and at small expense.

AMERICAN CONDUIT MFG. CO.
MAKERS OF WIREMOLD AND WIREDUCT
AT NEW KENSINGTON, PA.

The Temple of Wings

By LAURA BETHELL

December 1918

INDIVIDUAL members of families have, from time to time, attempted the simple life in one or more of its phases, with more or less regard to scientific laws of diet, clothing and housing, and have pursued the practice with more or less persistency. But it has remained for an entire family to practice for a period of four years, continuously, to their complete satisfaction, a scientific system of simple-life-living in *all* of its phases, with gains in health, happiness and usefulness. This experience, the Boynton family of Berkeley, California, claim for themselves, and claim it exclusively, so far as they know.

I wanted some of the details, so I asked the man of the family, Charles C. Boynton, who is an attorney, if by following their food schedule they had gained any advantage in these days of climbing prices.

"Yes," he told me, "we have solved the problem of living for these times of high cost. But, better still, we have solved it for all times. Our menu consists of California fruits and nuts: raisins, dried figs, prunes, almonds, English walnuts, peanuts, and fresh fruits in season. Besides these, it includes cheese, honey, milk and galleta, an Italian hardtack. We cook but one article of food: we roast peanuts, a fifteen minutes' task daily. Our fuel bill does not exceed $1.50 a month, and of course we do not employ a cook. Our food sustaining a family of ten costs less than $70.00 a month.

"And this 'simple diet' life is no dream of a faddist," he continued. "We have actually lived it out for four years. The food nourishes, and we do not tire of it. Other food tastes to us just the same as it always did, and wherever we are, as healthy mortals, we eat and relish anything and everything that is set before us. But no other meals satisfy like our own, for ours offer everything the system needs."

I sought Mrs. Boynton for her opinions. I found her at their Berkeley home—a stone palace without walls, built on a height facing the bay and the Golden Gate.

"My profession," Mrs. Boynton explained, "is motherhood. The inspiration came to me to build an outdoor home where the family could live free from domestic drudgery and convention in dress. We have named our open-air home of two circular porches 'The Temple of Wings,' and we have dedicated it to the democracy and freedom of women."

She stood in one of the great "wings," where she had been instructing a circle of girls in correct body movements, while they held pictures of Greek friezes. Sunlight streamed through the Corinthian columns and fell upon the group seated on the flagstoned floor. Beyond, in the companion wing-porch, boys were at play. Just outside a tot of three years was paddling in a pool built in the center of a sand pile.

"The open-air home is a product of our study," said Mrs. Boynton; "here adequate provision had been made for an entire family to live the simple life in dress, in diet and in occupation."

The structure of the "wings" backs against a hill; a grove of eucalyptus trees in front breaks the force of the daily trade winds. The "wings" are canopied, the blue of frescoed domes meeting the blue of heaven through center skylights. The flagstoned floor is heated to comfortable temperature by means of hollow earthen tubes. Awnings hang, undrawn, between thirty-four columns, promising protection from the rains of winter. A central concrete fireplace having four openings, with downward suction draft and chimney, promises cheer for winter, from four open faces. At the base of the towering fluted columns, and outlining the circle they form, fixed cabinets serve as bookcases, secretaries, tables and divans by day, and as beds by night.

At the rear a stone pantry tunnels the hill. Between the two wings, and under a third canopy, stretches a long balcony of curtained dressing-cabinets, from which hang vines and flowering plants. Under the balcony other cabinets serve as lavatories and bathrooms, with chests of drawers and the other conveniences of a modern home.

The dress worn by Mrs. Boynton and her children is a one-piece garment, buttoned at the shoulders and falling away in free lines, leaving the arms and shoulders bare. Referring to her reforms in dress, Mrs. Boynton said: "I wish that women would adopt the classic dress and free themselves and the coming generation from many useless problems."

From my observations, the first and the last impression received is that abounding life is manifest in each member of the Boynton family. The five ruddy-cheeked boys, bronze-limbed and sturdy, attest it as they roam the hills in search for the family cow, or dangle by their toes from high swings or trees, or bunch their heads together over bee-culture books, bought with "paper-route" money of their own earning. Rich life is apparent, too, in the grace, vigor, and wholesome charm of two daughters just entering womanhood, fellow-workers with their mother in writing and staging classic plays for the entertainment of hundreds who gather in the Greek Theater of their home hills.

Many observations of details incident to the simple life thus lived may be mentioned. There are no morning orders to give the butcher, the grocer, the vegetable vender and the baker; no milk carts and no delivery wagons rattle up the hill; no greasy utensils or dishes are to be washed; no milk vessels to be cared for (milk is used fresh from the milking); no stove to brighten (the cabineted electric roasts the peanuts); no floors to polish; no furniture to move for cleaning day; no windows to wash; no drapes or curtains to send to the laundry or to renew; no laces, ruffles or tucks to iron; no servant problems to meet; and only a few seams to sew when a new garment is required, to say nothing of the freedom from the tyranny of dress-maker engagements and "fittings."

There is time to enjoy the rows of books, among them a shelf of the classics in the original. There is time for the mother in the home to carry on her violin study. There is time for her to attend some of the lectures down in the university halls, and to do her part in club work. There is reserve strength and zest for the interests of the daughters, the sons and the husband, as the family gather at the close of the day, as there has been strength and zest for the demands of the three-year-old, taking her kindergarten training at home with her mother.

"I did not realize how far we had left behind us the life others live," Boynton remarked, "until a week ago, when I accompanied Mrs. Boynton to a meeting of one of her clubs. The women, experienced mothers, were considering ways and means to meet the high cost of living. In the two hours of discussion I did not hear mentioned a single article of food which, speaking selfishly, mattered a rap to me whether it went up or down." #

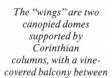

The "wings" are two canopied domes supported by Corinthian columns, with a vine-covered balcony between

Filming the Phantom

By Leland J. Burrud

November 1919

CRATER LAKE is very difficult to photograph. No matter how fine an apparatus you may have, no matter how famous an artist you may be, it is very hard to photograph this lake. It's the same way with all the National Parks. You have to have a strictly up-to-the-minute attachment to your camera, in the form of the permit which the regulations require. It's against the rules to take the Lake's picture otherwise and when I arrived at the edge of this marvel, with my carefully appointed truck and my elaborate outfit I found that my equipment lacked the one essential of photographic success in this region.

Judge, then, of my satisfaction in finding that the name of *Sunset*, hyphenated with my own modest name, was the open-sesame to this sapphire treasure of the Cascades.

The manager of the hotel there, one Parkhurst, a venturesome soul, kindly consented to act as skipper of a six-foot rowboat with an "every-once-in-a-while" one-lung motor suspended by a coat-hanger over the after-deck. (If this be unnautical make the most of it.) I loaded twenty-three hundred dollars' worth of moving-picture equipment into the stern-sheets and started round the lake. As you know, the blooming lake starts in to be a mile deep ten feet from shore. Along in the afternoon, when we were at the middle of the lake, one of those all-of-a-sudden thunderstorms came up, out of seemingly cloudless sky. From a peaceful mill-pond to a running sea was a matter of ten seconds. The lightning played round the edges of the water to shame the finest firework celebration anyone ever saw. And some angel, some leave-over from Lucifer's renegade bunch, in a cloud-bombing machine, began pegging at us with hailstones the size of eggs, while our palatial yacht was doing a tail-spin.

Finally the storm stopped, as quickly as it had started. The most solid thing I saw during those exciting moments, with one arm encircling my camera and tripod, was the famous "Phantom Ship" island. However, if we didn't have a thrill now and then, all the barbers in the country would be making moving pictures—it looks so easy when you sit in an opera chair and go sightseeing on the screen. #

Sunset's Rodeo of Literary Lions

April 1919

ON Wednesday, February 19th, a remarkable group of nationally-known Western writers was gathered together as guests of SUNSET MAGAZINE. The party was entertained at the Bohemian Club, world famous as a club of writers, artists, and others. The decoration of the supper table was novel enough to be recorded here. The table was bright with the delicate colors of spring: violet, jonquil and green, but there was not a flower in the decorative scheme. A six-foot centerpiece of uncancelled stamps, one-cent for green, three-cent for violet and ten-cent for jonquil, and dozens of ink wells in which stood quills dyed in the spring colors, with streamers of typewriter ribbons, officiated as flowers. Each of the literary guests was represented by a published work, bearing his name, many of which had been first published in SUNSET MAGAZINE. Among these were Stewart Edward White's "Rules of the Game," Peter B. Kyne's "The Long Chance," Camilla Kenyon's "Spanish Doubloons," George Sterling's "Evanescent City," and others. The guests in the picture are as follows:

Standing, from left to right—Robert C. Newell, Lloyd Osbourne, Stewart Edward White, Peter B. Kyne, Harry Leon Wilson, Walter V. Woehlke, Witter Bynner, George Sterling, Charles K. Field, Sam Blythe, Charles H. Woolley, Leland W. Peck, Peter Clark Macfarlane, Wilbur Hall.

Seated, from left to right—Mrs. Newell, Mrs. Osbourne, Mrs. White, Mrs. Kyne, Miss Hodgdon, Mrs. Wilson, Mrs. Woehlke, Mrs. Lillian Ferguson, Miss Miriam Michelson, Irvin S. Cobb, Mrs. Camilla Kenyon, Mrs. Woolley, Miss Estelle Wentworth, Mrs. Peck, Mrs. Hall, Mrs. Macfarlane. #

"Makes Cooking Easy"

This New Range Is A Wonder For Cooking

Although it is less than four feet long it can do every kind of cooking for any ordinary family by gas in warm weather, or by coal or wood when the kitchen needs heating.

The Coal section and the Gas section are just as separate as though you had two ranges in your kitchen.

Note the two gas ovens above—one for baking, glass paneled and one for broiling, with white enamel door.

The large oven below has the Indicator and is heated by coal or wood.

See the cooking surface when you want to rush things—five burners for gas and four covers for coal.

When in a hurry both coal and gas ovens can be operated at the same time, using one for baking bread or roasting meats and the other for pastry baking—It "Makes Cooking Easy"

Gold Medal
Glenwood

Write for handsome free booklet 157 that tells all about it.

Weir Stove Co., Taunton, Mass. Makers of the Celebrated Glenwood Coal, Wood and Gas Ranges, Heating Stoves and Furnaces.

Woman and Her War Loot

By MARY AUSTIN

February 1919

AMONG the many items which distinguish this war from other wars, there is one which maintains itself superior to all question. It is the fact that this war is the only war in which women, as women merely undistinguished by class or country, have gained anything. Suddenly after two hundred and fifty thousand years of militarism, they find themselves as a sex emerging from war with a share of the loot as well as the losses.

There is rather a widespread idea that the principal part of the woman's loot consists in the number and variety of new occupations annexed by her during war stress. But as a matter of fact the eruption of women into all sorts of untried industry is only an acceleration of a process going on for the past generation.

To the feminist nothing is more significant or important than the fact that even in conservative Great Britain it has been clearly established that woman is two-legged, and that when she is engaged upon two-legged business there is no impropriety in saying so.

As late as 1914 it was still in order in England if a young woman appeared in Hyde Park in riding breeches, or even in divided skirts, if she rode astride, to write to *The Times* about it. As late as 1917 in New York it was almost obligatory for young working women to go to their work in skirts cut to display as much ankle as possible and to call attention to the line of the hips, with peekaboo waists and other accouterments which cried aloud at every rustle—Look, I am a woman! And a good part of the difficulty of that young woman in industry was to know what to do with the men who responded to the call of her dress and conducted themselves to her as to a woman rather than as a fellow worker. Today London excels all other cities in the number of bifurcated styles for women's wear, and in any American city can be seen on the poster of the Y.W.C.A., an organization devoted to the conservation of all that the world most cherishes in its young women, an American girl clad unabashed in cap and overalls.

Feminist advocates have always recognized the necessity of eliminating femininity from women's working clothes if we were to make any progress in essential womanliness. Vance Thompson even went so far as to say, in his book called *Woman,* that complete political equality between men and women could not be hoped for until women in general had rid themselves of the over-emphasized sex dress. A Chicago employer, one of the foremost to put his five hundred young women employees in uniform, reports as a first fruit of the experiment that the men workers "treated them with more respect." . . . "Not in a moral way, but in regard to the work," he explains clumsily, probably realizing for the first time that there is a kind of respect due from men to women which has nothing to do with private virtue. This sort of personal equity in work is just what feminists have been fighting for, and failed to secure while they continued to emphasize differences in dress which have long been recognized as the greatest hindrance to true democracy between the sexes.

Until the eventful year 1917, the age at which women workers went to the discard was thirty-five, just the age at which the sheltered woman begins to be of use to society. But actual tests of women workers by women very quickly determined that one single cause out-weighed all the rest. This was the judgment of foremen, influenced perhaps unconsciously but nevertheless definitely influenced, by appearances. It is a fact that at the age of thirty-five few women who have worked since the age of sixteen for day's wages present that appearance of "pep" upon which very largely their efficiency is determined. And a very large factor in their appearance is the failure, through waning interest or a growing need to save, to dress attractively. Put these women in uniform, designed of itself to increase their own

*The uniform, skirtless working dress has merged
men and women into one common rating as
workers; it has brought about a new
personal equity between workers*

*Women save the state best when they are doing
productive work, such as farming and food
raising, for women must see something
grow and develop under their care*

sense of fitness, and the unconscious estimate
of efficiency rises with it.

In Europe, especially in England, perhaps
the most important war gain of women is equal
pay for equal work. This battle had been so
generally won in the United States that we are
likely to overlook the fact that equal pay for
women was actually opposed in England in the
beginning of the war by laboring men. In the
early stages of the war, when delegates from
Birmingham or Manchester conferred with
labor unions in New York, they would enlarge
fervidly on the domestic insubordination which
they thought sure to result from the equal pay
program. They were particularly eloquent on
the subject of the extravagances into which
English working wives and daughters were
plunged by having for the first time in their
lives the whole pay envelope to spend.

Actually the situation of women, as women
merely, is more critical than it has been since
the time of Charlemagne. Never since then has
the disequilibrium of population in civilized
countries been so great as·it is now. Official
estimates give us ten million as the number of
men whose lives have been laid down on sea
and land. Ten million women cut off from
home and husbands and children.

The movement to have unmarried women
retain their war jobs in offices and factories is
not enough. Working at the same things men
work at isn't by itself enough. Working for the
same wages won't do it. Women, to be at home
in the world, must produce. They must see
something grow and develop under their care.
In other words, they must be psychologically
accommodated.

So far the only practical attack on this
problem has come from two sources. It has
come from England where plans are being
made to utilize the productive energy of women in food raising. Mrs. Pankhurst, being
statesmanly to the highest degree, knows that
women serve the state best when they are
taking care of something.

Schools for women farmers are flourishing
and plans for providing unattached women
with land are maturing.

Farming, more than any other occupation,
gives scope for the nursing instinct of women.
That is why I emphasize the skirtless dress as
the chiefest, the most unquestioned of our war

gains, because of its relation to the likeliest outlet for woman's productive energy.

Other opportunities to utilize the surplus mother-energy of the world will undoubtedly grow out of the new appreciation of the value of children to the state, and the practical value of public health. In Europe the stigma of illegitimacy, which was the greatest curse ever visited by civilized peoples on innocent childhood, practically disappeared during the first year of the war. The right of fatherless children to full care and thoughtful attention has been conceded not as a sentimental theory but as a matter of practical administration.

The only other practical suggestion for utilizing the surplus woman population comes from Germany, and is one of the reasons why the war has been fought. It is a proposal to keep the women at their work of child-bearing either by raising the status of the unmarried mother or by creating a new form of "lateral marriage" which is a practical polygamy.

There is a collection of documents at Washington illustrating the German attitude on the problem of restoring their own equilibrium of population which is in its way as appalling as their method of decimating the populations of the occupied countries. It begins with the edict of a German general in a Polish city by which the German Government offered to buy boys at one hundred and fifty marks and girls at one hundred—note the thrifty Teutonic distinction of value—and to accelerate sales, turned a hundred thousand families out of their homes. The list concludes with two or three other little edicts on the increase of the population, not possible to reprint.

A year ago, the Young Women's Christian Association sent out a questionnaire to various women's colleges to discover what phases of reconstruction work most interested the young American woman. It was arresting, though perhaps not surprising, to find that this question of unmarried motherhood was one of them. And nobody was answering it. Partly because our women leaders are too much taken up with problems of organization and specific policies, and partly because of our tendency to think of it as a point of morals and as such ruled out of discussion. The proper approach to this question of the surplus woman is sociological.

Whether you argue for or against unmarried motherhood, it is impossible to escape the evidence of history that whenever, and to the degree, that monogamy has been threatened it has meant loss of dignity, loss of power and loss of freedom to the women of that country.

Already American women have scored a point in the superior "socio-physical" morale of their sons in the army and navy. I have to invent that word to express exactly what I mean, certainly not meaning that American men are any braver, more patriotic or trustworthy than European men. But on the whole, they are cleaner. It has been impossible to escape the impression this has made on the European press. One of the favorite English pictures of American boys is a group of Jackies, all agrin to show their beautifully kept and perfect teeth. Our daily tooth-brush drill is commented on as something quite surprisingly worth adopting. Their clean skins, and their clean language on topics on which most European men permit themselves a great deal of laxity, has surprised even such a widely acquainted and observant man as Mr. Rudyard Kipling. And Mr. Kipling is entirely frank in attributing this to the fact that American boys are "brought up by women." You gather that heretofore Mr. Kipling has not considered it an unmixed advantage to be brought up by women. He is surprised, with true British bluntness, to find that it has not impaired their fighting qualities, and that an American soldier can efficiently kill a Hun for a piece of beastliness of which he speaks, as Mr. Kipling says, "choosing his words like a girl."

The American woman has placed herself before the world in a position to take the lead in all solutions of post-war problems which have to do with the home and the family. For the moment this is of more importance than that she has made so many million Red Cross bandages or collected so many shiploads of old clothes.

On the whole, women are agreed that the sense of spiritual community is the greatest of their war gains, and it would seem that the next greatest would be their own strategic position in the unprecedented opportunity to influence the world spirit. It is to be hoped, it is expected, that they will rise to it as efficiently as to the earlier more practical occasion. #

Bobbie's Good Judgment

"Whoop-e-e!" Bobbie says. "I'm glad it isn't that old shortcake."

Whether Bobbie's preferences are shared by Betty and Nan or not, their approval of the Jell-O is plain enough. They know what they like and mamma knows what is good for them.

Just now she is serving Orange Jell-O, which is a delightful change from the fruit itself, as the other flavors of Jell-O are.

If you cannot get strawberries you can have Strawberry Jell-O, which is wonderfully enjoyable these warm spring days.

And there is Raspberry Jell-O, beautiful to see and delicious to eat—raspberries in a lovely new form.

And Cherry Jell-O that looks like the richest of the fruit and tastes like it.

And the other three flavors of Jell-O—Orange, Lemon and Chocolate—cool, sparkling, flavorful.

All these can be made into "plain" desserts or the more substantial Bavarian creams that women and children are so partial to and men find so satisfactory that they always want more.

To Make Bavarian Creams

Everybody knows, of course, that a plain Jell-O dessert is made by dissolving a package of Jell-O in a pint of boiling water and letting it cool and harden, but everybody doesn't know how to make Bavarian creams in the easy Jell-O way; so we will tell you how if you will kindly read on.

JELL-O

For a strawberry cream, chop or cut fine with a knife half a box of strawberries, sprinkle with half a cup of sugar and stand in a colander to drain. Dissolve a package of Strawberry Jell-O in half a pint of boiling water. When cool, measure strawberry juice and add enough cold water to make half a pint and turn into the dissolved Jell-O. Whip until of thickness of whipped cream and then fold in the cut strawberries. Serve in sherbet glasses. Garnish with fresh berries. Any fresh or canned fruit can be used instead of strawberries.

For a perfect pineapple Bavarian cream dissolve a package of Lemon Jell-O in a half pint of boiling water and add a half pint of juice from a can of pineapple. When cool and still liquid whip with an egg-beater to the consistency of whipped cream and add half a cup or a cup of shredded pineapple from the can.

Never overlook the fact that Jell-O can be whipped with an egg-beater in the same manner as cream, and that whipping Jell-O changes it fully as much as whipping cream changes that.

The six flavors of Jell-O are Strawberry, Raspberry, Lemon, Orange, Cherry, Chocolate. Grocers and general storekeepers sell them two for 25 cents.

In the latest Jell-O Book there are recipes for dainty salads as well as desserts, and a great deal of information that will save money for the housewife and make her work easier and pleasanter.

THE GENESEE PURE FOOD COMPANY,
Le Roy, N. Y., and Bridgeburg, Ont.

"Unto the Least of These"

By HERBERT HOOVER

February 1920

I KNOW of no greater deed ever done by one nation to others than the service and sacrifices of the American people in caring for the children of Europe. Nor is it unappreciated. I have a letter, out of many thousands, that sums up this story. It comes from a town in Esthonia of which probably few of SUNSET'S readers have ever heard, and is addressed simply to the people of the United States, as follows:

"Dear Friends:

"The children whom you feed in the different kitchens wish to express their appreciation and thanks.

"The levies made by the great War and German occupation in Esthonia impoverished our homes, and later the Russian Bolsheviks in hordes plundered and robbed what was still left us. Some of our fathers became victims of the war, while others were unable to earn our daily bread, fighting on the battlefields and defending our country. In a short time our supplies became exhausted and the lack of food was felt greatly. Very little bread was to be had; sugar, rice and milk entirely missing; our eyes grew dull, our cheeks blanched and hollow; happiness, joy and games were all forgotten, and listlessly we watched the passers-by in the streets, and some of us had to stretch out our tiny hands to ask for alms. Then your country thought about us and your magnificent generosity found a way across seas and lands to this little spot where so many suffered. You brought us food that made our eyes bright again, gave us courage to become good and obedient in thoughts and deeds at home and at school.

"We praise God in our souls that He sent America and ask Him to bless, guard and protect your mighty country and everything it undertakes."

This letter is signed by three hundred children in Reval.

The feeding of ten millions of Belgian and French people was the first attempt ever made anywhere, so far as I know, at the mass feeding of a whole nation. There were no experts in the problem, but we sought such scientific advice as was to be obtained. We soon found, however, that the children were failing on a ration that should be ample for the adults. The number of debilitated children up to ten years of age greatly increased. The number of adolescent children developing tuberculosis increased to a disheartening degree. We at first attempted to deal with this problem by the establishment of feeding centers for debilitated and ailing children where, under careful treatment, they could be restored to normal. We soon found that the pressure on these services was increasing to an alarming degree, and thus it was that we took the resolution to feed the children *en bloc,* apart from their parents. We believed that if we could subject all the children to medical inspection, that if we could give them one meal a day adapted to their needs, that we would have entered into the province of prevention from the province of cure. Something over 1,200,000 children of the Belgian and French towns and cities were thus put under systematic inspection and feeding, and this was continued during the last three and one-half years of the Occupation. If you will go to Belgium today and if you will examine the public health statistics, you will find that the disease mortality among children is less than the pre-war normal, in spite of nearly five years of continuous famine.

At the time of the Armistice we were confronted with two hundred million underfed people who had been under German domination. Due to denudation of cattle by the German army at the point of the bayonet, milk had been practically unknown for years. So that in considering this problem of the great famine that confronted Europe, one of our first duties was to develop a method of saving the children. It appeared to us that the distant future of these nations would lie in the immediate rescue of the greatly debilitated children. Here, again, we attacked the problem both by prevention and by cure. The feeding of the children in the public schools in many of these countries was organized under their governments, and milk and other supplies were furnished for this purpose. Aside from these measures, we established a special service for debilitated children and through the acute period last spring we had as high as four millions of such children receiving special care. This great nursery was carried on by the United States Government until the first of July. Since that time it has been carried on through public charity of many nations.

One feature of organization in these matters is outstanding—that the responsibility of organization has rested almost entirely upon the women. Those American men who had to do with this work can claim but little credit except in initial organization and for the physical provision and distribution of food supplies into the hands of this multitude of devoted women.

This treatment of the problem on so large and so wholesale a scale has, I believe, made a deep impression upon those people and governments in Europe where it has been undertaken. American charity and American direction have been withdrawn from Belgium, Rumania and Northern France, yet the impress of the work has been to a great extent incorporated into public life and polity. #

The Lady of Tamalpais

By KATHLEEN NORRIS

May 1920

About her generations come and go,
    A hundred hearths are warm upon the slopes,
Child voices fill the valley far below,
    And lovers pray their prayers and hope their hopes.

But her mute mouth and her sweet shuttered eyes
    Warm not to the vain kisses of the West,
Her unbound hair like a blown mantle flies
    And her locked hands are still against her breast.

Indifferent to the shy march of the spring
    Creeping across the ridges warm and green,
Unwarmed by June and her mad burgeoning
    Left by the storms of winter still serene—

Though night may bind a mist about her eyes,
    And though the opal raptures of the dawn
May storm the very tomb whereon she lies,
    The lady of the mountain slumbers on!

"*You've come all the way from New York to San Francisco without a blowout?*
Those must be some tires you have!"

"*They are. Kelly-Springfields, you know.*"

Lodge-Fires

By LAFAYETTE MAYNARD DIXON

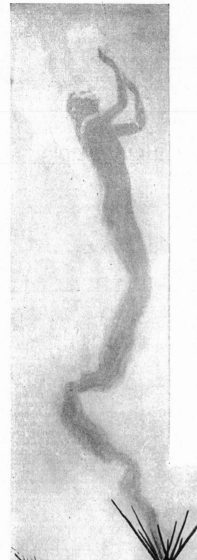

September 1919
In this humble smoke-brown tepee,
Apart in a hidden depression of prairie,
Here, as of old, is the pipe,
(Legends of mystery-power and war)
And the ceremonial block for tobacco,
The sacred sweet-grass and charcoal,
The mysterious medicine-bundle with fringes depending,
The robes and the blankets and beadwork,
The gun and the rawhide and saddle,
And (silent witness) a moccasin-print in the ashes.
Lying here, gazing up where the lodge-poles cross
Against the bright inscrutable sky,
I follow the smoke of this lonely lodge-fire rising,
A pale blue visible sigh,
A vague passing spirit exhaling—
(O ancient lodge-fire, where are your many brothers?
O ancient pipe, where are the smokes of council?)
The dim and wandering ghost of wilderness tribes
Exhaling into the blue and formless ether.

An Englishman Discovers The Real West

By W. L. George

November 1922

AN Englishman setting out for the Far West carries in his baggage a certain load of preconceptions. He has read a work of Mr. Zane Grey, and seen a few Broadwest films. He has a vision of bronzed men clad in hairy trousers, wearing sombreros, who ride about madly in all directions and readily draw bowie-knife and six-shooter for the sake of the pure, pure heroine, or the little child with the golden, golden hair, that has wandered into the camp, shack, adobe hut, ranch, as the case may be. It is a highly colored dream, which the journey confirms only in part. At last, in a sudden burst of sunshine, he comes upon Canaan, upon California.

One trouble is that the man from Europe continually thinks that at last he is reaching the West, only to discover that this is not yet the West, that it lies yet another thousand miles beyond his eyes. I remember my impression as I reached Nebraska, as I began to see cattle and horses being driven along the roads. Such a sight, so different from that of Chicago and its eastern hinterland, suggested that this must be the West. But it wasn't. It was only the Middle West. Not the magnificent Middle West of Chicago, of my beloved Chicago, fumous, flame-spattered, roaring through her own streets, wild with physical energy, Chicago, the bronco city. It was another Middle West, scrubby, dingy, barely begun, and lacking in promise. It was not the West. When we reached Lincoln, a dusty city grown like a sickly mushroom in the light, my wife began a speculation that amused us all the way: what can a bride feel when she is brought here from the east? to these sketched out roads, to this cluster of gasometers, oil pumping stations, and smokestacks? She must feel wretched. Here was a place where there was nothing to do except work: to a European this is a horrible idea.

So it was not until my awaking eyes peered under the blind of my sleeping berth that I discovered myself in another West, perhaps the real West this time, Colorado. I had gone to sleep on the prairie; I awoke in a fantastic land of mountain and stream, of nature formidable and still untamed, in the midst of a loneliness that would have felt savage if the sunshine had not irradiated the hills with purple, puce, and striating emerald.

I think again of the Royal Gorge, between its towering rocks splashed with mauve and gold, of the tumbling torrent that goes, furious and fast, down from Cañon City. A chaplet of tunnels, a bridge perilously suspended upon two clefts in the rock, now wooded heights, then again the bitter land of rock. It goes on all day as we climb and climb toward the Tennessee Pass, higher into the snow upon which the setting sun now throws the sheen of old copper.

This is the West at last. The real West. First of all I miss the ever present automobile of the east; here and there, along the trails, go men on horseback, rough-looking men, who sit their horses differently from the way in which they are sat in Central Park. It is the West because here the few settlements which hide in the valleys strike one always as unfinished. Here are wooden shacks: it is quicker to build of lumber than of stone, and there are no bricklayers in this land. Everything is improvised. Here are hedges made partly of wire, partly of hurdles, partly of sticks tangled with brushwood. Here, too, the yards of houses are choked with rubbish thrown aside while the pioneer gets on with a more urgent job, or which he leaves behind as he goes westward upon the trail. Here also cattle rather than ploughed fields, cattle in herds which astonish the eastern eye. This is still a pastoral land at a stage earlier than cultivation.

Once again we play the bride game. What would she feel in Colorado, this young lady from Manhattan? She would feel very lonely; she would miss the movies and the drug store, but my wife considers that something fine and bracing would fall from these towering cliffs. Here everything is alive: men are making trails through the woods; they are laying new railroads; we encounter a large coach which carries and houses the pioneers of the track: women and children have somehow occurred in the traveling camp. Here are no bungalows, but loghuts fit to breed a Lincoln. But man prevails, for here are small cornfields and even orchards. Everything is beginning; here is being done what thirty years ago was being done a thousand miles east.

I picture the first Westerners coming out of this glowing wilderness into the happy valleys, into the deep arable land of Utah which was to give birth to Salt Lake City.

It does not last long, the relief of Salt Lake City, its broad streets, the trees and well-laid pavements which surround the Temple. The Westerner who came out here had not gone very far towards the promised land. There was lying before him so much more agony, so much more peril, that one wonders how he passed through the desert, on a march so much longer than forty days in the wilderness. He who has not seen the bitter desert of Utah and Nevada can not hope to imagine what it cost a man to pioneer. One does not understand at first, as he looks out over this dry country that lies flat, rising toward the horizon to gray hills, splashed with silver, crowned with violet, and in the evening showing crests like blackened teeth. One does not understand because he does not know how long this will last. It is only by degrees that it strikes me that here grows only a little heather or some heath, bitten gray with frost. It is cold here. Then, a little later, not far from the track, I see twelve dead sheep, frozen stiff in strange attitudes, like wooden toys. They lie under their immense coats; even the sheep freeze, for the desert does not deal with life.

Sometimes there are no hills, but only on the horizon a faint range which hardly breaks the emptiness of space. This is the West, really the West; the Rockies were well enough, but the European has his Switzerland. The desert of Nevada, its bleakness, the appearance of the

land burnished by the sun, cracked by the frost, nothing of this does he possess. To equal that he must go to Arabia Deserta, to Asia and the desert of Gobi. At night, when the moonlight falls like silver spears upon the mountains that grow blue, he thinks of the mountains of the moon. Little by litle I grow used to the desert. There is so much of it. Still more frozen fields, still more purple hills. I begin to escape it: the telegraph posts help me, for man after all has set his mark even here. Men have come here, men gone through it. And an idea comes to me: what about the women who, following their men, somehow reached California? San Francisco has erected a monument to the pioneer mother, but it seems to me that the Far West is her monument. We do not hear enough about her, but only of the men who did while she endured. I have a vision of that woman as she went through the desert, settling for a short time where there was a spring, a little grass where the cattle might graze, some lumber with which to make a hut. It freezes hard. She is sick; there is no doctor within five hundred miles. Nobody will ride toward her with quinine. She must get over her fever if she can. About her her children, vigorous, sunburnt, happy, but always clamoring that she should cook for them, mend for them, wash them, tell them stories, dry their tears, join in their games. She must teach them, too, for there is no school-master here. They grow up, she thinks crude and savage, unlike her playmates in distant Illinois. Her man is happy, successful; she is his lover, his cook, his adviser, his servant.

I met two pioneers in Nevada, and they summed up today all that is tragic in the past. The man was about fifty-five, very big, very handsome, in magnificent health. Seldom have I seen a man more vigorous, more willing to laugh, taking his food with greater pleasure. Beside him his wife, probably younger, but so old. Bent by continual scrubbing, having found in the desert no help, no support; too poor in the early days to buy a stove, her new comfort has failed to teach her to desire a vacuum cleaner, a laundering machine; too far from electricity to get help from that; broken by excessive child-bearing; starved of pleasure. She was fifty perhaps, and so old, so thin, her hair so poor, her wretched hands so twisted and blackened about the nails, her clothes, good

"When a Feller Needs a Friend"

Drawn by Will James

Our cowboy artist explains that this scene from actual range life illustrates by a dramatic moment the
reason why a cowpuncher carries a gun

enough, but shabby because she was shabby,
because she had been worn too long, as if the
stones had rubbed her freshness off, as if her
beauty had been taken by the crackling frost,
the devouring sun. It is a good land for men; it
makes them big, courageous, enduring. But of
women it makes a wreck, the wreck of
womanhood, the wreck of beauty and of the
graces. It is not only of gravel that trails are
made, but of dead skin and powdered bones.

Then, cherry blossom, with an extraordinary
effect of suddenness, as if on the stage a back
sheet had been dropped before my eyes. After
one has unsuspectingly wandered down the
Feather River cañon, its precipitous slopes,
harsh with stone, clad with pine, one is in
Canaan. As I write, this vision of cherry blossom oppresses me after so many days in the
wilderness, for it comes without warning. Before me lies a land of soft swelling hills, clad
in pines and firs. No more gray surfaces; now
all is green as Ireland. There is an air of
kindliness and comfort. No longer does the

land roll to an empty horizon into an empty
sky. Here are houses, roads, bridges, wired
fields: extraordinary!

I think it was at Oroville that I first felt
California. It was enough to see the railroad
station built in the Spanish style, with its deep
arcade and the hint of a patio behind. It is not
often you see a beautiful railroad station, but I
suppose that it isn't difficult to be made beautiful when built in a grove of palm trees, by
the side of a plot where California, rightly
vainglorious and anxious to show herself to the
stranger has planted orange, lemon and grape
fruit trees which carry their fruit in the soft air.
Near by acacias are flowering, bending under
heavy yellow blooms; from the marsh a crane
rises in a leisurely fashion. One has a sense of
fatness, of richness, of deep earth, abundant
water.

I suppose it is natural enough, though
perhaps tedious to the Californian ear, that the
foreigner should above all be impressed by the
richness of the vegetation of this distant coast.
Perhaps the natural beauty should impress him
more, but an almost sensual delight may be
found in the thickness of stems, the abundance
of leaves, the color of blooms. I think of the
feathery pepper tree, like a gay green peacock,
of great heliotropes, puritan in color, but
queerly ardent in a secretive way, of the labur-
num that in languor drops its wells of fire, the
japonica, so red and saucy, like a flapper with a
doubtful present and an undoubted future.
Most beautiful of all, the listless eucalyptus,
that most negligent of trees, which droops its
shiny, fleshy leaves in fragrant weariness. And
swollen figs, and oranges that glow, palms from
New Zealand or Africa, swollen with sap,
shining, outlining themselves like strips of metal upon the softer sky. Everything is growing.
There is in it a continuing excitement. In
California life is vivid, in the plants as much as
in the beasts.

The thing which first impresses in San Francisco is the variety of its architecture. It is not a
city built in a hurry on a readymade eastern
plan, or out of frames. Here the houses arose by
degrees and were houses to live in more than
houses to sell. Hence individual taste, sometimes fortunate, sometimes not, but always
various. At first San Francisco irritates the
stranger, because the plan is awkward when

compared with the rigidities of New York. It takes a little time to understand other people's difficulties, to realize that since almost the whole of San Francisco is built on hills, the result of a quadrilateral plan would have been that no horse and hardly a car could have gone straight up a hill. Incidentally I suspect that bad motorists go to San Francisco when they die, to drive without brakes down hills of forty-five degrees gradient. The San Franciscans who kindly drove me about their city have no idea of my continual state of terror as their automobiles casually hurled themselves down streets which in England we would call precipices. I said nothing. I kept the Union Jack flying. But within my heart it wasn't flying: flapping was the most it could do.

After Market street and its four streetcar lines it does one good to discover something of the San Francisco that was, that is still the real San Francisco, the Mission Dolores. To pass under the mild archway of this little fane, after glancing at its frontage, Moorish and Corinthian, helps one to forget much that modernity has spoilt. Here is something real, something permanent, something not quite forgotten. Here indeed America has a long past, and here for a moment hitches her chariot of petrol to the patient mule team of the Spanish fathers. All through California I was haunted by the feeling of the missions, not only Dolores, but the others, San Miguel, San Carlos del Carmelo, so small, so delicately laid of adobe and plaster, so very much there, not stranded and lost in the middle of shunting yards and canning plants. The missions still mean something. They are of the country, like the oranges which ripen in its fields.

As one goes South the feeling of California is enhanced. San Francisco is intensely Californian, but to me California really means battering sun blasts, warmth, and everywhere intense blue, golden, intense, almost African color. You do not perceive this everywhere, but it filters into the cities. Los Angeles for instance. One might not think that a big modern city would allow California to penetrate, but California is an atmosphere, as well as a place. Here in Los Angeles, in spite of the banks and the big stores, you still find Spain. It is only at Hollywood, perhaps, that you get away for a moment into modern industry, into that strange industry of evolved showmen. At Hollywood everything seems unfinished, or better still, just begun. Here I had the good fortune to encounter Mr. Douglas Fairbanks, who was kind enough to show me his studio, the designs of his new film, and, staggering to a European, an almost complete Norman castle which he was building. Here America appears, overlying California, the America which does not hesitate to erect a building some hundreds of feet long, to decorate it with towers sixty feet high, to pull it down tomorrow when its purpose is served. Mr. Fairbanks, I gathered, proposed to dive into the moat from one of those sixty foot towers. Unfortunately the rehearsals had not begun.

And still I go South, until I strike San Diego, among its orange and lemon groves, between plantations of olive trees, thick with silver leaves. Here it is hotter, and the Pacific rolls bluer on the other side of Coronado. It is real California, casting toward Pacific Beach and Oceanside her hills of blue and rose. Here is a foreign land in its fatness. I meet Mexicans, swarthy and thin. At La Jolla I gaze in a garden at an immense banana tree. Fatness and wealth, warmth, color, ease.

Ease! That is what I always come back to when I think of California. First it is ease of life in this fertile land; then it is the ease of social relations among people who trouble little about forms; now I find another ease: California shares with the South the honor of not working too hard. One of the few things which have upset me in America is the intensity of labor in the East and the Middle West. I can but admire it, for ambition, physical energy, devotion to the task, those are virtues, but I have always felt myself to be different from people who give themselves so entirely to their work that nothing is left them to enjoy. That is not the case in San Francisco or in any part of California: California has not lost her pleasures. You will imagine that, coming from the Middle West, it was staggering to find all the big stores and many of the small ones closing at half past five. Things get done in California, but they do not, as happens elsewhere, get done a little faster than they need.

At last I leave California, and once again I understand her better, as if I realized her most in comparison with less fortunate lands. After a few hours the land dries. The oranges and lemons become scarcer, barren fields appear, as the railroad takes me into Arizona toward New Mexico. Here once more a land of crimson sandstone, beautiful and terrifying. A lonely land of sandy desert where nothing grows but stunted palms, fantastic varieties of cactus; here are occasional cattle, mysteriously fed, shacks made of poles and dry palm leaves, about which circulates a small population of brown children, fine men. Here are the women, always the tragic women, out of whom the desert is being made into civilization. We are far now from the soft breezes of the sea. Here is heat and dust. A hissing wind carries sand and powdered alkali into my eyes. The immense loneliness begins to unroll, the loneliness of gorge and treeless slope, where no birds fly. There is no promised land on the other side of this desert; the promised land lies behind. #

Help Preserve God's Greatest Cathedral

June 1921

"THROUGH all the eventful centuries since Christ's time, God has cared for these trees, saved them from drought, disease, avalanches and a thousand storms; but He can not save them from sawmills; this is left to the American people."

Thus wrote John Muir. Did he have in mind the storm which last winter swept over the Olympic peninsula in Washington, leaving in its wake a thousand square miles covered forty feet deep with twisted, torn and up-rooted forest giants? In a night last winter magnificent forests three and four hundred years old were destroyed by wind. Against the storm man's puny hand could not protect a single tree. From such storms as these benign Providence saved the majestic redwood trees of northern California, preserved them and handed them over to a generation of Americans able to appreciate the beauty and dignity of a forest that was ancient when Charlemagne ruled over their ancestors.

But this generation of Americans seems unable to preserve this priceless heritage from the blade of the ax and the saw. The National Park dams that have aroused the indignation of Eastern nature lovers can be torn down at any time, pipe and transmission lines can be removed, but when a redwood tree thirteen hundred years old is felled, chopped up into ties and grape stakes and shingles, no effort, no money can replace it.

Thanks to the work of the Save the Redwoods League, the ax and the saw have been stayed—for a few months. Some of the finest, most accessible groves will not be cut this summer. They will never be cut if you imitate the example of Dr. J. C. Phillips, of Wenham, in faraway Massachusetts, who gave $12,000 for the purchase of a grove to be dedicated to the memory of Colonel R. C. Bolling, first officer of high rank to give his life for his country in the late war.

Perhaps you can not afford to erect so wondrous a temple to the memory of the son who fell in the war; but you can send a hundred or five hundred dollars to Robert G. Sproul, Treasurer Redwoods League, 431 Library, University of California, Berkeley, California, asking to have one of the titanic trees dedicated to the memory of your loved one. And the least you can do is to send two dollars for a membership in the organization that is trying to preserve a heritage which can not be replaced with all the money in the world a year or two hence. #

*An everyday gathering of Los Angeles residents at
the opening of a new subdivision*

Roots of Los Angeles' Astonishing Growth

By WALTER V. WOEHLKE

April 1924

THE main reason for the remarkable continuous growth of Los Angeles and its surrounding territory is the fact that Karl Marx was wrong. He predicted the concentration of all wealth in a few hands, the speedy disappearance of the middle class and the division of the population into those few who owned everything and the masses who owned nothing except the ability to work. Had the Marxian prediction come true, Los Angeles would still be a semi-Spanish country town dozing somnolently between the sun-flooded slopes of the Sierra Madre and the blue sea. But Marx turned out to be a false prophet. The middle class declined to disappear; instead, it increased in numbers and wealth, especially in the upper basin of the Mississippi and its tributaries.

Then came to pass an entirely new phenomenon in American economic and social history. There had been many rushes for gold, free land, timber and other resources and invariably the men who had gone out in thousands to take possession of these resources had been the young and the strong, the adventurous and the hardy. But the rush into

Southern California was made up principally of the middle-aged, of men and women who had made their more or less modest stake, whose simple needs were provided for out of rents, interests and dividends and who sought not opportunity but comfort and health in a mild climate amid beautiful surroundings. They transplanted themselves bag and baggage, kit and kin, became all-year residents and enthusiastic Californians.

Until the middle-aged middle class of the Middle West rose en masse and migrated to California's southern third there had been winter resorts and winter residences, but they had been patronized and maintained almost exclusively by the upper crust. The substantial, God-fearing, hard working Middle Westerners had considered it almost a sin to nullify the will of Providence by dodging the blizzards and spending the winter in milder climes; also, the frugal, thrifty population of the Middle West objected to the expense. But when it was discovered that the dollar actually went farther in Los Angeles and San Diego than in Keokuk, when it was found out that a cow, a chicken, a bee and half an acre of irrigated land heaped

*"Come on ladies and gentlemen, these lots will
double in value in six weeks."*

They first came in the '80s when the Santa Fe was completed, but the railroad boom soon dried up in the heated air. The real hegira did not begin before McKinley's first term and it continued without interruption until 1915, bringing with it the subdivision of nearly all the vast Spanish ranchos, increased agricultural productivity, constantly rising land values, moderate oil development and a very high general level of prosperous well-being.

After the four hard war years when the influx of population ceased almost completely, when real estate values dropped and vacant houses abounded, a sudden tidal wave of humanity swept in from the East. The 1920 slump did not stop it, the 1921 depression did not give it pause. It kept right on coming, clamoring for houses and apartments to live in, for stores in which to buy, for automobiles to ride in, for roads on which to run the automobiles. But the horde of newcomers no longer increased the productivity of the soil. It couldn't. The limit of water development for agricultural purposes had almost been reached.

What did all these umpty-ump thousands per month want? What did they find to do?

"Take in each other's washing," I've heard scores of outsiders say. Sure, That's being done, has to be done in any rapidly growing community. When a thousand families with

high with climate would materially reduce family expenses, there was no holding 'em.

Incidentally their industry transformed the arid valleys into the country's most intensively cultivated orchards and gardens; they blazed the trail in the coöperative marketing of fruit; they made of horticulture a science, built model irrigation systems, led in water and forest conservation and altogether turned out to be most valuable, high-minded, intelligent community builders, albeit a little narrow in their views.

*This is a new development in the real estate world, a subsidiary business center on a street without a car line. Auto
traffic lifted values on this through street from $50 to $1000 and $2000 a front foot almost overnight.
The spectacular rise launched the lot speculation that was superimposed on
the normal activity of the Los Angeles real estate market.*

independent incomes arrive in California to make their homes, they at once call for the services of a thousand carpenters, plasterers, plumbers, roofers, grocers, bakers, manicurists, furniture makers and dozens of other trades who in turn call on lumber yards, cement plants, packing houses, soap factories and flour mills for increased supplies. Making money in an active, constantly growing market is fairly easy, given sound business judgment; with the profits derived from the home market many enterprising manufacturers step out, invade distant markets, increase their output and enlarge their payroll. And every worker added to the force immediately stimulates the building industry, the dry goods, cafeteria, creamery, candy and clothing business.

Do you get the idea? Constant additions of new residents with incomes provide trade and employment to a larger number of business, professional and laboring men whose growing needs in turn call for still more workers. Given a certain momentum, a growth of this character is like an avalanche—it keeps on getting bigger the farther it travels.

Add a tremendous oil boom to these basic ingredients; sprinkle them with an ever increasing summer-and-winter tourist business; pour over them a generous dose of Hollywood movie sauce; spice them with greatly enlarged manufacturing, shipping and jobbing business, and you have a perfectly legitimate growth warranting a healthy movement of real estate and rapidly rising land values. From 1919 to the end of 1921 these factors were in full operation, but there was comparatively little speculation.

Then something new and unexpected happened.

It had been a real estate axiom that subsidiary business centers with their high front-foot values could develop only along car lines, and that the highest values would be reached on and near the crossing of two car lines. This axiom was smashed in Los Angeles and the automobile did the smashing. When a broad north-and-south thoroughfare was opened on Western avenue and an ever increasing motor traffic poured over this street, it suddenly, almost overnight, blossomed out as a subsidiary business street and land values went up with a tremendous bang. #

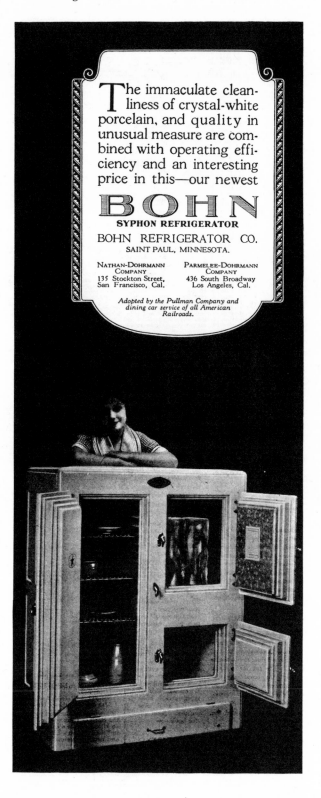

Lake Tahoe, California—showing Rubicon Point. In the distance is Freel Peak—elevation 10,000 feet. This mountain is about four miles southwest of the boundary between California and Nevada.

RED CROWN GASOLINE

Beautiful Lake Tahoe

The Gasoline of Quality

LAKE TAHOE lies on the California-Nevada line in the Sierra Nevada Mountains—fifteen miles south of Truckee and two hundred miles east of San Francisco. The marvelous color of Tahoe varies from the deepest indigo to brilliant emerald. Surrounding the lake are lofty peaks—from seven thousand to over ten thousand feet high.

The motorist may reach Tahoe by many routes, and whether you go from the east, west, north or south, you will always find a service station or garage displaying the Red Crown sign.

Look for that sign when you need gasoline. It is your assurance of getting an all-refinery gasoline—with a continuous chain of boiling points.

STANDARD OIL COMPANY
(California)

When you have a home on wheels you save railroad fares and hotel bills

An Auto Home

December 1921

R. C. JOHNSON of San Francisco wanted to see America, but the idea of a three-year pleasure trip with his wife and child in stuffy railroad trains and hotels did not appeal to him as healthful or as a wise expenditure of money. Why not navigate his own course with an auto de luxe on the nutshell plan? He knows automobiles. His friend William Norrington knows how to build whatever goes on wheels. The result is pictured herewith.

The auto home is an interesting example of ingenuity, compact, convenient, practical, equipped for actual housekeeping. It has two sections, one being the driver's compartment, the other containing a dresser, two Pullman-like beds, a mirror, electric fixtures, clothes-presses and many devices for convenience of the occupants. Folding glass doors divide this room from the driver's, which is also the kitchen. The auto home has at least eliminated the servant problem.

Independent of time-tables, selecting their objective points with regard to personal preference only, the occupants of the traveling domicile will enjoy the advantages of an extended tour with the added pleasure of perfect freedom. #

Two beds are operated Pullman-style.
This comfortable
couch serves as a bed at night. An upper berth folds
down from the ceiling

Interesting Westerners:
Mother Curry

By ARTHUR F. AGARD

August 1922

ANY housekeeping woman will contend that the preparation and serving of a dinner for company, with all the detail of planning and timing, is a stunt taxing her talents to the utmost. All domesticated men will agree, without contention, that a spring house-cleaning, even in a three-room flat, is the limit of the strenuous life.

Multiply these small cataclysms and think in terms of eighteen thousand visitors dropping in to a summer camp in a remote region—sometimes twelve hundred in a day, mostly without notice. This is what Mrs. Jennie Curry looks forward to in the spring and lives through in the summer; and because she accomplishes it with grace is the reason why she is esteemed as a superwoman in the Department of the Interior and in all the National Park Service of the United States. She is a pioneer in the practical work of making the parks known to hundreds of thousands of people as their own intimate possession.

When David Curry died in 1917, lovers of the great spaces of the Sierra and all Californians who knew him felt as though a robust Sequoia Gigantea had fallen. Something big and hearty and wholesome, intensely virile, measuring in its human way with the walls and forest stretches of the Yosemite, had gone. People wondered what would happen to the Yosemite hostelry, because Mr. and Mrs. David Curry had built up a great public utility in the real sense of the term—Camp Curry in the Yosemite Valley. There are complex business systems that can go on almost of themselves after the initial impetus has been given and perfect organization has been effected, but a summer camp to make a home for thousands of people in a valley which is snow-covered in winter and at all times inaccessible

by railroad is scarcely self-continuing. The yearly miracle must be accomplished of erecting tents while the Valley is yet powdered with snow or dripping in the spring thaw, of securing endless supplies of food and household equipment, of persuading leisurely railroads and stages to deliver them, of hiring responsible help and, finally, making everything seem as fresh as if it had always been there, just waiting for the chance guest.

In 1892, when Mr. and Mrs. Curry wished to explore the Yellowstone, they found that their salaries as school teachers in Utah did not permit of journeyings, so they harnessed the horses, took a few friends and went gypsying and each year more people went with them. Two years later they made a trip to California and were eager to see the Yosemite, for both the Currys were enthusiastic geologists and nature lovers, but hotel rates were impossible for them. So in 1899, after they had settled in California, when the Yosemite was still a journey of a day and a half by stage from the nearest railroad, they harnessed the horses and moved to the Valley, put up seven tents, and by the end of the season were amazed that two hundred and ninety guests had found that inexpensive simple democracy with Mr. and Mrs. Curry was the solution for the problem of Yosemite.

"I did a little of everything, one time or another," she says. "I have made soap and I have put up the tents. I've been baker and head waitress, postmistress and pantry woman. I've put up lunches and looked out for the babies and it didn't hurt my pride, any of it."

It is nearly a quarter of a century from the seven tents in 1899 to the six hundred and twenty-seven tents, thirty cottages, the warehouse and pavilion, swimming-pool, laundry and clubhouses of 1922, but through all the years the directing intelligence, the personal force that have made the camp known the world over have been Mrs. Curry's in large measure. Hers also the risk and the high courage, for each year the entire profits have been invested in camp equipment.

The guests see a little woman with white hair, eyes large and blue, a slender and active figure clad in soft grays or lavender. The last loiterer at the campfire sees her at work with endless correspondence; the morning hiker sees her superintending the six o'clock breakfast. Mrs. Curry has never had the leisure to grow old. She possesses the knack of being everywhere at all times through the day. When anything needs deciding or adjusting, somehow she is on hand with the best solution.

They all come to her: officials of the Valley for conference; stage drivers seeking a word of authority; the autoist who couldn't do the Sierras on high and who wants his carburetor adjusted immediately; the tent-girl who has misplaced two towels; poor people who haven't money enough to stay the desired day longer; the geologist who seeks a terminal moraine; the hiker who has lost her camera on the trail and wants to borrow cold cream; the teacher collecting flowers for the school herbarium; the soprano who wishes to entertain with "The Rosary;" the man who insists on a tent to himself when hundreds are being turned away; the lady who dislikes cornmeal in her muffin; the baker whose supplies have not arrived; the waitress who has bad news from home; the man who doesn't approve of governmental policies in the parks; the youth and the maid whose eyes are a little dazzled by moonlight shining in lonesome and lovely places. For each, Mrs. Curry has a swift unerring answer of gentle reasonableness, and the questioner goes away feeling that he is to be commended for bringing the matter to light and that this is the best of all worlds. They all think of her as Mother Curry because they hear the college boys and girls who work about Camp call her Mother Curry. To them she is the mother of two universities. Employes, almost without exception students from Stanford or California, have made her such—not in any official capacity but as the maternal adviser of thousands whom she has helped to work a way through college. Family wealth or poverty, fraternities, social honors count for nothing in the good democracy of service in this summer camp. From her they get understanding, friendship, incentive, and they feel with her the joy and dignity and comradeship of labor. The interval when the college youths went to the army or hospitals was a time of trial in getting employes but boys and girls from the high schools gave willing help. Now the high schools have little groups who look to Mrs. Curry as Mother.

To be the clear-headed and forceful executive of a complex business organization, to be a good mother to her own family, a faithful church member and the most efficient worker in camp, whether at packing lunches or transacting business with the Department of the Interior—to be Mother to thousands of young men and women!

How does she do it? #

The Maybeck
One-Room House

By MIRA ABBOTT MACLAY

July 1923

TO smooth a few wrinkles out of the complexity of modern life, Bernard Maybeck of Berkeley, California, creator of the San Francisco Palace of Fine Arts and internationally known architect, has come forward with a scheme for a one-room house.

The Maybeck plan in a nutshell is a scheme to incorporate the house and garden into one home entity, concentrating the expense of the house, measured in terms of time and effort as well as money, upon one large, beautiful living-room, supplemented by several utility rooms, so small and insignificant as far as space goes that they do not justify the name of room. They are merely alcoves or additions. Dressing-rooms, bath and kitchen come under this head.

The architect who designed the famous Palace of Fine Arts in San Francisco is using his genius to simplify yet beautify the important art of creating small houses. Here is an example, a one-room studio home with mezzanine floor

There is no rigidity about the Maybeck scheme but a most delightful flexibility and freedom. The home, Maybeck has always maintained, should be an individual expression, and the one-room house gives as great scope for personal tastes and preferences as a six-room bungalow or a millionaire's villa.

Any material—wood, concrete, plaster, brick—may be used to develop it. Almost any period or type of architecture may be bent to its requirements. It follows that the cost is equally elastic.

The large main room may be of any size or proportions, almost any shape the owner desires, for there is no need of a room forever conforming to the rectangular or square. This room may be furnished in any desired style, period-Colonial, Mission, Louis the some steenth or other, Italian—it does not matter. But concentrating the main furniture expense upon one room permits of its furnishings being better and more beautiful.

Wall beds, which like the old Dutch beds may be so beautifully carved as to become real works of art, are to be built into the main room. They should be so constructed as to open either inside or outside the room, thus providing for out-door or in-door sleeping, according to weather conditions or the fancy of the sleeper. Wardrobe space can be contrived at the end of these beds, while closets off the individual dressing-rooms will take care of further needs along this line.

A mezzanine floor can be successfully introduced when desired. The children's beds can be arranged here and such a floor gives admirable space for individual workshops. The housewife can be provided with a cabinet that tidily encloses her prosaic sewing-machine when not in use and gives a place for her sewing materials. The equally unpoetical typewriter and materials for writing or drawing can be disposed of in a similar manner. Lacking a mezzanine floor, cabinet spaces for these purposes can be arranged on the main floor.

The kitchen, which Maybeck dubs the "stomach of the house," can be arranged in an alcove. It should be equipped with the best labor-saving devices, for the one-room house is servantless and the place of the "hired girl" can to a large extent be taken by electrically-operated mechanisms. An electric stove of the type that destroys automatically all cooking fumes, an electric dishwasher, washing-machine and compact cabineting complete its conveniences. The sink, a necessity, should be so arranged that dishes can be washed and vegetables peeled from either indoors or out-doors. A French door properly provided will contrive this and give the housewife the op-portunity of spending health-building hours out of doors that are usually spent on the cold north side indoors.

A fireplace, the "soul of the house," Maybeck claims, should never be omitted. Ad-ditional heat may be required. A furnace will give this, or even a heating stove that can be tucked away out of sight in the kitchen alcove.

The table for dining can form part of the living-room furnishing. It may be rolled to the entrance of the kitchen alcove for setting, then either rolled out of doors, through the French door by the sink, for out-door dining when the weather is fine, or be pushed back into the living-room for that cosiest of meals by the fireplace.

A store-room, an expansion of the garage, is an integral part of the scheme. This room is to be supplied with lockers of an inexpensive variety, bins, cabineting a-plenty. Such a room will absorb and neatly take care of the overflow of the house in every direction. Surplus supplies of all sorts, extra clothing, even or-naments, pictures and objects of art, can be kept here in an orderly manner and taken into the house when needed.

Many doors are recommended by Maybeck as another essential. They bring the warmth, fragrance and vitality of the out-of-doors into the house and weld the house and garden into a unity in the most effective manner. The garden should be planted in harmony with the house and Maybeck advocates a hedge surrounding both house and garden, making for privacy and completing the home unit.

"The children of this house" he says, "will scarcely know the inside from the garden without. It will all be home." #

Do You Give the Tramp a Ride?

By An Open-road Hobo

May 1925

NINETEEN out of every twenty auto-mobiles on the highways leave the tramp tramping—the twentieth car gives him a lift. I know for I have done a lot of tramping.

Some drivers never stop, some always stop, others stop sometimes. If the one in twenty should suddenly stop stopping, the highway borders would return to their pristine glory of dandelions, tin cans and cracker boxes undebased by the plebian heels of the indolent.

But that twentieth car will stop, so there are the tramps.

By choice and practise I am an expert ride moocher. Is it the thrill of adventure that leads me on? There may be a thrill or so but the real reason is the same as that which caused the chicken to cross the road. I mooch rides to get somewhere.

You who drive along the highways will do well to use discretion in taking strangers into your cars, for some of my companions of the open road are worthy of the slang title "hard boiled." For your guidance I have written a few useful hints:

1. Never pick up more than one man at a time unless your party is the stronger. But do not be afraid of picking up a dozen, one at a time. Murder, arson, robbery or mayhem plots are not concocted on the spur of the moment between strangers. Your second guest is a pro-tection against the first.

2. Never pick up a man in overalls and jumper with the sleeves and legs turned up several inches. This means the garments are bought large to cover other clothes. The other clothes may be full dress or a prison uniform. The average honest hobo does not own two suits. If he has overalls, he has the proper size.

3. Never put a heavy force of the enemy in the back seat behind you and drive down a lonely road. Why invite attack?

4. Never pick up a stranger on a country road after dark. You may lose your money,

your car and your life.

And now—perish the thought—you may, some day, be down but not out, and find yourself walking along the highway. Here are a few rules to aid you in such an emergency:

1. Dress as well as possible. No driver will pick up a man who inspires either fear or disgust; shabby clothes inspire both.

2. Put yourself where it is convenient for the driver to stop. No driver will stop from a 50 mile speed for your sake. Linger near the sharp corners, poor pieces of road, road intersections or filling stations, but do not stop walking.

3. Always keep on walking. When you stand or sit you become a native of the district and

lose your identity as a tramp. I have never known of a tramp being picked off of a fence by a kindly autoist.

4. Never ask or signal for a ride. Despite many authorities to the contrary, you get more rides by not asking, as the average driver prefers to pick out his own objects of charity. You can take it for granted the autoist suspects you want a ride.

5. Always travel alone. The one driver, your best chance, prefers to have an even break, at least.

Follow these rules and you will get rides—on Sunday from one car in 150; on Monday morning from one car in ten when traveling men are scurrying about to get to their fields. On other days the ratio is one out of twenty. The statistics are my own.

The low Sunday average is due to the fact that many family parties are out for the day. The average American family, from appearances, is always just large enough to fill the family car.

I have never been offered a ride in a car driven by a chauffeur, and seldom in a car which indicated either extreme wealth or hopes toward aristocracy.

Outside of traveling men, the bulk of rides are offered by laboring men or the moderately well to do.

If a tramp picks his rides properly, he can go long distances without change. I have frequently made it from Seattle to Portland, or from San Francisco to Los Angeles in a single free ride and in a single day. That, you will admit, is traveling.

I consider it part of the bargain to be either talker or listener as my host wishes, so that is why I like traveling men. They like to talk, thus forcing me into a passive part.

And traveling men, I have found, do not tell snappy stories—at least not to tramps. As a rule they talk about their homes, or politics or the news of the day.

There are good souls to whom it is a shock that a plain hobo can talk and understand English. They expect a tramp jargon, and bless their hearts, I give it to them, with frills which lose nothing in being spontaneous and entirely original. There is no such thing as a tramp dialect, but nevertheless, almost any honest tramp will talk one for you, if he sees a chance for profits ahead. #

A New 4-Passenger Coupe

This car is Dodge Brothers response to a definite demand—

A high grade coupe of moderate weight and size that will seat four adult passengers in genuine comfort.

The body is an admirable example of fine coach building. Low, graceful, smartly upholstered and attractively finished in Dodge Brothers blue, it reflects dignity and distinction in every line.

Above all, the 4-passenger coupe is characteristically a Dodge Brothers product. It possesses all the attributes of construction and low cost service for which more than a million Dodge Brothers Motor Cars are favorably known throughout the world.

The price is $1375 f. o. b. Detroit

DODGE BROTHERS

Make the world's grandest "Hole-in-One" on your Hawaiian Holiday!

FOREVER after, you'll laugh at the puny "mental hazards" on your course at home. *You've* sailed a ball in a perfect drive—out, and down, and down, till it was swallowed in Kilauea Volcano's fuming throat. You've made the world's grandest Hole-in-One. Scorch your scorecard at a smoking crevice nearby to prove it!

Each year thousands view the awesome grandeur of Kilauea in perfect safety. And *every* day in Hawaii is filled with experiences as strange—shopping for brasses and South Sea treasures in quaint Oriental bazaars; trips in a native sampan to troll for fighting tuna, swordfish and *ulua*; golf on Hawaii's dozen scenic courses; surf-boarding, swimming, outrigger-canoeing 365 days in the year; visiting colorful canyons, extinct craters, secluded tropical beaches on the idyllic islands of Kauai, Oahu, Maui and Hawaii.

About you are all the luxurious comforts of modern travel. Ten million dollars have been newly spent for additional steamship and hotel facilities. Yet the emerald surf of Waikiki breaks in the sunlight just as it did when Stevenson dreamed on this very beach—and at night, when the moon rises above the palms and *hau* trees, the native boys sing the same slow-cadenced Hawaiian melodies that he loved.

Easy to Go—and Inexpensive

Ocean liners from Los Angeles, San Francisco, Seattle or Vancouver will carry you to far-off exotic Hawaii in the same time it would take just to cross the Atlantic. Come by one route—return by another—enjoy the scenic Pacific Coast as a part of your trip.

Your local railroad, steamship or tourist agent will book you direct from home, without passports or formalities. He can tell you what a travel bargain it is—four thousand miles, in all, of delightful sailing on the sunny Pacific, first class steamer fares both ways, two weeks at Hawaii's world-famed hotels, inter-island trips and sightseeing—and the cost need be no more than $400.

Plan for it now. See your nearest ticket agency—and today, while you think of it, send this coupon for "The Story of Hawaii," a 24-page illustrated booklet in colors, and a copy of "Tourfax".

Hawaii
The World's Island Playground

*She wasn't exactly beautiful, but if you were
alone with her you kept looking at her,
and you wished she didn't belong
to a man you were afraid of.*

Ber-Bulu

By Dashiell Hammett

March 1925

SAY it happened on one of the Tawi Tawis.
That would make Jeffol a Moro. It doesn't
really matter what he was. If he had been a
Maya or a Ghurka he would have laid
Levison's arm open with a machete or a kukri
instead of a kris, but that would have made no
difference in the end. Dinihari's race matters as
little. She was woman, complaisant woman, of
the sort whose no always becomes yes between
throat and teeth. You can find her in Nome, in
Cape Town, and in Durham, and in skin of any
shade; but, since the Tawi Tawis are the lower
end of the Sulu Archipelago, she was brown
this time.

She was a sleek brown woman with the
knack of twisting a sarong around her hips so
that it became part of her—a trick a woman has
with a potato sack or hasn't with Japanese
brocade. She was small and trimly fleshed, with
proper pride in her flesh. She wasn't exactly
beautiful, but if you were alone with her you
kept looking at her, and you wished she didn't
belong to a man you were afraid of. That was
when she was Levison's.

She was Jeffol's first. I don't know where he
got her. Her dialect wasn't that of the village,
but you couldn't tell from that. There are any
number of dialects down there—jumbles of

Malay, Tagalog, Portuguese, and what not. Her sarong was a gold-threaded *kain sungkit,* so no doubt he brought her over from Borneo. He was likely to return from a fishing trip with anything—except fish.

Jeffol was a good Moro—a good companion in a fight or across a table. Tall for a Moro, nearly as tall as I am, he had a deceptive slimness that left you unprepared for the power in his snake-smooth muscles. His face was cheerful, intelligent and almost handsome, and he carried himself with a swagger. His hands went easily to the knives at his waist, and against his hide—sleeping or waking—he wore a sleeveless fighting-jacket with verses from the Koran on it. The jacket was his most prized possession, next to his *anting-anting.*

His elder brother was datto, as their father had been, but this brother had inherited little of either his father's authority or his father's taste for deviltry. The first had been diluted by the military government, and Jeffol had got most of the second. He ran as wild and loose as his pirate ancestors, until Langworthy got hold of him.

Langworthy was on the island when I came there. He hadn't had much luck. Mohammedanism suited the Moros, especially in the loose form they practised. There was nothing of the solemn gangling horse-faced missionary about Langworthy. He was round-chested and meaty; he worked with dumb-bells and punching-bag before breakfast in the morning; and he strode round the island with a red face that broke into a grin on the least excuse. He had a way of sticking his chin in the air and grinning over it at you. I didn't like him.

He and I didn't hit it off very well from the first. I had reasons for not telling him where I had come from, and when he found I intended staying a while he got a notion that I wasn't going to do his people—he called them that in spite of the little attention they paid him—any good. Later, he used to send messages to Bangao, complaining that I was corrupting the natives and lowering the prestige of the white man.

That was after I taught them to play blackjack. They gambled whenever they had anything to gamble for, and it was just as well that they should play a game that didn't leave too much to luck. If I hadn't won their money

the Chinese would have, and, anyway, there wasn't enough of it to raise a howl over. As for the white man's prestige—maybe I didn't insist on being *tuaned* with every third word, but neither did I hesitate to knock the brown brothers round whenever they needed it; and that's all there is to this keeping up the white man's prestige at best.

A couple of years earlier—in the late '90s—Langworthy would have had no difficulty in getting rid of me, but since then the government had eased up a bit. I don't know what sort of answers he got to his complaints, but the absence of official action made him all the more determined to chase me off.

"Peters," he would tell me, "You've got to get off the island. You're a bad influence and you've got to go."

"Sure, sure," I would agree, yawning. "But there's no hurry."

We didn't get along together at all, but it was through my blackjack game that he finally made a go of his mission, though he wouldn't be likely to admit it.

Jeffol went broke in the game one night—lost his fortune of forty dollars Mex—and discovered what to his simple mind was the certain cause of his bad luck. His *anting-anting* was gone, his precious luck-bringing collection of the-Lord-knows-what in a stinking little bag was gone from its string round his neck. I tried to buck him up, but he wouldn't listen to reason. His security against all the evils of this world—and whatever other worlds there might be—was gone. Anything could happen to him now—anything bad. He went round the village with his head sagging down until it was in danger of being hit by a knee. In this condition he was ripe fruit for Langworthy, and Langworthy plucked him.

I saw Jeffol converted, although I was too far away to hear the talk that went with it. I was sitting under a cottonwood fixing a pipe. Jeffol had been walking up and down the beach for half an hour or more, his chin on his chest, his feet dragging. The water beyond him was smooth and green under a sky that was getting ready to let down more water. From where I sat, his round turban moved against the green sea like a rolling billiard-ball.

Then Langworthy came up the beach, striding stiff-kneed, as a man strides to a fight he counts on winning. He caught up with Jeffol and said something to which the Moro paid no attention. Jeffol didn't raise his head, just went on walking, though he was polite enough ordinarily. Langworthy fell in step beside him and they made a turn up and down the beach, the white man talking away at a great rate. Jeffol, so far as I could see, made no reply at all.

Facing each other, they suddenly stopped. Langworthy's face was redder than ever and his jaw stuck out. Jeffol was scowling. He said something. Langworthy said something. Jeffol took a step back and his hand went to the ivory hilt of a dris in his belted sarong. He didn't get the kris out. The missionary stepped in and dropped him with a hard left to the belly.

I got up and went away, reminding myself to watch that left hand if Langworthy and I ever tangled. I didn't have to sit through the rest of the performance to know that he had made a convert. There are two things a Moro understands thoroughly and respects without stint—violence and a joke. Knock him round, or get a laugh on him, and you can do what you will with him—and he'll like it. The next time I saw Jeffol he was a Christian.

In spite of the protests of the datto, a few of the Moros followed Jeffol's example, and Langworthy's chest grew an inch. He was wise enough to know that he could make better progress by cracking their heads together than by arguing the finer theological points with them, and after two or three athletic gospel-meetings he had his flock well in hand—for a while.

He lost most of them when he brought up the question of wives. Women were not expensive to keep down there and, although the Moros on that particular island weren't rolling in wealth, nearly all of them could afford a couple of wives, and some were prosperous enough to take on a slave girl or two after they had the four wives their law allowed. Langworthy put his foot down on this. He told his converts they would have to get rid of all except the first wives. And of course all of his converts who had more than one wife promptly went back to Allah—except Jeffol.

He was in earnest, the only idea in his head being to repair the damage done by the loss of his *anting-anting*. He had four wives and two slaves, including Dinihari. He wanted to keep her and let the others go, but the missionary said no. Jeffol's number one wife was his only real wife—thus Langworthy. Jeffol almost bolted then, but the necessity of finding a substitute for his *anting-anting* was strong in him. They compromised. He was to give up his women, go to Bangao for a divorce from his first wife, and then Langworthy would marry him to Dinihari. Meanwhile the girl was turned over to the datto for safe keeping. The datto's wife was a dish-faced shrew who had thus far prevented his taking another wife, so his household was considered a safe harbor for the girl.

Three mornings after Jeffol's departure for Bangao we woke to find Levison among us. He had come in during the night, alone, in a power-yawl piled high with wooden cases.

Levison was a monster, in size and appearance. Six and a half feet high he stood and at a little distance you took him for a man of medium height. There were three hundred pounds of him bulging his clothes if there was an ounce—not counting the hair, which was an item. He was black hair all over. It bushed out from above his low forehead to the nape of his neck, ran over his eyes in a straight thick bar, and sprouted from ears and great beaked nose. Below his half-hidden dark eyes, black hair bearded his face with a ten-inch tangle, furred his body like a bear's, padded his shoulders and arms and legs, and lay in thick patches on fingers and toes.

He hadn't many clothes on when I paddled out to the yawl to get acquainted, and what he had were too small for him. His shirt was split in a dozen places and the sleeves were gone. His pants-legs were torn off at the knees. He looked like a hair-mattress coming apart—only there was nothing limp or loose about the body inside of the hair. He was as agile as an acrobat. This was the first time I had seen him, although I recognized him on sight from what I had heard in Manila the year before. He bore a sweet reputation.

"Hello, Levison," I greeted him as I came alongside. "Welcome to our little paradise."

He scowled down at me, from hat to shoes and back, and then nodded his immense head.

"You are—"

"I'm not," I denied, climbing over the side. "I never heard of the fellow, and I'm innocent of whatever he did. My name is Peters and I'm not even distantly related to any other Peters."

He laughed and produced a bottle of gin.

The village was a double handful of thatched huts set upon piles where the water could wash under them when the tide was in, back in a little cove sheltered by a promontory that pointed toward Celebes. Levison built his house—a large one with three rooms—out near the tip of this point, beside the ruins of the old Spanish block-house. I spent a lot of time out there with him. He was a hard man to get along with, a thoroughly disagreeable companion, but he had gin—real gin and plenty of it—and I was tired of *nipa* and *samshu*. He thought I wasn't afraid of him, and that error made it easier for me to handle him.

There was something queer about this Levison. He was as strong as three men and a vicious brute all the way through, but not with the honest brutality of a strong man. He was like a mean kid who, after being tormented by larger boys, suddenly finds himself among smaller ones. It used to puzzle me. For instance, old Muda stumbled against him once on the path into the jungle. You or I would simply have pushed the clumsy old beggar out of the way, or perhaps, if we happened to be carrying a grouch at the time, knocked him out of the way. Levison picked him up and did something to his legs. Muda had to be carried back to his hut, and he never succeeded in walking after that.

The Moros called Levison the Hairy One (*Ber-Bulu*), and, because he was big and strong and rough, they were afraid of him and admired him tremendously.

It was less than a week after his arrival when he brought Dinihari home with him. I was in his house when they came in.

"Get out, Peters," he said. "This is my dam' honeymoon."

I looked at the girl. She was all dimples and crinkled nose—tickled silly.

"Go easy," I advised the hairy man. "She belongs to Jeffol, and he's a tough lad."

"I know," he sneered through his beard. "I've heard all about him. The hell with him!"

"You're the doctor. Give me a bottle of gin to drink to you with and I'll run along."

I got the gin.

I was with Levison and the girl when Jeffol came back from Bangao. I was sprawled on a divan. On the other side of the room the hairy man was tilted back in a chair, talking. Dinihari sat on the floor at his feet, twisted round to look up into his face with adoring eyes. She was a happy brown girl. Why not? Didn't she have the strongest man on the island—the strongest man in the whole archipelago? And in addition to his strength, wasn't he as hairy as a wanderoo, in a land where men hadn't much hair on face and body?

Then the door whipped open and Jeffol came in. His eyes were red over black. He wasn't at home in Christianity yet, so he cursed Levison with Mohammedan curses. They are good enough up to a certain point, but the climax—usually pig—falls a bit flat on western ears. Jeffol did well. But he would have done better if he had come in with his knives in his hands instead of in his twisted sarong.

The hairy man's chair came down square on its legs and he got across the room—sooner than you would think. Jeffol managed to loosen a kris and ripped one of Levison's arms from elbow to wrist. Then the Moro was through. Levison was too big, too strong, for him—swept him up, cuffed weapons out of hand and sarong, took him by arm and thigh and chucked him out of the door.

Dinihari? Her former lord's body hadn't thudded on the ground below—a nasty drop with the tide out—before she was bending over Levison's hairy arm, kissing the bleeding slit.

Jeffol was laid up for a week with a twisted shoulder and bruised back. I dropped in to see him once, but he wasn't very cordial. He seemed to think I should have done something. His mother—old toothless Ca'bi—chased me out as soon as she saw me, so my visit didn't last long. She was a proper old witch.

The village buzzed for a day or two, but nothing happened. If Jeffol hadn't gone Christian there might have been trouble; but most of the Moros held his desertion of the faith against him, and looked on the loss of Dinihari as just punishment. Those who were still Christians were too tame a lot to help Jeffol. His brother the datto washed his hands of the affair, which was just as well, since he couldn't have done anything anyway. He wasn't any too fond of Jeffol—had always been a bit envious of him

*Levison was a monster in size and appearance. Six and a half feet he stood; there were three
hundred pounds of him not counting the hair, which was an item. He was black hair all over.
Below his half-hidden eyes, black hair bearded his face in a ten-inch tangle and furred
his body like a bear's. The Colt in Jeffol's hand was too large
and too steady for even a monster like Levison to jump at.
Dinihari was the only one of us who moved.*

—and he decided that in giving up the girl at the missionary's request, Jeffol had surrendered ownership, and that she could stay with Levison if she wished. Apparently she did so wish.

Langworthy went to see Levison. I heard of it a few minutes later and paddled like mad out to the house. If the missionary was going to be smeared up I wanted to see it. I didn't like the man. But I was too late. He came out just as I got there, and he limped a little. I never found out what happened. I asked Levison, but if he had done all the things he told me the missionary wouldn't have left standing up. The house wasn't upset, and Levison didn't have any marks that showed through his hair, so it couldn't have been much of a row.

Jeffol's faith in Christianity as a substitute for an *anting-anting* must have been weakened by this new misfortune, but Langworthy succeeded in holding him, though he had to work night and day to do it. They were together all of the time—Langworthy usually talking, Jeffol sulking.

"Jeffol's up and about," I told Levison one day. "Better watch your step. He's shifty, and he's got good pirate blood in him."

"Pirate blood be damned!" said Levison. "He's a nigger and I can handle a dozen of him."

I let it go at that.

Those were good days in the house out on the point. The girl was a brown lump of happiness. She worshipped her big hair-matted beast of a man, made a god of him. She'd look at him for hour after hour with black eyes that had hallelujahs in them. If he was asleep when I went out there, she'd use the word *beradu* when she told me so—a word supposed to be sacred to the sleep of royalty.

Levison, swept up in this adoration that was larger than he, became almost mellow for days at a time; and even when he relapsed into normal viciousness now and then he was no crueler to her than a Moro would have been. And there were times when he became almost what she thought of him. I remember one night: We were all three fairly drunk—Levison and I on gin, the girl, drunker than either of us, on love. She had reached up and buried her brown fists in his beard, a trick she was fond of.

"Hold on!" he cried, kicking his chair away and standing up.

He reared up his head, lifting her from the floor, and spun round, whirling her through the air like a kid swinging on a May-pole. Silly, maybe. But in the yellow lamplight, his beaked nose and laughing red mouth above the black beard to which her fists clung, her smooth brown body slanting through the air in a ripple of gay waist and sarong, there was a wild magnificence to them. He was a real giant that moment.

But it's hard for me to remember him that way: my last picture of him is the one that sticks. I got it the night of Jeffol's second call.

He came in late, popping through the door with a brand-new service Colt in one hand and a kris in the other. At his heels trotted old Ca'bi, his mother, followed by broken-nosed Jokanain and a mean little runt named Unga. The old woman carried a bundle of something tied up in nipa leaves, Jokanain swung a heavy *barong*, and Unga held an ancient blunderbuss.

I started up from where I was sitting cross-legged on the floor.

Unga centered the blunderbuss on me.

"Diam dudok!"

I sat still. Blunderbusses are wicked, and Unga had lost twelve dollars Mex to me three nights before.

Levison had jerked to his feet, and then he stopped. The Colt in Jeffol's hand was too large and too steady for even a monster like Levison to jump at. Dinihari was the only one of us who moved. She flung herself between Jeffol and Levison, but the Moro swept her out of the way with his left arm, swept her over into a corner without taking eyes or gun from the hairy man.

Old Ca'bi hobbled across the floor and peeped into each of the other rooms.

"Mari," she croaked from the sleepingroom door.

Step by step Jeffol drove Levison across the room and through that door, Ca'bi going in with them. The door closed and Unga, holding me with the gun, put his back against it.

Dinihari sprang up and dashed toward him. Jokanain caught her from behind and flung her into her corner again. Beyond the door Levison roared out oaths. Ca'bi's voice cackled excitedly in answering oaths, and in orders to her son. Bind (*ikat*) and naked (*telanjang*) were the only words I could pick out of the din. Then Levison's voice choked off into silence, and no sound at all came from the sleeping-room.

In our room there was no motion. Dinihari sat still in her corner, staring at her feet. Unga and Jokanain were two ugly statues against two doors. The chatter of flying foxes busy among the cottonwoods and the rustling of thatch in a breeze heavy with the stink of drying *tripang* were the only things you could hear.

I had a dull, end-of-the-road feeling. A Moro is a simple son of nature. When he finds himself so placed that he can kill, he usually kills. Otherwise, it runs in his head, of what use is the power? It's a sort of instinct for economy. I suspected that Levison, gagged, was being cut, in the Moro fashion, into very small bits; and, while my death might be less elaborate, I didn't doubt that it too was on the cards. You don't last long among the Moros once you let them get the bulge on you. If not tonight, some young buck will cut you down tomorrow night, just because he knows he can do it.

Half an hour or more went by slower than you would think it could. My nerves began bothering me: fear taking the form of anger at the suspended activity of the trap I was in; impatience to see the end and get it over with.

I had a gun under my shirt. If I could snake it out and pot Unga, then I had a chance of shooting it out with Jeffol and Jokanain. If I wasn't fast enough, Unga would turn loose the blunderbuss and blow me and the wall behind me out into the Celebes Sea, all mixed up so you couldn't say which was which. But even that was better than passing out without trying to take anybody with me.

However, there was still gin in the bottle beside me, and it would make the going easier if I could get it in me. I experimented with a slowly reaching hand. Unga said nothing, so I picked up the bottle and took a long drink, leaving one more in it—a stirrup cup, you might say. As I took the bottle down from my mouth, feet pattered in the next room, and old Ca'bi came squeezing out of the door, her mouth spread from ear to ear in a she-devil's grin.

"*Panggil orang-orang,*" she ordered Jokanain, and he went out.

I put the last of the gin down my throat. If I

were going to move, it would have to be before the rest of the village got here. I set the empty bottle down and scratched my chin, which brought my right hand within striking distance of my gun.

Then Levison bellowed out like a bull gone mad—a bellow that rattled the floor-timbers in their rattan lashings. Jeffol, without his Colt, came tumbling backward through the door, upsetting Unga. The blunderbuss exploded, blowing the roof wide open. In the confusion I got my gun out—and almost dropped it.

Levison stood in the doorway—but my God!

He was as big as ever—they hadn't whittled any of him away—but he was naked, and without a hair on him anywhere. His skin, where it wasn't blue with ropemarks, was baby-pink and chafed. They had shaved him clean.

My gaze went up to his head, and I got another shock. Every hair had been scraped off or plucked out, even to his eyebrows, and his naked head sat upon his immense body like a pimple. There wasn't a quart of it. There was just enough to hold his big beaked nose and his ears, which stood out like palm leaves now that they weren't supported by hair. Below his loose mouth, his chin was nothing but a sloping down into his burly throat, and the damned thing trembled like a hurt baby's. His eyes, not shadowed now by shaggy brows, were weak and poppy. A gorilla with a mouse's head wouldn't have looked any funnier than Levison without his hair; and the anger that purpled him made him look sillier still. No wonder he had hidden himself behind whiskers!

Dinihari was the first to laugh—a rippling peal of pure amusement. Then I laughed, and Unga and Jeffol. But it wasn't our laughter that beat Levison. We could only have goaded him into killing us. Old Ca'bi turned the trick. The laughter of an old woman is a thing to say prayers against, and Ca'bi was very old.

She pointed a finger at Levison and screeched over it with a glee that was hellish. Her shriveled gums writhed in her open mouth, as if convulsed with mirth of their own, her scrawny throat swelled and she hopped up and down on her bony feet. Levison forgot the rest of us, turned toward her, and stopped. Her thin body shuddered in frenzies of derision, and her voice laughed as sane people don't. You could almost see it—metal lashes of laughter that coiled round his naked body, cut him into raw strips, paralyzed his muscles.

His big body became limp, and he pawed his face with a hand that jerked away as if the touch of the beardless face had burnt it. His knees wobbled, moisture came into his eyes, and his tiny chin quivered. Ca'bi swayed from side to side and hooted at him—a hag gone mad with derision. He backed away from her, cringing back from her laughter like a dog from a whip. She followed him up—laughed him through the sleeping-room door, laughed him back to the far side of the sleeping-room, laughed him through the thin wall. A noise of ripping as he went through the thatch, and a splash of water.

Dinihari stopped laughing and wiped her wet face with her sleeve. Her eyes were soft under Jeffol's cold gaze.

"Your slave (*patek*) rejoices," she cooed, "that her master has recovered his *anting-anting* and is strong again."

"Not so," Jeffol said, and he unbent a little, because she was a woman to want, and because a Moro loves a violent joke. "But there is much in the book of the Christian (*neserani kitab*). There is a tale the missionary (*tuan padri*) told me of a hairy one named Sansão, who was strong against his enemies until shorn of his hair. Many other magics (*tangkal*) are in the book for all occasions."

So that damned Langworthy was at the bottom of it!

I never saw him again. That night I left the island in Levison's yawl with the pick of his goods. He was gone, I knew, even if not in one of the sharks that played round the point. His house would be looted before morning, and I had more right to his stuff than the Moros. Hadn't I been his friend? #

Driving Home at Night

By MEDORA V. PETRIE

October 1921

Swift as we fled along the road, the twilight followed faster,
   It veiled the sky and foothills with its dusky, silver smoke.
The painted rose and gold were gone; the artist sun, their master,
   Had sunk behind the mountains and the far small stars awoke.

Our headlights' flaming pencils went to meet the moon before us,
   And now and then the raucous horn spat out a blurted word,
But soothing all the stillness with a whispered, chanting chorus
   Of perfect parts at work within, the eager motor purred.

Now hushed at widely circling curves where gravel drummed the fender,
   Now singing up across the hills, or checked and throbbing slow,
When golden eyes of homing cars we met and passed, would render
   The roadway all uncertain with their sudden, stabbing glow.

So held entranced in motion's spell upon a magic highway,
   Through velvet-fingered darkness of the summer night we sped,
Until remembered palm-trees beckoned down a shadowed byway,
   And through its depths we saw the little lights of home ahead.

Conserving the Covered Wagon

By ALDO LEOPOLD

March 1925

ONE evening I was talking to a settler in one of those irrigated valleys that stretch like a green ribbon across the colorful wastes of southern Arizona. He was showing me his farm, and he was proud of it. Broad acres of alfalfa bloom, fields of ripening grain, and a dip and a sweep of laden orchards redolent of milk and honey, all created with the labor of his own hands. Over in one corner I noticed a little patch of the original desert, an island of sandy hillocks, sprawling mesquite trees, with a giant cactus stark against the sky, and musical with the sunset whistle of quail. "Why don't you clear and level that too, and complete your farm?" I asked, secretly fearing he intended to do so.

"Oh, that's for my boys—a sample of what I made the farm out of," he replied quietly. There was no further explanation. I might comprehend his idea, or think him a fool, as I chose.

I chose to think him a very wise man—wise beyond his kind and his generation. That little patch of untamed desert enormously increased the significance of his achievement, and conversely, his achievement enormously increased the significance of the little patch. He was handing down to his sons not only a piece of real estate, but a Romance written upon the oldest of all books, the land. The Romance of The March of Empire.

It set me to thinking. Our fathers set great store by this Winning of the West, but what do we know about it? Many of us have never seen what it was won from. And how much less will the next generation know? If we think we are going to learn by cruising round the mountains in a Ford, we are largely deceiving ourselves. There is a vast difference between the days of the "Free Tourist Campground—Wood and Water Furnished," and Covered Wagon Days.

"We pitched our tents where the buffalo feed,
Unheard of streams were our flagons;
And we sowed our sons like the apple seed
In the trail of the prairie wagons."

Yes—sowed them so thick that tens of thousands are killed each year trying to keep out of the way of each other's motors. Is this thickness necessarily a blessing to the sons? Perhaps. But not an unmixed blessing. For those who are so inclined, we might at least preserve a sample of the Covered Wagon Life. For after all, the measure of civilization is in its contrasts. A modern city is a national asset, not because the citizen has planted his iron heel on the breast of nature, but because of the different kinds of man his control over nature has enabled him to be. Saturday morning he stands like a god, directing the wheels of industry that have dominion over the earth. Saturday afternoon he is playing golf on a kindly greensward. Saturday evening he may till a homely garden or he may turn a button and direct the mysteries of the firmament to bring him the words and songs and deeds of all the nations. And if, once in a while, he has the opportunity to flee the city, throw a diamond hitch upon a packmule, and disappear into the wilderness of the Covered Wagon Days, he is just that much more civilized than he would be without the opportunity. It makes him one more kind of a man—a pioneer.

We do not realize how many Americans have an instinctive craving for the wilderness life, or how valuable to the Nation has been their opportunity of exercising that instinct, because up to this time the opportunity has been automatically supplied. Little patches of Covered Wagon wilderness have persisted at the very doors of our cities. But now these little patches are being wiped out at a rate which takes one's breath away. And the thing that is wiping them out is the motor car and the motor highway. It is of these, their uses and their abuses, that I would speak.

Motor cars and highways are of course the very instruments which have restored to millions of city dwellers their contact with the land and with nature. For this reason and to this extent they are a benefaction to mankind. But even a benefaction can be carried too far. It was one of Shakespeare's characters who said:

"For Virtue, grown into a pleurisy
  Dies of its own too-much."

To my mind the Good Roads Movement has become a Good Roads Mania; it has grown into a pleurisy. We are building good roads to give the rancher access to the city, which is good, and to give the city dweller access to recreation in the forests and mountains, which is good, but we now, out of sheer momentum, are thrusting more and ever more roads into every little remaining patch of wilderness, which in many cases is sheer stupidity. For by so doing we are cutting off, irrevocably and forever, our national contact with the Covered Wagon days.

Pick up any outdoor magazine and the chances are that on the first page you will find an article describing the adventures of some well-to-do sportsman who has been to Alaska, or British Columbia, or Africa, or Siberia in search of wilderness and the life and hardy sports that go with it. He has pushed to the Back of Beyond, and he tells of it with infinite zest. It has been his Big Adventure. Why? Because he brought home the tusk of an elephant or the hide of a brown bear? No, fundamentally no. Rather because he has proved himself to be still another kind of man than his friends gave him credit for. He has been, if only for one fleeting month, a pioneer, and met the test. He has justified the Blood of the Conquerors.

But have these well-to-do travelers in foreign wilds a monopoly on the Covered Wagon blood? Here is the point of the whole matter. They have not. In every village and in every city suburb and in every skyscraper are dozens of the self-same blood. But they lack the opportunity. It is the opportunity, not the desire, on which the well-to-do are coming to have a monopoly. And the reason is the gradually increasing destruction of the nearby wilderness by good roads. The American of moderate means can not go to Alaska, or Africa, or British Columbia. He must seek his big adventure in the nearby wilderness, or go without it.

Ten years ago, for instance, there were five big regions in the National Forests of Arizona and New Mexico where the Covered Wagon blood could disport at will. In any one of them a man could pack up a mule and disappear into the tall uncut for a month without ever crossing his back track. Today there is just one of the five left. The Forest Service, the largest custodian of land in either State, has naturally and rightly joined with the good roads movement, and today has built or is helping to build good roads right through the vitals of four of these five big regions. As wilderness, they are gone, and gone forever. So far so good. But shall the Forest Service now do the same with the fifth and the last?

Round this last little remnant of the original Southwest lies an economic empire without any wilderness playground or the faintest chance of acquiring one. Texas, Oklahoma, and the rich valleys and mines of Arizona and New Mexico already support millions of Americans. The high mountains of the National Forests are their natural and necessary recreation grounds. The greater part of these mountain areas is already irrevocably dedicated to the motorized forms of recreation. Is it unreasonable or visionary to ask the Forest Service to preserve the one remaining portion of unmotorized wilderness for those who prefer that sort of place?

Would it be unreasonable or visionary to ask the Government to set aside similar remnants of wilderness here and there throughout the National Forests and National Parks? Say one such area, if possible, in each State?

As a matter of fact, the officials of the Forest Service are already seriously considering doing just that. Colonel William B. Greeley, Chief Forester, in addressing a meeting of the American Game Protective Association, put it this way:

"We all recognize what the forest background of the United States has meant to this country—how it has given stamina and resourcefulness and mental and physical vigor to every oncoming generation of Americans. We must preserve something of that forest background for the future. It seems to me that in the National Forests, while we are building roads, as we must; while we are developing areas for the utilization of timber, as we must; while we are opening up extensive regions for the camper, the summer vacationist, and the masses of people who have the God-given right to enjoy these areas—we should keep here and there as part of the picture some bit of wilderness frontier, some hinterland of mountain and upland lake that the roads and automobiles will have to pass by.

"The law laid down for the guidance of the Forest Service was that these public properties must be administered for the greatest good of the greatest number in the long run. When Secretary Wilson laid down that rule, probably he was thinking more of timber and water and forage than anything else, but today the same rule applies just as clearly as it did in the time of Roosevelt in 1905. I think we can all agree that the greatest good of the greatest number of American citizens in the long run does require that in their own National Forests there should be preserved some bits of unspoiled wilderness where the young America of the future can take to the outdoors in the right way."

But let no man think that because a few foresters have tentatively formulated a wilderness policy, that the preservation of a system of wilderness remnants is assured in the National Forests. Do not forget that the good roads mania, and all forms of unthinking Boosterism that go with it, constitute a steam roller the like of which has seldom been seen in the history of mankind. No steam roller can overwhelm a good idea or a righteous policy, but it might very readily flatten out, one by one, the remaining opportunities for applying this particular policy. After these remnants are gone, a correct wilderness policy would be useless.

What I mean is this: The Forest Service will naturally select for wilderness playgrounds the roughest areas and those poorest from the economic standpoint. But it will be physically impossible to find any area which does not embrace some economic values. Sooner or later some private interest will wish to develop these values, at which time those who are thinking in terms of the national development in the broad sense and those who are thinking of local development in the narrow sense will come to grips. And forthwith the private interests will invoke the aid of the steam roller. They always do. And unless the wilderness idea represents the mandate of an organized, fighting and voting body of far-seeing Americans, the steam roller will win.

At the present moment, the most needed move is to secure recognition of the need for a Wilderness Area Policy from the National Conference on Outdoor Recreation, set up by President Coolidge for the express purpose of coordinating the many conflicting recreational interests which have arisen in recent years. If the spirit of the Covered Wagon really persists, as I firmly believe it does, its devotees must speak now, or forever hold their peace. #

How Long Will Our Gasoline Supplies Last?

August 1922

TWO years ago this summer gasoline on the Pacific Coast was doled out by the spoonful. Hundreds of cars were stranded now and then for lack of fuel in certain localities and long discussions of the impending oil famine filled the papers.

Less than a year after the famine certain oil producers asked for a stiff duty on imported crude oil in order to protect them against the "ruinous foreign competition" of the Mexican oil fields. The market was glutted with oil.

Now the demand for oil, crude and refined, is picking up again. But there won't be a famine. Many wells in every Western field are still shut in, stocks are large and the distribution system has been improved. Henry's output has no terror for the oil industry. If one source of supply is exhausted a new one is opened up. Ten years ago, for instance, not a drop of "casing-head" gasoline reached the market. This fuel is produced by wringing it out of natural gas through compression or by absorption. In 1921 the output of this natural-gas gasoline, reached nearly half a billion gallons, enough to keep all the ten million automobiles moving at their average rate for nearly six weeks.

We'll exhaust our present oil supplies by-and-by. That's as certain as the continuance of the income tax. But there will be new though more expensive sources, among which the oil-shale deposits of the Far West will play the leading role twenty or thirty years hence. #

My Radio

By WALTER ANDREWS

January 1926

IN the beginning, let me frankly confess that I am not a radio expert. I know little about hook-ups, wave-traps or grids. I wouldn't know a variometer if I met it on the street. Electrons and amperes do not move in my social circle.

Some months ago I bought a crystal set to please the boy. It worked, and I became mildly interested in listening through the earphones to the more or less faint music that came from local broadcasting stations. Soon I bought a two-tube set, largely because of my curiosity to see "what it would do." It did it; but in a week I traded it for a four-tube set—to see if I couldn't hear John Wanamaker's pipe organ in the city I came from—Philadelphia. In this desire I was disappointed, though I did hear a pipe organ in San Francisco and an orchestra in Chicago. In two more weeks I traded again, this time for a powerful five-tube neutrodyne set warranted to get anything "within reason." Evidently that Philadelphia pipe organ is not within reason, for as yet I have not been able to hear even a faint note from it. Nor have I heard London or Cuba or Mars.

But oh, the things I have heard over that blessed set! Springfield, Mass.; Schenectady, N. Y.; Pittsburgh, Pa.; Chicago; Cleveland; Hastings, Neb.; Davenport, Iowa; Denver, San Antonio, Texas; Calgary, Canada; Los Angeles, Portland, Oakland, Salt Lake City, and dozens of other places that maintain powerful broadcasting stations.

I have heard, and am still hearing, music from the best singers and orchestras in the country. I know all the latest songs and dance steps. The world of music comes trouping into my modest living-room every night, the evenings have grown surprisingly short, life has taken on a new meaning for me, a new zest, a new inspiration. And the cost has not been much more than for a new set of automobile tires.

Some evenings my wife and I find a good program somewhere, tune in, put on our slippers, pull our chairs closer to the fire, and settle down for a whole evening of enjoyment—the loud speaker doing all the work, without pay or without attention. It may be raining or snowing outside, but that doesn't hurt the music, and even adds to our comfy feeling. The worse the night the brighter our fire and the sweeter the music.

Now and then we enjoy a three-act comedy or drama from Oakland, or a Sunday evening church service from San Francisco or Calgary. Often we hear notable speakers in far-off cities, men and women of prominence whom we have read about but never expected to have in our home. Twice have we had President Coolidge in our living-room—so clear, loud and life-like we shall always feel he has really been with us.

Some other evenings I just sit in a chair in front of the radio, and play with it—taking a snatch of music here and a snatch there—from Seattle to Chicago—as the mood grips me, making the music soft or loud as my fancy dictates, like a musician at the key-board of some mighty pipe organ.

On still other evenings, when Millie is getting dinner and the house is quiet, I love to sit down by my radio and "go fishing," all by myself.

Fishing was my chief sport when a boy, but lately I have discovered a new kind of fishing —a glorified sport that beats the other all to pieces—fishing for uncharted, unknown, unfound radio broadcasting stations! And when I make a strike I get a thrill that takes twenty years off my back.

For instance, when I first hooked Cleveland

the other evening (I was born and reared there but have not seen it for more years than I like to remember), I let out a shout of joy that brought Millie running from the kitchen in an instant. She grew up in Cleveland, too, so when I told her where the music was coming from, we hugged each other delightedly, and listened to some home-town melodies that brought the tears to our eyes. But they were happy tears.

On Christmas morning I awoke at my usual hour—seven—which I am sure to do on a holiday. Got up. Found the house cold. Dressed. Fixed the furnace. Built a fire in the fireplace. Put on the tea kettle. Looked for the morning paper on the front porch. Pitch dark. Felt lonesome. No paper. Came in house and hurriedly shut door. Cold. Tried not to look at Christmas presents spread out on table. Not fair. Just then happened to think of an item I had read in the paper the night before—about some early carols to be sung and broadcasted from KGO, Oakland, California, at 7 o'clock Christmas morning.

Without stopping to turn on the light, guided only by instinct and the blaze from the fireplace, I turned the radio dials to the right places, switched on the current, and—

Out of the stillness and blackness of that cold Christmas morning came the soft melody of fresh young voices singing that old favorite hymn of mine, "Silent Night—Holy Night." It touched me inexpressibly. I am not ashamed to say that my eyes were wet, as if I were a boy again in the days when tears were nearer the surface. I bowed my head and listened, entranced. There was something uncannily sweet about that Christmas carol coming to me a thousand miles through the air, over mountains and rivers and valleys, out of the darkness, to cheer my heart.

The fire crackled more merrily; Millie in another room, awakened by the music, threw on a dressing gown and came out to me, wondering. Together we listened—carol followed carol—dawn peeked in the windows as the last strain died softly away. We looked at each other and-well, there was love in our hearts for those far-off singers, for KGO, for the Christmas day just beginning, and for the marvel of radio.

My son-in-law says that a radio set is the most glorified toy for grown-ups ever invented. I think he is right. Anyhow, it is the only toy I have had in many a year. It takes me out of myself, makes me forget the daily grind and the

humdrum of life. It is a recreation, an education, an inspiration.

At first Millie hinted in her gentle way that perhaps I had been a little extravagant, hadn't I? in spending so much money (about $200) on a mere toy or amusement. But I notice this viewpoint of hers is steadily changing. The other evening when I arrived home somewhat earlier than usual I found her sitting in front of the radio, working the dials like an old hand. She looked like a happy kitten caught in the cream, and admitted finally that when I was away it "kept her from being lonely." Bless its heart, it surely can do that same little thing. Who could be lonely when the world sweetly comes in when you bid it and sings to you? Who could be down-hearted when the joy of music and human voices is on tap with the turn of the spigot?

I am frequently asked: "Wasn't it hard to learn how to operate your set?" And, "Did you get an expert to show you how?"

My answer to both these questions is, "No." The dealer brought out the set and installed it, showed me how to work the various dials and controls, and said, after this five-minutes' course in A B C, "I'll come out any evening this week and teach you how to operate—just phone when you want me."

He left me with an instruction booklet. In two days I was picking off musical bouquets from a half a dozen stations. I have never phoned him and he has never had to come out. #

Road Pals

By EVE EGLESTON HOYT

July 1922

You at the wheel and I at your side
(Always beside you) we ride and ride.
Even the roads that we know so well
Lure us on with their magic spell,
But oh, the roads that are new and strange!
The far-flung highways beyond our range!

This old car, with her well-worn leather,
Her paint the worse for sun and weather,
Seems to pause of her own free will
Where past years' shelters beckon still;
Seems to see old campfires' embers,
Gray ashes now, but she remembers.

Yet, I believe, when I feel the surge
Of her fifty horse-power, that the urge
That drives us on to the untried road,
Fills her with scorn of weather or load;
Never a grade that she wouldn't climb,
Never a pulse-beat out of time.

The three of us, if we had our way,
Scarcely from sun to sun would stay,
For she was born with rolling wheels,
And we with wings on our restless heels;
Traveling only feeds the fires
That burn in us both and speed her tires.

Arm-chair and lamp, and kettle on hob
Lose their charm when we hear the throb
Of her eager engine; then we must go,
Whether it shine or rain or blow.
Pal, you shall drive her and I will ride
Mile after mile after mile at your side.

CHEVROLET

for Economical Transportation

for
Everybody, Everywhere *!*

The Coach
$595
f.o.b. Flint, Mich.

The Sedan
$695
f.o.b. Flint, Mich.

The Touring Car
$525
f.o.b. Flint, Mich.

The Roadster
$525
f.o.b. Flint, Mich.

The Imperial Landau
$780
f.o.b. Flint, Mich

The Sport Cabriolet
$715
f.o.b. Flint, Mich

The Landau
$745
f.o.b. Flint, Mich

The Coupe
$625
f.o.b. Flint, Mich.

Among the eight beautiful Chevrolet passenger car models there is one particularly suited for every driving preference—a Chevrolet for everybody everywhere.

This notable achievement in fine car building touches every cross-section of American life.

The family seeking an all-purpose automobile—women and men who require personal cars of unquestioned smartness—the business man who demands combined economy, utility and fine appearance — owners of high-priced automobiles who wish to enjoy the advantages of additional transportation without sacrifice of quality or prestige—

—all find in Chevrolet exactly the car that meets their needs at a price whose lowness reflects the economies of gigantic production!

Whether you intend to purchase a smart two-passenger roadster, or a five-passenger enclosed car of the most distinguished individuality and style, visit the nearest Chevrolet dealer and learn how Chevrolet combines beauty, utility, amazing performance, economy and low price as does no other car in the world!

CHEVROLET MOTOR COMPANY
DETROIT, MICHIGAN
Division of General Motors Corporation

QUALITY AT LOW COST

Beyond the Limit

By ERLE STANLEY GARDNER

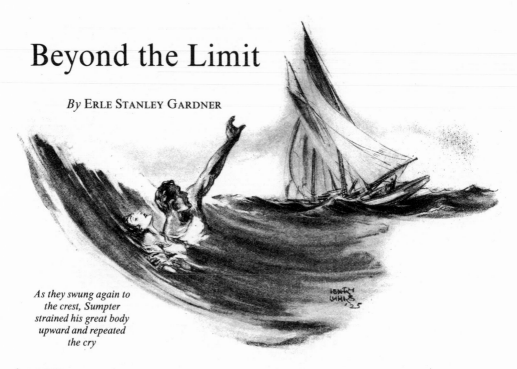

As they swung again to the crest, Sumpter strained his great body upward and repeated the cry

April 1925

FOG—gray, silent, dripping fog slipped over the smooth surface of the slumbering ocean. A yacht lazily rose and fell on the long swells, her huge, white sails stretching up into the thick mist—calm, silent, majestic. Occasionally a faint noise was swallowed up by the enveloping walls of silence—the "slap", "slap", of waves against the bow—the slow creak of a block—the "drip", "drip", of moisture from the boom—

Suddenly a hoarse siren boomed through the vapor—again, louder, nearer—there sounded the muffled throb of engines, the hissing of a mighty prow cutting the water; the curtain of mist parted before the towering bow of a great steamer, slicing through the water at terrific speed—a hoarse shout from a lookout, a jangling of bells, the great sides of the ship, studded with port-holes raced by and was swallowed up in the fog. A swirl of water swept upon the little yacht, rocked it violently, then subsided and once more the boat nodded upon the long, lazy swells.

On board the yacht a man of about fifty, alert, well-knit, walked aft, his keen, gray eyes twinkling with excitement.

"Well, Jan, that was a close call. She sure was travelin'—full speed ahead, fog or no fog."

A slender, graceful girl with short bobbed hair, white duck shirt open at the throat, trousers of the same material, feet neatly encased in white, rubber-soled shoes, turned a pair of flashing black eyes toward the man.

"I tried to get her name, but the fog was too thick. To think of a captain driving a ship through a fog like this at full speed! Why—it's a crime! He missed us by inches!"

The man laughed.

"Not quite that close, Jan, but too close for comfort. Funny we didn't hear her siren before. Not that we could have got out of her way."

Harrison G. Colton, retired millionaire, yachting enthusiast and adventurer, did not seem to share his daughter's indignation.

"Forget about it, Jan. She missed us, that's enough. I wonder if—"

He stopped and peered intently into the fog.

His daughter, holding the wheel, turned and followed his gaze.

Something black floated upon the surface of the water, progressed toward the yacht in a series of steady, rhythmic lunges—the head of a swimmer. A moment more and the shoulders could be discerned swinging in a powerful, unhurried stroke.

The man, clad in a suit of light underwear, caught the rope the yachtsman threw to him, clambered up the side of the boat, easily, gracefully and stood dripping on the deck, a huge figure of a man, powerfully muscled, heavy of chest, lean of waist, steady, gray eyes calmly scrutinizing the world from beneath a pair of black brows.

The girl, unembarrassed, regarded him with frank interest, eyes shining, lips slightly parted.

"Why, you must—must have jumped overboard from that steamer." The man smiled, a slow, good-natured smile.

"Can I borrow some clothes and work a passage?" he asked of the owner.

Mr. Colton had been keenly scrutinizing the newcomer.

"Come below and I'll fix you up as to the clothes. As to the passage—we're bound for nowhere in particular, are provisioned for four months, and I'll be hanged if I put in to port for any man—I'm sick of civilization, and I'm on this cruise to get the taste out of my mouth."

The man nodded, a grave, dignified nod of acquiescence.

"Thank you," he muttered ambiguously, and followed the owner below.

Janice Colton, left at the wheel, looked up into the gray fog.

"Of *all* things!" she said.

The man looked strangely incongruous in Mr. Colton's clothing. His wrists and ankles seemed fairly to burst forth. He gave his name as George Sumpter, his occupation as a "freelance adventurer" and beyond that gave no information whatever.

"Of course," he said, "I shall take the first opportunity to leave the yacht. I wouldn't think of spoiling your trip, and I certainly realize that if you had wanted any guests on this cruise you'd have invited them."

It was very evident that he was a gentleman. It was equally evident that he desired to make no explanation concerning the reason which prompted him to jump overboard from the steamer and trust himself to the heaving waters of the Pacific, some fifteen miles from the California coast.

"My daughter and I were speculating as to what steamer that was," ventured Mr. Colton. He paused.

"I didn't get her name," drawled Sumpter.

Harrison G. Colton, shrewd student of character, smiled a bit quizzically and dropped the subject. Janice, however, failed to notice the significant reticence of the reply.

"Why, you must have purchased a ticket and secured reservations!" she exclaimed.

Again a slow, good-natured smile.

"As it happened, Miss Colton, I wasn't bothered about transportation or reservation. Those details were carried out for me with rare consideration, and I simply stepped aboard."

This time Janice noticed Sumpter's unwillingness to be questioned, noticed and resented it.

"Oh yes! I see," she flared, "and so, fearing the trip might prove monotonous, you stripped to your, er, underwear and stepped overboard. How delightfully simple—and logical."

"Janice!" reproved her father.

Sumpter again smiled.

"A sure cure for ennui. And so you're on a four months' cruise, Mr. Colton?"

The millionaire hesitated a moment, then, apparently deciding that Sumpter's secretiveness could not be better rebuked than by answering the question at length, made a brief outline of the reasons which had brought about the unusual cruise.

"I said we were provisioned for four months. I don't know that I'll take a cruise of that length, but I do know that I won't put into port until I get good and ready. Civilization makes me sick. Automobiles, dictating machines, telephones, street cars, banks, and money, money, money. Every one is money-mad, selfish. Here I am worth—well worth enough so that I can do what I want to, and I've been a slave to my money. The very extent of my property interests has caused me to be constantly on the go. A secretary at my elbow, a private wire to the stock exchange—

"Why, my daughter here is almost a stranger to me. Ever since her mother died she's been in boarding school and college. Now that she's graduated, I just made up my mind that I'd quit. I've finished with the whole money-grubbing system. That is, until I get tired of resting

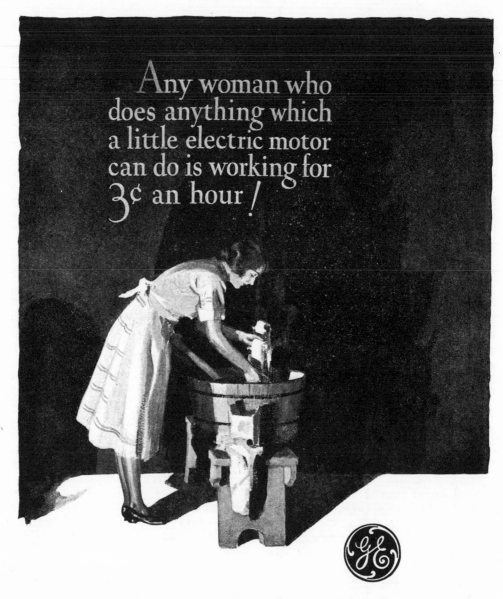

Any woman who does anything which a little electric motor can do is working for 3¢ an hour!

There are few hard tasks left in the home which electricity cannot do at trifling cost. You will find the G-E monogram on many electrical household conveniences. It is a guarantee of excellence as well as a mark of service.

Ask your electric company or dealer to help you select the labor-saving electrical appliances best suited for your home.

GENERAL ELECTRIC

and watching nature. The wireless receiving set is my only link with civilization. I've violated all maritime rules by changing the name of the yacht after I put out to sea, and nobody even knows where I am, they don't have any idea that I'm aboard a yacht at all. My secretary thinks I'm in a sanitarium somewhere with a nervous breakdown threatened."

Sumpter scanned the yacht with the eye of an expert.

"Looks like it might be a little risky for just you two out here like this. Must be pretty hard to handle in heavy weather."

Colton laughed. "We don't handle her in heavy weather. We aren't trying to get anywhere, and if it gets stormy we'll throw out a sea-anchor, heave to, and let it blow. I used to do a lot of sailing, and Janice is no novice, but we're not expecting anything very heavy this time of year." Janice had been an attentive listener.

"Now that we all know all about each other, we seem quite well acquainted, Mr. Sumpter, don't we?"

Sumpter laughed a deep, boyish laugh, and threw up his hands, acknowledging that the sarcasm had hit home.

"Kamerad!" he said.

As it happened, Janice's curiosity was not destined to remain long unsatisfied. That evening, as the three sat in the main cabin, Colton tuned in his magnificent receiving radio, and the party listened to a concert from one of the big broadcasting stations.

Following a musical number, the announcer stated that the next feature would be the news events of the day. There followed several paragraphs of national news, and then, startlingly clear, the voice from the loud-speaker reported:

"Suicide or Escape? George L. Sumpter, who was recently arrested in San Diego for murder, and who was being taken by a posse of officers to San Francisco for trial, jumped overboard from the *Sea Queen* some time between eleven this morning and one in the afternoon. He worked his way through the porthole of a locked stateroom while the boat was some fifteen miles from land. It is presumed he committed suicide; but he is a wonderful swimmer, and it may well be that he was able to swim ashore, or that some small yacht was waiting for him at a designated spot. There was a thick fog at the time of the discovery of Sumpter's escape, and Captain Anderson refused to alter the course of the boat or to make any search.

"Sumpter is about twenty-five years of age, tall, well-muscled, black hair, gray eyes; weight, two hundred and ten. If he has escaped and is not a suicide he will be very desperate, and persons who may meet up with him are warned to take no chances."

The speaker then branched off into news of international politics. Within the little cabin the eyes of the owner and his daughter turned to their guest.

In Janice's eyes was a look of startled incredulity—a look which finally became one of suspicion—and then melted into one of sympathy.

Her father's eyes expressed a certain hard, quizzical humor, a look which became more pronounced as the cabin clock ticked off the seconds and Sumpter made no attempt to deny or explain.

At length Colton arose and shut off the radio.

"Sumpter, eh?" he muttered meditatively, "George L. Sumpter, wanted for murder—and aboard *my* yacht."

"Daddy, I don't believe it!" exclaimed Janice warmly.

Sumpter flashed her a quick look, impulsively drew in his breath as though about to speak, then hesitated, looked at Mr. Colton—

"I presume I may smoke?" he said reaching toward the box of cigarettes which lay open upon the table.

Colton nodded, his eyes still upon Sumpter's face and still retaining their look of whimsical humor.

Sumpter tapped the cigarette gently upon his thumb nail, struck a match and inhaled a long draught of smoke which he gently exhaled through his nostrils.

With something of a flourish, the owner arose, returned to the radio, pressed a button, and stepped back to his chair, apparently giving his entire attention to the music which came pouring into the cabin through the horn of the loud-speaker. Plainly his action showed that he considered the subject closed.

For more than an hour they sat.

Colton listening to the radio, absorbed in it; Sumpter smoking intermittently, maintaining absolute silence. Janice watched the two men with wide eyes, silent, thoughtful.

At length the concert came to a conclusion. Colton escorted Sumpter to his stateroom with all the courtesy which one would show to an honored guest. The boat, well out of the steamer lane by this time, sails lowered, gently rose and fell on the long swells.

Sumpter slept well and late. When he awoke the yacht was jumping and plunging like a live thing. He could tell by the feel of the boat that she was under shortened sail and headed into a choppy sea. Hastily dressing he climbed to the deck.

Colton sat at the wheel, covered in oilskins, a short pipe gripped in his teeth, upon his face a look of fierce enjoyment. From out of the northwest there came an endless procession of plunging, choppy seas, cold, gray and relentless. The yacht quivered and throbbed as she smashed into those sullen seas. A wind shrieked and howled through the taut rigging. Spray dashed upward from the bow, hung suspended for a moment, and was then swept back across the deck in cold showers.

Sumpter made his way aft.

"I'll take her," he yelled to the owner, "you go get yourself a cup of coffee."

Colton nodded, indicated the course and approximate position of the yacht upon a chart which was weighted down upon a shelf under a canvas weathershield, relinquished the wheel, and stood aside to observe the way in which his guest handled the wheel. For several minutes he stood there, critically watching. The yacht rose as lightly as a bird on the waves, hesitated a moment at the crest, then plunged downward. A huge wave would appear in front of the bow, rise to such a height that it would seem to tower over the deck, then the bow would start upward, there would be a crashing impact, a cloud of spray would dash up high in the air, and the yacht would rush swiftly upward to the crest of the new wave.

At times there would come a sea much higher than its companions. Upon its top would appear a curling crest of tumbled white. At such times Sumpter would deftly twist the wheel. The deck of the yacht would slant and

right—quickly, firmly Sumpter would spin the wheel—the comber would slip easily astern, the yacht would nod slightly as if in approval and again roll on her way.

Colton smiled, nodded, knocked the ashes from his pipe, placed it in his pocket and inched his way along the slippery, slanting deck. Carefully working from handhold to handhold he disappeared down the companion-way.

A moment and the figure of Janice, slim, active, girlish in spite of the enveloping slicker, appeared on the deck. She stepped forward, saw Sumpter at the wheel and threw up her hand in greeting.

As she did so there came a staggering lurch, her feet slipped out from under her on the slippery deck, she crashed to the rail, her handhold torn loose—there came a swirl and a torrent of greenish white, boiling water mounted the bow and roared down the deck. There was a flutter of a white hand, a dark spot on the ocean as the slicker, pushed up by the air beneath it, bellied up on the surface, and—the deck was empty!

With a quick slash of his knife Sumpter ripped loose a life preserver, poised for a second and hurled it outward and to one side. A second or two and he had torn off his coat and outer garments and slipped into the tumbled, angry waters.

At the moment he released the wheel the boat quivered, lurched; there came the terrific slatting of canvas, sounding like the reports of a hundred rifles and the anxious face of Harrison G. Colton peered from the companion-way. In a flash he took in the significance of the empty deck, the slatting sail—scorning handholds, he raced for the wheel. Quickly, deftly he brought the yacht up, gathered headway, spun the wheel, turned about and began anxiously to scan the tossing crests.

Powerfully, swiftly, as surely as a huge seal, Sumpter slipped through the waters. In an incredibly short space of time he was beside the struggling figure of Janice, helped her as she struggled and ripped loose from the enveloping garments, gazed into her startled, white face with its wide eyes, clumsily, yet tenderly pushed back the wet hair from her eyes, placed her arm over his shoulders, and—smiled.

There was only the faintest response in those wide, terror-filled eyes. Sumpter turned, waited until they were pushed to the crest of a wave, and looked for the yacht—she had turned and was zigzagging back within two hundred yards. With the eye of an expert Sumpter noticed the tumbling waves, drew a deep breath into his great lungs as they slipped down the side of the wave, threw back his head as they once more raised upward, and, on the very crest of the sea, threw his great body upward, waved his long arms and emitted a bellow which sounded above the roar of the gale like a fog-horn.

Four times he repeated his attempt to attract the attention of the yacht. Four times his efforts were in vain; she had passed by them. The fifth time his voice, borne downwind, carried above the noise of the seas and Colton turned, caught a glimpse of the waving arms as they sank back into the blue waters, and frenziedly spun over the wheel. There ensued anxious minutes, careful maneuvering, shouted directions, and a long, black rope snaked out over the ocean.

With marvelous dexterity Sumpter caught the rope, turned in the water and knotted the hemp under Janice's arms—a long minute and the pair were alongside. At a signal from Sumpter, Colton twisted the rope about a stanchion, and the big man, seemingly without effort came hand over hand up and over the rail. Together they pulled Janice from the water—unconscious.

Fifteen minutes later the yacht lay, hove-to, a sea-anchor thrown out. Janice, wrapped in warm blankets, a hot water bottle at her feet, sighed, fluttered her lids, and opened her eyes. Colton turned and placed his hand upon the bare shoulder of his guest, his eyes filled with tears.

Instantly Sumpter became conscious of his soaked underwear, his missing clothes.

"I guess you'll have to stake me to another outfit," he remarked. "I seem to be pretty hard on your wardrobe."

Colton did not answer for a moment. His eyes were fastened upon an object which protruded from beneath Sumpter's left shoulder, an object which showed clearly through the wet underwear—apparently an envelope wrapped in oiled silk and strapped across the man's chest.

Sumpter noticed the other's gaze and quickly twisted the packet back into place beneath his left arm.

"At your convenience," he said, and his voice had suddenly become hard and deadly.

Colton started.

"I beg your pardon, Sumpter," he turned toward his own cabin. "Right this way, please."

By noon the wind had abated, the seas had smoothed out, and the ocean glinted a deep blue in the warm sunlight. Janice, fully recovered from her experience, but wrapped in warm clothes reclined in a deckchair in the sun on the lee side of the cabin. Colton was below, Sumpter again at the wheel.

"Put," "put," "put," "put," "put," came downwind. A long, powerful launch came slipping through the water, a huge bow-wave parting gracefully on each side of the cleaving prow. A figure came forward, carrying a megaphone. He crouched in the bow, waiting—studying the yacht through binoculars.

Janice looked enquiringly at George Sumpter at the wheel. He did not return the glance. He was watching the oncoming boat, his face set in a grim mask, jaw thrust forward, hands clenched tightly on the spokes of the wheel.

"Ahoy! Ahoy the yacht!"

Sumpter did not reply. He was studying the man at the bow. There were three men on the launch. The helmsman, and, in addition to the man at the bow, a huge, heavy-set man who stood by the rail. The latter went forward and spoke to the man with the megaphone. Instantly this man dropped the megaphone and raced back to the man at the wheel. In a few seconds the powerful launch was running within a few feet of the yacht.

The heavy-set man, and the one who had held the megaphone came to the rail.

"Heave-to," ordered the heavy-set man. "You've the man there we want. We're coming aboard."

With that he threw a grappling iron, watched his chance and jumped to the deck of the yacht. In a moment he was joined by the other. Together they started for Sumpter.

Janice advanced and stood directly in the path of the men.

"The idea of you thinking Mr. Sumpter is guilty of that awful crime!" she exclaimed. "You make me tired, you, you great big bullies!"

"Here now, sister, none o' that. Just can that line o' chatter," growled the man of the bull neck and thick lips. "We're here on business, an' before we leave we're goin' to find out how much you know about this."

With the words George Sumpter stepped forward with the light step of the trained athlete. He poised himself easily on the balls of his feet, his shoulders slightly weaving, jaw stuck forward in an expression of grim, desperate determination—

There was a crash of broken glass, the tinkle of slivers as the broken pane showered upon the deck. The muzzle of a high-powered rifle slipped through the cabin window.

"Never mind, Sumpter," snapped Harrison G. Colton, his gray eyes gleaming along the barrel of the rifle. "I'll take care of this."

The smaller of the men jumped back, his right hand dropping significantly.

"Stop right where you are or you're a dead man," came the icy tones of the millionaire yacht owner. "You fellows just remember that we're beyond the three mile limit and that I'm master of this ship. If I think there's a criminal aboard I'll take steps to see he doesn't escape and surrender him to the authorities when I make port; but I will surrender him to no man on the high seas."

There was a calm deadly earnestness in the tone which caused the two men to glance apprehensively at each other. A moment they wavered, then the heavy-set man took charge of the situation.

"I'm a special deputy, and if you interfere with me you're going to be guilty of a crime."

"You're a liar," immediately rejoined Colton, squinting along the sights as he spoke. "I'm on to your little game, and if you don't get off this yacht at once I'll proceed to interfere with you in a way you'll remember."

A sneer came to the face of the man, distorting his heavy features. His thick, flabby mouth twitched spasmodically.

"All right then. Have it your own way. We'll stay alongside until you make port, and then we'll turn you in for aiding and abetting a murderer."

"Sounds reasonable," came from the cabin. "Go ahead. I'll even go you one better. We'll put into port right now. I'm just going to call your bluff. We're only twenty-five miles from Monterey, and we'll see which one of us gets in jail."

The leader turned to his companion and conferred in a whisper. "He's right, Bill. As long as he's outside the three mile limit we've got no right to enter his boat and take off a man.

Sumpter stepped forward. There was a crash of broken glass and the muzzle of a rifle slipped through the window.

*With a series of ripping
explosions, the launch
seemed to shoot forward
in the water.*

We'll let him think we're going in to Monterey, then, when we get within the three mile limit we'll board him again. He won't dare to resist us then, and we've got a launch that'll run circles round this old tub. He can't give us the slip."

Aloud he said: "All right. If you want to spend the night in Monterey jail go ahead. It's nothing to me. This man Sumpter is the man I want."

Almost unconsciously Janice had taken a position beside Sumpter, her hand on his arm—clinging to him instinctively for protection.

Colton noticed and smiled.

"One real man," he muttered to himself.

The boarders withdrew, cast loose their grappling iron and followed along beside the yacht, which, in turn, headed for Monterey Bay. Colton ordered the men to stand off sufficiently to give him "elbow room," and began to make sail. Aboard the launch the men laughed surreptitiously as they watched the yacht crowding on canvas.

The man at the wheel joined in the conversation.

"The poor fool," he sneered, "wonder if he thinks he can give us the slip. We're runnin' on less than half speed right now."

Upon the yacht Colton turned to his guest.

"I've got to give you up, Sumpter. That is, unless you can convince me of your innocence. I'd stand by an innocent man, but I couldn't afford to protect the guilty."

Sumpter shook his head.

"I can tell you that this whole thing is a frame-up; but I can't go any further. I can't give you details. You see—well, it's not my secret."

This time Janice made no effort to conceal the hand which clutched his arm.

"Please—oh, please," she begged.

Sumpter shook his head although his eyes grew infinitely tender as they looked down into the girl's.

Suddenly Colton laughed, a short, hard laugh. Picking up his rifle he suddenly threw the wheel round. The yacht spun upon her wake and headed toward the west and the great stretch of gleaming Pacific.

Immediately the launch let out a roar of ripping explosions and seemed to shoot forward in the water. She heeled over, swung to port and easily drew abreast of the yacht. Colton stood on the side, the rifle in his hand, watching. Janice had taken the wheel. Sumpter stood stupefied.

"Hey, you," bawled the man on the launch, "What d'ye think you're doin'. You can't run away from us with that old tub. Turn about and head back to Monterey."

"I've changed my mind," yelled Colton. "I'm still on the high seas, and I've determined to take a cruise. You can trail along if you want."

Again there was a whispered conference on the launch.

"Say, Jim, is he right?" asked the man who had been addressed as Bill.

"Hell's bells," retorted the other, "I don't know. I'm no sea lawyer. It sounds like it's law, an' he's got a rifle an' b'gosh, I believe he's got the guts to use it. We've got revolvers, but what're they against a rifle. We aint in no position to start nothin' anyway. We'll just trail along until we strike some other boat. He's just bluffin' about that cruise anyway."

For an hour the two boats sailed along, side by side, the yacht heeling over in the fresh wind and slipping through the waters at high speed, the launch keeping up with her easily, although using more throttle than earlier in the day.

It was the man at the wheel who first sounded the alarm.

"Say, fellows, the gas is gettin' low. That bird's sailin' along on wind. We're usin' gas an lots of it."

There followed another conference, then the big man once more came to the rail.

"Ahoy the yacht," he shouted, "where the hell do you think you're goin'?"

Colton lost no time in replying.

"I just decided to go to China," he called back across the heaving, blue waters. "The wind's just right, and my daughter has never seen the Orient."

The other spat out a curse.

"All right. You think you're smart. We're goin' on back and have every port watched for you, an' what's more we'll have a revenue cutter on your trail inside of ten hours. Then we'll see where you're goin'."

Colton waved his arm.

"Go ahead. The ocean's free. We're still beyond the three mile limit. You can do anything you damn please."

The three figures stood grouped on the deck of the yacht as the launch faded out of sight below the eastern horizon.

"Daddy, you're going to get in trouble," said Janice and there was a slight catch in her voice. "But, Oh Daddy, I think you're just too wonderful for words!"

Her father smiled.

"Now I'll tell you a story," he said. "Once upon a time there was a message that was to be delivered from Mexico involving the location of some very valuable oil lands. The man who was the man behind the scene ordered the president of a big corporation to get a messenger who was all nerve, a man who knew no fear, to go and get that message, and to bring it safely back into the hands of the president of the corporation.

"That man got the message, but he was followed. After he landed in San Diego he was arrested on a faked charge and rushed aboard a boat to be taken to San Francisco. He managed to conceal the papers somewhere, or if the others ever got them, he managed to retake possession of them, strapped them under his arm, watched his chance and jumped overboard from the steamer when he saw a small yacht lying becalmed in the fog.

"He hadn't counted on the enemy boldly announcing that he was wanted for murder. He was bound by oath not to disclose his mission to any one, or to part with the possession of the papers; for that reason—"

Sumpter jumped back, his face working in surprise.

"For Heaven's sake how do you know all this?"

Colton smiled.

"Partly by deduction, and partly because I happened to be the man behind the scenes who ordered the president of the corporation to send one George L. Sumpter after those papers."

There was a moment's silence.

"But, Daddy," said Janice, "why didn't you tell Mr. Sumpter and save him from all that worry?"

The millionaire smiled.

"Because I was testing Mr. Sumpter, Jan. I wanted to see if he would weaken, if he would violate his oath and tell his mission."

Janice frowned.

"Still I don't see."

"Well," added her father, with one of his rare smiles, as he reached forward and grasped Sumpter's hand, "I commenced to think I had something else for Mr. Sumpter, and I wanted to look him over pretty closely."

"What else," asked Janice.

"Oh, just another job," answered her father with a smile as he turned and went back into the cabin, leaving the couple alone on the deck. #

The Log of the Gladiator

A Famous Western Author's Account of
Deep Sea Fishing off Avalon

By ZANE GREY

April 1926

OWING to the Galapagos Island trip we are late starting at Avalon this season. I will not be able to begin fishing until probably July.

R. C. and Captain Mitchell started in today, the former in the *Gladiator,* and the latter in one of my small boats.

R. C. reported seeing several school of tuna. He had two strikes. Captain Mitchell saw a few fish on surface, but did not get near them.

The last few days have been warm, with high fog and little wind. A number of broadbill have been sighted, three on two occasions. I see some bait working up the channel. No tuna caught as yet this month. That is a bad sign.

August 12th.

Clear bright day that promised wind, but turned out to be fine. Ran ten miles straight off Avalon. Sid sighted swordfish. With mackerel bait R. C. took the rod and we ran round him, not very close, still not very far. As the bait crossed in front of the fish he turned away. We gave up and said things. Suddenly he whacked the bait mightily. R. C. was surprised. He yelled. We were all excited and elated. Again the fish hit the bait, and then again. Next he took it and ran off easily. This was as we wanted it. Presently the swordfish started to run, then he came up on the surface with a crash. R. C. jerked and wound hard. The hook caught solidly.

Then to our amazement the broadbill charged on the surface directly at us. It was manifest that he was furiously enraged. We got out of his way. Again he followed. R. C.'s line went slack. The fish lashed the surface white, and churned the water. We ran away from him. When the line came taut R. C. had some tremendous strain to endure. I saw the fish lift him out of the chair. We were all so excited at the menace of the swordfish that we scarcely knew what to do. Sid handled wheel and clutch. Bob reached out with the long gaff. I had a camera ready and failed to use it upon several marvelous occasions. We had to keep away from this broadbill. He was unquestionably bent on destruction. Finally he sank down on a long line, and R. C. went to work on him, whipping him in something like two hours.

It was the shortest swordfish we every saw, very heavy and round, with small tail. He weighed 343 pounds.

August 17th.

The best swordfish day this year so far. We ran out straight from Avalon for ten or twelve miles, and at nine-twenty I sighted the first broadbill, a huge fellow that made me thrill. His length was enormous, likewise his fins. We ran down to him and Sid went too close. He sounded on us. But he came up again, and would not look at our bait. I got a good view of him, and was struck dumb at his size. Fully 900 pounds.

We gave him up, and soon saw another, a small one. He was not hungry. Then we sighted two more, but could not work them. In the next hour we saw three more, all fair size, and worked one of them pretty well.

A little before eleven o'clock I saw a swordfish jump two miles distant. We ran down and I picked him up. We made a perfect presentation of the mackerel, at least three hundred feet from the boat. He went down, and sailed for it. He hit it too, once, twice, three times. Then he ran off steadily, but soon took to a rush. Then I hooked him.

He put up as versatile and hard a battle as any I ever *caught,* punishing me severely the first several hours. Then at last he took to weaving round and under the stern. We saw him often, also the mackerel bait close to his head. We figured he was hooked in the corner of his mouth. The last hour and a half was terrible. But as I weakened so did he, and at last by repeated and superhuman efforts I drew him to the boat. Sid gaffed him, and we tied him up and towed him back to Avalon. Fifteen miles!

He was alive when we got to the dock. A tremendous crowd awaited us, and saw the fish landed and stripped of gaff, hook, ropes, etc. The hook had caught on the outside near the corner of mouth, and the leader had tangled round a pectoral fin. Both hook and leader stuck, marvelous to see! His pectoral and anal fin were badly split and lacerated by the fine wire.

He was a beautiful specimen, with magnificent bill and tail. He weighed 369 pounds, which was a considerable surprise to me. I spent four hours, fifty minutes getting him.

August 25th.

Same kind of morning as yesterday. It was great to run out on the dark cool level sea. We took a different direction, knowing that a dozen boats would go to the California mainland where so many swordfish were seen yesterday, and four caught.

Twelve miles out we ran into a fleet of Japanese bait boats heading for Clemente. Evidently a new run of albacore was on. About the same time R. C. missed one of the flying fish teasers that we always drag after the boat. A marlin swordfish had slipped up to steal one from us.

The fog lifted, the sun shone wanly through, the sea brightened until it resembled a moonstone. Birds magnified by the strange atmosphere deceived us. At nine-twenty I sighted my first broadbill, and we were soon on the way to give him a bait. We had a fresh barracuda. Bob had found a new trick for fastening the bait to the hook yet leaving it hang free. We used a long leader of different kind of wire, heavier and not so pliable.

I fed the bait from the crow's nest, letting out a hundred yards of line while we circled the fish fully two hundred yards distant. But as we circled we gradually drew the bait closer. I could see the barracuda shine white and silver. I could discern every move of the swordfish. He milled round some, then took a straight course.

This was my opportunity. I wound in some line. Then when I had gauged the distance between bait and fish, and the movement of each, and had brought the bait almost even with where the swordfish was heading, I called for Sid to throw out the clutch. The *Gladiator* slowed down, glided on slower and slower. My bait followed suit. When the swordfish reached to within one hundred and fifty feet of the bait I saw him distinctly, a very large fish. He flipped his tail and slid under. I saw his purple mass going for the bait.

"Boys, he's after it. Look out!" I yelled.

Presently he disappeared. I waited in tense expectancy, thrilling all over.

Suddenly the line whipped up, and whizzed off my reel. We all yelled. R. C. came running to take the rod.

"He just hit the bait and didn't tangle. All O.K." I said. As I lowered the rod to R. C. the swordfish hit the bait again. R. C. ran forward on the top of the deck and I dropped out of the crow's nest to run to the cockpit. R. C. handed the rod down to me and I sat down to put the butt in the rod-socket. Just at that moment the swordfish struck again, not so violently. Presently the line began to slide off the reel.

"Boys, it's a perfect strike," I exulted.

We were all elated, as that seldom happens. Faster and faster the line reeled off, until I had to shut down on the drag, and try to hook him.

"Hand it to him!" cried R. C. from above.

I jerked with all my might, and felt a solid live weight that lifted me out of my chair. I struck half a dozen times. We all were sure I had hooked the swordfish. He began to take line in sharp irresistible pulls. I had never felt a heavier swordfish. I settled down to wind the reel and pump on him. All of a sudden the line slackened. I felt a peculiar break, a loosening, a freedom from that tremendous live weight.

"Aw!" exclaimed Sid, in dismay. We all knew what had happened. The swordfish had pulled away from hook and leader. In an instant we were plunged from thrilling excitement to blank disappointment.

I reeled in the line. The bait was gone. The cord that had held the barracuda on the hook had been forced clear along the curve of the hook to the notch of the barb. Nothing but the bill of the swordfish could have done that. In some way he had slipped his sword into the curve of the hook; and then, of course, when he turned towards us his bill had slipped free.

"Hard luck!" said R. C. shaking his head. #

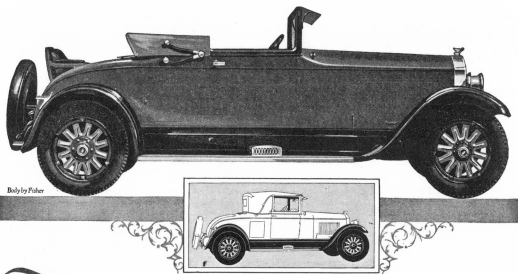

Body by Fisher

The Convertible Coupe

˅ ˴ a new and very charming
version of *Buick Beauty* ˴ ˵ ˵

A car in a thousand, is this prince-ly new open-enclosed Buick—the Convertible Coupe.

The name describes its adaptabil-ity and versatility. The top lowers for fair days. It raises in a moment, when the weather blusters. An open car today. Tight, closed-car comfort tomorrow.

Either way, the Convertible Coupe is a very charming motor car—style for those who ask for the grace of the thoroughbred in the car they drive.

The colors of this newest Buick are in Coronation Duco—the year's smartest custom effects; the upperstructure is of Lenox grey, dual-texture top-weave; the upholsteries are of hand-buffed leathers, in tones to match the body colors; the windows raise even though the top is folded, and serve as wind deflectors.

The Convertible Coupe is built on the Series 128 chassis—and the engine is *vibrationless beyond belief*.

The performance, style, utility, and moderate price of this ex-quisite new Buick will win your warm approval.

BUICK MOTOR COMPANY, FLINT, MICHIGAN
Division of General Motors Corporation

The GREATEST  EVER BUILT

Herbert Hoover—Then and Now

By CHESTER H. ROWELL

November 1927

THE editor of SUNSET asks for an article on "Hoover Then and Now" —meaning, apparently, an answer to the question why Herbert Hoover could have been an ideal but unstrategic candidate for President in 1920, and yet be the most strategic candidate now, even from the standpoint of the most practical politics.

For an active supporter of Mr. Hoover, who desires and expects his election and hopes to contribute to it, the assignment is not easy. It means violating the rule of political publicity, "claim everything, and concede nothing"; to analyze the evident practical disabilities of the Hoover campaign of eight years ago, and to point out some of the difficulties which confront it even now. But no other sort of article would be worth writing. So let us make the choice of frankness and take its risks. That is, after all, usually the best policy.

Eight years ago, Hoover was a political amateur, and his supporters were largely idealists. Now they are still inspired by an ideal, but they are practical men also, and Hoover himself has graduated far beyond the amateur class. The Hoover candidacy then was outside the established scheme of things political; now it is at its very center. To nominate him then would have been contrary to all the rules of the game; now it is precisely the regular thing to do. And the idealism of his candidacy, which was against the stream then, is with it now. So, without losing the qualities which made it appeal to the foresighted then, Hoover's candidacy now appeals to the hard-headed also. The transition spells precisely the difference between an ideal and its realization.

When, with little more than passive acquiescence on his part, Mr. Hoover's friends proposed him for President in 1920, they were launching their idealistic crusade at precisely the least propitious moment in recent American history. The very fact that the convention which might have nominated Hoover did nominate Harding, sufficiently reflects the spirit of the time.

The American people were tired, and wanted, above all things, a rest. It was only two years after the armistice, a year after the Peace of Versailles, and in the very midst of the bitter contest to prevent American membership in the League of Nations. America was bent on getting completely out of the war, into which, spiritually, it had never fully entered. It was at the very bottom of a reaction from an emotional exaltation which had been largely an artificial product. We had elected Woodrow Wilson on the slogan, "he kept us out of war," and we had been divided even in our sympathies. We were united only in self-congratulation that we were out of it. When circumstances made our participation inevitable, we dutifully followed the President, ruthlessly imposed compulsory conformity on each other, and worked up war hatreds which increased in intensity with our distance from the front. One brief summer our soldiers participated in the actual hostilities. The rest of us obeyed Hoover's orders on what to eat and President Wilson's orders on what to think. Then we blew off the whole tension in the shouting of Armistice Day, and settled down to the comfortable assurance that our world was once more as it had always been.

President Wilson of course knew better, and sought to readjust human relations to the new conditions. He succeeded with the world, but failed with his own country. Politicians made partisan opportunity out of the world's travail, and rode the growing reaction against President Wilson as the symbol of all we wanted to forget. It was the bottom of the slump in Europe also. Our convention came the very year when it was uncertain whether all Europe would go Bolshevik. Europe was frightened and revolutionary; America indifferent and tired.

Into this dreary time came the idealists, crying in the wilderness the name of Hoover and the cause of a new and better world. There was instant response from the still-idealistic element. A series of votes, straw-ballot and official, in Michigan, illustrated it. Hoover carried the faculty of the University of Michigan something like forty to one, and the students two or three to one, but he was defeated in the popular primaries, and he had no supporters at all among professional politicians of the state committee. There were similar results elsewhere. Hoover's support came chiefly from those who are usually some years ahead of the times.

It was an admirable but premature movement—an attempt to rally the people to a world figure when they wanted to forget the world; to offer them a leader when they wanted to stand still, and a thinker when they wanted to forget. They had had too much of these things from Wilson already. Why offer them still more, from an even abler leader, who had already demonstrated his capacity to stir them to effort and sacrifice?

A Pullman smoking room story of the time illustrates the state of the public mind. One man praised Harding. "What has he ever done?" asked another. "Nothing!" protested a third. "Then I'm for him," exclaimed a quiet stranger in the corner. "Nothing" was exactly what a weary people wanted.

In this situation, when the flaccid torpor of the people left the political gamesters in full control, Hoover was a candidate outside all the rules of their game. Personally, he scarcely knew that there were such rules. Though one of the best-informed and practically capable men in the world, on most of the major concerns of life, he was less than an amateur in the chess game of practical professional politics. At first he did not even know to which party he belonged. That, to be sure, was a disability which he shared with George Washington, and the time was one in which the philosopher from Mars might well have stumped the party leaders by asking them what, after all, was the difference between them; but to the practical politicians, who always knew their party affiliations, even when they knew nothing else, it was supreme and unthinkable ignorance. Worse still, when asked his political views, he

described himself as a "liberal." The politicians did not understand what that meant, but, on looking the word up, they discovered that there was a party named "Liberal" in England. Horrors! Here was a man who not only did not know what American party he belonged to, but did belong to a British one. Looking further, they learned that Hoover, during the time when he had charge of his firm's business in Europe, had taken a house in London, and had given it as his address. His world-wide acquaintance included very few whom the politicians knew, and his vast knowledge covered too many things which they did not know, and therefore suspected. And his most recent public service, as food controller, had been as a loyal worker under a Democratic administration. What mattered it that Hoover was one of the most famous and best-tested men in the world; the Quaker who had headed the great peaceful and constructive services of the war and the reconstruction; who had ruled whole nations and expended billions without criticism; who had saved more lives than guns had destroyed, and manifested an executive capacity unequaled by any military leader? He was a person completely and unimaginably beyond classification by any rules they knew. The whole proposition was simply outside their horizon.

As the convention approached, other friends of Hoover who did know, in a limited way, the rules of the game, took charge and conducted primary campaigns, in regular form, in some states. Hoover became a regular candidate for the regular Republican nomination—to have his case decided by a convention ruled by men to whom he and all his sort were an incomprehensible enigma. The result, of course, was predestined by the very conditions. Hoover had indeed met, as no other man, the great tests of war and restoration. He had inspired his fellow-workers with a frantic personal loyalty, and his very name had become a noun and a verb in the language of the people. No other man in the world had shown, under test, greater powers of popular leadership. But he was outside the standards by which this convention measured men.

So the Senatorial oligarchs nominated Harding for his faults—the mildest-mannered Senator that ever took a program. He was to fulfill the ideal of the smoking-room story, and do "nothing." And then, to their dismay, Harding developed virtues. Genially recognizing his own limitations, he braved Senatorial protest by putting into his cabinet men who could supplement them—Hoover, to regulate the business which Harding's sponsors did not want regulated; Hughes, to conduct the foreign affairs which they wanted ignored, and Mellon to handle on business principles the financial affairs which they wanted dealt with on political principles. With one-half of his now-aroused character, Harding gave the country the intelligent and vigorous administration he had been picked to prevent. With the other half, to be sure, he was faithful to his old cronies, with results which are tragic history; but the total result was not merely the "normalcy" for which a jaded people had longed, but also much real progress and constructive accomplishment.

In this, Secretary Hoover played a loyal and characteristically able part. Appointed Secretary of Commerce, he regenerated a perfunctory department into the real center of the nation's economic life. The law gave him little power over business, and he was chary of exercising even that. He preferred to have business regulate itself. Here he showed his unique quality of personal leadership. By sheer persuasion, he induced business to do things which it would have been scarcely possible to impose by law. He pulled American industry, almost by its bootstraps, out of a slough of unemployment. He introduced simplifications and standardizations which have saved literally billions of dollars. He organized a worldwide service of information and aid to American foreign commerce. He was a member of the commission which arranged the payments of the debts owed us by European governments. He became practically dictator of radio. When the Mississippi floods came, it was a matter of course that Hoover should be sent, to meet the disaster of the century. Big jobs naturally gravitate to Hoover. These are only a few of the things which distinguished his service as a member of two administrations. And, in them all, he manifested that fine quality of loyalty to the administrations which even the politicians could appreciate. This is the one virtue which is valued in our feudal political system, even among those who comprehend no others.

So Hoover grew, in years, in governmental experience, and in skill in handling men under the difficult conditions of politics and public administration. He is one of the few great business men who understand the difference between the ways things have to be done in government and in business, and who is nevertheless efficient in both. Just for these reasons, some of the more visionary of the idealists grew lukewarm toward him. From a world leader, haloed in the clouds, Hoover had become a practical man, doing a job. He had, in fact, been just this, nearly all his life. But the picture did not fill their souls with the accustomed glow. They remained for him, as still better than any one else in sight, but they were less fervent about it. But, by the same process, the practical men came flocking to him. The spectacle of great practical efficiency in government, regardful of the interests of producers and consumers alike, but indifferent to political buncombe, was something refreshingly startling to them. Business men no longer feared him, though he ran them an intellectual pace which must have dazed them. The people grew to trust him, as one "highbrow" who was never alien to the common touch. And those who came in contact with him personally were staggered by the tremendous intellectual as well as practical capacity of the man. "It has been part of my business," said one, "all my life to come in close contact with some of the ablest men in the world, and I have found among them many brilliant minds, but never until I knew Herbert Hoover did I feel any actual awe before any of them. With him you feel the presence of something stupendous."

Then came the sudden "I do not choose" by which President Coolidge renounced a nomination and election which were his for the acceptance. Instantly, the Hoover candidacy made itself; this time not as the vain aspiration of idealists, but as precisely the first force in practical politics. It was Hoover against the field. The time had come. The people are no longer tired, but are eager for a new and vigorous leadership. They are even capable of thrills, as the Lindbergh episode showed. The work of "normalcy" is done. Harding got us back on the track, and Coolidge has put the machinery in shape. Now we want to go somewhere. It is not yet time for the great emotional crusade of another Roosevelt, if there were one, but it is time to set our house in order for it. If there is a great progressive movement looming just round the corner, we need first to equip the structure of government to bear it. This is the next great task, and Hoover, by common consent, is the one man for it. He is as timely for the present situation as he was premature before.

Even to the chess-players of politics, Hoover has now become the most important figure on the board. An outsider before, he is now the very center of the inside. It would have smashed all the rules of the game to have nominated him before; now it would strain them to do anything else.

In the first place, Hoover has learned the game himself. He will never be a champion at it, of course, and he is handicapped, in the eyes of the ultra-practical, by the scruples natural to a gentleman of honor. But he does know the game, its rules and its players, in far more than an amateur way. He might be beaten at it, but not fooled.

And on the sheer arithmetic of it, which is what the politicians figure on, he now outclasses everybody else. For the nomination, he is now the strongest candidate in more states than all the other visible candidates combined. Business and finance, which are the power behind conventions; the people, whose votes win elections; and the men of thought and vision, who give significance to historic movements, all are for him, as shown by widespread and representative declarations from them.

This strength, in fact, is Hoover's only weakness. Any candidate who leaps too soon to first place thereby tempts the others to combine against him. Some of the manipulators, who fear Hoover because he has too much brains and character for their purposes, and who, in any event, if he must be the nominee, would rather have him chosen by convention deals than by popular stampede, are seeking to divert the movement into scattered "favorite son" trading delegations. There is little indication, so far, of their success. In the East, the South, the West, and a considerable fraction of the Middle West, Hoover stands incontestably first.

Without organization, campaign, or even an announced candidacy, the natural forces of the situation and of public opinion have already crystallized him into the principal place.

For the election, the situation is likewise unique. The Democratic nominee is evidently going to be that party's only strong, and yet most vulnerable candidate, Governor Al Smith, of New York. The Republican candidate must be some one who can beat him. Hoover is not only the strongest candidate in the largest number of debatable but normally Republican states, but he is the only one who would be strong in the normally Democratic states where Smith is weakest. Hoover could break the Solid South—not its border states merely, but some of the states at its very core. That would mean more than merely winning this election. It would be an epoch-making service, to restore nationality to American public life. It is an unprecedented opportunity for the Republican party and the nation.

For the presidency itself, after the election—something the politicians commonly ignore, except as a source of patronage—the hope of seeing Herbert Hoover in the White House is enough to restore enthusiasm to even the most cynical. Here would be a real man, an American for Americans to be proud of, an example of all that is best and most inspiring in American life, plus a genius for the exact responsibilities of the place, at this time, such as happens only once. There are those who fear that this last qualification is a political disability—that supreme intellect and too high and independent character are not what democracy will put in high place. Whether that turns out to be so is a test of us, and of democracy.

For California, there is of course no question. That any faction or interest in California should even hesitate to rise to an opportunity so unique, for the advantage of the state and of the nation, is unthinkable. There will be a loyal Hoover delegation from California, without doubt. It should also be without contest.

These, only too briefly and incompletely, are some of the differences between the "Hoover then" who ought to have been President but could not be, and the "Hoover now," who still ought to be President—and, in the writer's opinion, is going to be. #

What a Surprise They Had in Store for Mr. Hoover!

The Art of Forging Cattle Brands

By BARRY SCOREE

September 1928

A FEW days ago Mr. Herbert Clark Hoover of Palo Alto, Cal., had the surprise of his life. From the veranda of his modest bungalow he saw a number of automobiles approaching. From them emerged a crowd of formally dressed, solemn men and women who astounded Mr. Hoover by informing him that he had been nominated as its presidential candidate by the Republican party in convention assembled. Recovering rapidly from the shock of the surprise, Mr. Hoover accepted the honor in four or five thousand well chosen words even before he had consulted Mrs. Hoover.

Isn't it possible in this radio age to break with the traditions that originated in the horseback period? A century and a quarter ago it may have taken a notification committee several weeks of hard riding to tell the candidate that he has been chosen, but when the candidate's radio keeps him in instantaneous touch with the proceedings, when he knows the outcome of the voting as soon as the press gallery gets the result, the formal notification degenerates to a political vermiform appendix.

Economy in campaign expenditures is one of the modern issues; funds this year will be hard to get unless the bootleggers contribute handsomely to the campaign fund of the driest party. Why couldn't the expense of the anachronistic and obsolete ceremony have been dispensed with? Surely no presidential candidate of a major party needs a pretext for telling the voters what he thinks of national issues. #

April 1927

THOUGH in the old days there was a lot of sport and good-natured rivalry in originating fancy and complicated cattle brands, big and intricate branding was not merely cowboy's fun and nothing else. There was a genuine need of intricate, or large and heavy branding. For consider how a simple brand like LP could be and was altered by three brief applications of the red-hot iron to a Coffee Pot.

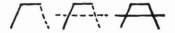

It behooved the owner to be more complex. A brand spread well over a cow's ribs, a brand that looked like a tarantula or a sky full of forked lightning could not be so easily doctored or blotted out. But a simple brand was known as a "rustler's delight." Such a one was that adopted by an eastern Kansas farmer who moved to the west and went into the cattle business. He took as his brand the simple two-line Backward Seven. And here is what a rustler did to it:

The rustler called it the Rail A brand. He had done his work so neatly that a jury, in court, failed to convict him. But everybody knew he was guilty, and after the trial the same jury rode the gentleman out of town on a rail—a wagon-tongue being the substitute for an actual rail in that treeless range country.

Just as a cowman took pride in originating a mark that would puzzle the rustlers to alter, so did the rustler have his pride in neatly changing anything that came his way. It is said that any rustler worth his salt could change almost any simple brand to a three-leaf clover. This is exaggeration but it points the fact that many brands could readily be changed to something more or less resembling the clover, as with the 7U or Y6, herewith:

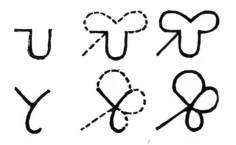

A big brand used to come out of Mexico—and so far as this writer knows it may have originated or been extensively used in the United States—that, while neither simple nor intricate, must have been impossible to alter satisfactorily, if at all. It has been called the "rebus brand" and it was usually burned well over an animal's ribs.

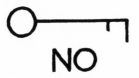

It was read "Keno," which was the name of a gambling game much played in the West. One can imagine the artists—the Rembrandts and Michael Angelos of brand altering days losing their rest trying to puzzle out a way to meet this competition and put over some pretty alteration that they could feel proud—and sure—about.

Perhaps the most famous brand-altering story in the West has to do with the well known XIT brand of the Panhandle of Texas. Whether the story is true or not, it is a cow-land classic. The story goes that a man was charged in court with altering the XIT to a five-pointed star with a cross in the center. The prosecuting attorney was not able to show the jury, by actual demonstration, how this could be done, and the jury turned the accused loose. Whereupon the man obligingly showed the court how the trick was turned. In the following illustration, which is supposed to be an imitation of what the man drew with a stub pencil on the back of an old envelope, the lines of XIT are left solid the better to show the correlation of old and new lines, but in practical brand-changing the essence of the art was to conceal the old lines by making them harmonize perfectly with the new, or vice versa.

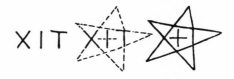

There are two other little classics of the range, among many, that are likely to be discussed anywhere in Cattleland where brand-altering yarns are being spun. One has to do with the changing of the Double-X to a six-pointed star, and the other with the joke that was slipped over on the Army when its horse brand US was changed to the "Two Dollars." The XX was made a star by the addition of six lines, and the US was altered by burning an S over the U and a U over the S. #

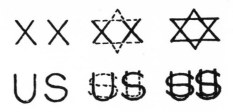

*A*s Sees *E*urope *Us*

By James Thurber

March 1928

SO far as Europe is concerned, America will never live down its Wild West. Even those enlightened Europeans who have traveled all over the United States, keep the legend of sombreros and gun-fanning bad men and riddled bar mirrors alive by jesting references to them. I recently heard, in a room in the Latin quarter of Paris, a distinguished English novelist discuss "Middle Westernism in Literature." He felt called upon to make several facetious remarks about the Wild West. In fact no discussion of anything American is complete without some humorous allusions to sheriffs and army Colts. It is a topic that never grows threadbare, for it is the mark of the sophisticated globe trotter. But many listeners to the lecture in question doubtless took the speaker seriously. Hence the legend of buffalo herds which stop trains may still be found current on the continent.

I know a little chasseur in a French hotel who fondly believes that ten hours ride out of New York takes you into a rough-timbered mining saloon whose puncheon floor is colorful with flapping chaps and red spangled ballet skirts mingling in the dance. Here one may find Douglas Fairbanks and William S. Hart idly shooting out kerosene lamps. Bill Hart, in fact, has taken up the perpetuation of the woolliness

of the West where Bret Harte left off. Obviously, say the French, the Americans would not and could not turn out bigger and better Wild West pictures every year if there were no Wild West. All you have to do is look at the sets and the background. They are palpably authentic.

A composite picture of the inhabitants of this wild country, made up from French and English stage conceptions, is interesting. The American man is tall and blustery, with horn-rimmed spectacles, and he is constantly shaking hands and saying, "Say-y, boy!" That much is English. He wears a straw hat and tan shoes on all occasions and has a penchant for engaging menials in small talk replete with allusions to his possession of large quantities of money. That much is French.

Three hundred thousand tourists from America, flooding France and England this year and exhibiting, for the most part, certain undeniable manifestations of twentieth century civilization, have no appreciable effect in changing these misconceptions. That is the French and English story and they will stick to it. Proof of advancing civilization in the United States doesn't mean anything. One knows and one's ancestors have known for years that if an American gets on a street car in his native land

and finds he has left his money in his other vest, he backs off at the next stop, firing as he goes and is pursued up alleys by the neighborhood posse, mounted on broncos and discharging sawed-off shotguns as they ride. If he is cornered he dies fighting, yelling "yip! yip! yay!" as he goes down.

I know an English lady who though she hasn't been to New York since Mrs. Leslie Carter hung on the bell clapper in "The Heart of Maryland," has nevertheless kept in close touch with conditions in America. She deplored the depths of corruption into which the police system in America has fallen. "I understand," she said, "that the officers never hit a criminal. They shoot at them, of course. But it is a mere formality. They never hit them." I wondered where she had picked up this piece of information. She said an American himself had told her. And I saw how it had been. He had jokingly referred to some instance in which a criminal had escaped, though fired upon by pursuing police. He had probably said, still in jest, "They never hit 'em." So she naturally believed it was a nefarious system that had grown up. It isn't true that the English can't see a joke, but it is true that they absorb much of the badinage of their American cousins without the necessary grain of salt. It is a good thing, therefore, that Joe Cook has never been invited to speak at the Pilgrim club's annual dinner. Think of the result! "My dear, have you heard that in America, President Grant has been known to consort with a common actor in a swimming pool or whatnot where the two of them have played quartets or something of the sort, on stupid Hawaiian fiddles!"

This same lady had been told that American society ladies have their teeth filled with diamonds. She asked me if it wasn't a strange sight. I told her I had never seen teeth of the first water in any mouth, American or otherwise. She was also much disturbed because the American people have adopted the German word "ja." This Teutonic affirmative had replaced the English "yes" altogether, she had been advised. It was a pro-German gesture that the English greatly resented so soon after the war. It was quite a task explaining to her that what her traveling friends had heard was merely the unfortunate American corruption of "yes" into "yeah."

I met a Scotchman on a train in Italy who intends to visit the Grand Canyon some day. To him America is all grand canyon. It is a spectacular canyon that reaches from any given part of the country to any other given part. It is quite a picnicking place for North Dakotans and residents of Miami. But he doesn't want to go until prohibition is killed off. That, he is informed, is merely a question of months. In this connection it may be said that certain journals published abroad in the English language are inclined to play up the errors and misfortunes of enforcement rather than its successful features. Things accordingly look brighter to the expatriated wets in Europe than to those living in the great American desert itself.

But if Europeans have their misconceptions of us, we have our own of them. This same Scot bought me two drinks in Milan! #

Dates of Advertisements

So the reader will not have to guess the dates of the advertisements reproduced in this book—amusing as this game may be—here is the key (page-month/year): 22-5/98; 33-2/07; 34-4/07; 41-1/07; 44-4/07; 53-4/05; 54-1/06; 60-4/05; 61-12/07; 66-5/07; 69-9/09; 70-2/10; 82, 83-10/08; 90-12/09; 93-12/09; 95-6/09; 98-7/08; 107-10/09; 131-9/11; 133-4/14; 134-5/14; 147-9/10; 149-7/11; 155-2/16; 164-1/09; 173-11/19; 178-4/19; 182-6/14; 185-6/20; 195-3/23; 196-6/21; 202-4/27; 203-4/24; 204-8/27; 219-4/27; 222-4/27; 231-1/27. Will James: 189-8/20.

Notes on Contributors

MARY AUSTIN (1860-1935). Celebrated writer on life in the Southwest. Best known: *Land of Little Rain* (1903).

WILLIAM ROSE BENÉT (1886-1950). Poet, novelist, magazine editor. Brother of Stephen Vincent Benét.

GELETT BURGESS (1866-1950). Humorist, essayist, novelist. Best known: *The Purple Cow, Goops and How To Be Them; Are You a Bromide?* Serious work: *War the Creator.* Editor of *The Lark.*

GALEN CLARK (1814-1910). Guardian of Yosemite 1866-80, 1889-96. Author of three books on Yosemite.

INA COOLBRITH (1842-1928). Editor, poet, librarian. Assistant editor of *Overland Monthly.* California's poet laureate, 1915. *Songs from the Golden Gate.*

MAYNARD DIXON (1875-1946). Illustrator and painter. Many of his canvases hang in distinguished galleries.

CHARLES K. FIELD (1873-?) Associate Editor of *Sunset Magazine* 1908-11, Editor 1911-25. Author of *Stanford Stories* (1900), *The Cave Man* (1910) and others.

ERLE STANLEY GARDNER (1889-1970). Lawyer and author. First mystery stories in the 1930s.

W. L. GEORGE (1882-1926). English novelist and lecturer. Commentary on America in *Hail Columbia!* (1921).

ZANE GREY (1875-1939). Famous author of Western stories, probably more widely read in the world than any other U.S. author.

DASHIELL HAMMETT (1894-1961). Railroad man, stock broker, detective, soldier. Author of numerous mystery stories.

BRET HARTE (1839-1902). Writer of short stories, novels, humorous verse; editor of *Overland Monthly.* Best known: *Luck of Roaring Camp, Outcasts of Poker Flat.*

THEODORE H. HITTELL (1830-1917). Author of four-volume history of California, 1885-97.

INEZ HAYNES GILLMORE (b. 1873) IRWIN. Novelist, author of girls' books; political activist. Author of *The Californiacs* (1966), *Angel Island* (1914), *Story of the Women's Party* (1921). Wife of Will Irwin.

WILL JAMES (1892-1942). Author, self-taught artist, first published in *Sunset.* Best known book: *Smoky* (1934).

DAVID STARR JORDAN (1851-1931). President of Stanford University, 1891- 1913; author of many articles on international affairs, *The War's Aftermath* (1914). Academic specialty: ichthyology.

PETER B. KYNE (1880-1957). Prolific writer of adventure stories. Best known: Cappy Ricks series, *Pride of Palomar* (1913), *Never the Twain Shall Meet* (1923). Published thirty books.

ALDO LEOPOLD (1887-1948). Forester, professor of forest management, conservationist. Best known book: *A Sand County Almanac* (1949).

SINCLAIR LEWIS (1885-1951). Novelist, newspaper reporter. Earliest novel: *Mr. Wren* (1914); best known: *Main Street* (1920), *Babbitt* (1922). Nobel prize 1935.

VACHEL LINDSAY (1879-1931). Author, illustrator; famous poet. Known for jazzlike rhythm, lyrical fervor. Best known: *The Congo, Lincoln Walks at Midnight.*

JACK LONDON (1876-1916). Famous short story writer and novelist; six stories in *Sunset,* 1903-19.

MIRIAM MICHELSON (1870-1942). Novelist, drama critic, writer for San Francisco and Philadelphia newspapers. *The Superwoman* (1912).

JOAQUIN MILLER (1841-1913), pseudonym of Cincinnatus Heine Miller. Playwright, fiction writer, poet of frontier life. Gold seeker, filibusterer with Walker.

JOHN MUIR (1838-1914). Naturalist, explorer, conservationist. Charter member of Sierra Club. Author, *The Mountains of California* and other well-known works.

CHARLES G. NORRIS (1881-1945). Noteworthy novelist of realistic school: *Salt* (1917), *Brass* (1921), *Bread* (1923), *Pig Iron* (1926), and others. Brother of Frank Norris.

KATHLEEN NORRIS (1880-1966). Novelist. First book on California theme, *Mother* (1911); best work: *Certain People of Importance* (1927). Wife of C. G. Norris.

CHESTER H. ROWELL (b. 1867). Political editor of San Francisco *Chronicle,* Fresno *Republican*; essayist and lecturer on political subjects. Prominent in Republican Party affairs.

GEORGE STERLING (1869-1909). Prolific poet—ten volumes of generally flamboyant, luxuriant and emotional poetry. Best work: *Wine of Wizardry* (1908).

CHARLES WARREN STODDARD (1843-1909). Author and professor of English at Notre Dame; correspondent for San Francisco *Chronicle.* Best known: *In the Footprints of the Padres* (much of it run in *Sunset), South Sea Idylls, The Leper of Molokai.*

JAMES THURBER (1894-1961). Humorist, novelist, affiliated with *The New Yorker* magazine.

HELEN WILLS (b. 1906) ROARK. Author of many articles and books; versifier, artist. National and international tennis champion.

WALTER V. WOEHLKE (b. 1881). German-born writer, editor; Managing Editor of *Sunset Magazine,* 1912-14; specialist in economics, labor, agriculture.

JOHN P. YOUNG (b. 1895). Managing Editor of San Francisco *Chronicle.*